THE REIGN OF KING EDWARD VI

HEADSTART LECTURE SERIES

THE REIGN OF KING EDWARD VI

DAVID LOADES

HEADSTART HISTORY
PO Box 41
Bangor
Gwynedd, LL57 1SB
GREAT BRITAIN

First Published in 1994

Copyright 1994 David Loades

Set by Richard Foulsham

Printed by Henry Ling Limited.
    The Dorset Press,
    Dorchester.

ISBN I 873041 02 0

Table of Contents

Preface

The reign of Edward VI has been subject to the vagaries of historical fashion. Generations of Tudor historians from Pollard to Elton passed it by with little more than a nod of recognition while they concentrated on the more compelling issues raised by the actions of Henry VIII or Elizabeth. Along with the reign of Mary, it was a period of weak and unstable government which served mainly to highlight the achievements of the "great Tudors". In the late 1960's and early 1970's, however, the period began to attract attention. Daunted, perhaps, by the massive scholarship of *The Tudor Revolution in Government* (1953) and *Elizabeth I and her Parliaments* (1955-7), historians began to explore the middle years of the century in earnest. In 1968 and 1970 W.K. Jordan published an imposing two volume history of the reign, *The Young King* and *The Threshold of Power*. In the latter years he also edited Edward's journal. In 1973 W.R.D. Jones produced *The Mid-Tudor Crisis, 1539-1563*. In 1975 M.L. Bush's brief but stimulating *Government Policy of Protector Somerset* appeared, and in 1976 D.E Hoak's *The King's Council under Edward VI*. B.L. Beer's study of Edward's second regent, John Dudley, duke of Northumberland, had also appeared in 1973, and there was a steady accumulation of learned articles. Since then, however, interest has waned again, until very recently. In 1992 Charles Knighton completed his invaluable and excellent new calender of the Domestic State Papers of the reign, and in 1993 Jennifer Loach has flagged a forthcoming major work with her Headstart Paper on *Protector Somerset*. Jordan, Bush, Beer and Hoak are all out of print, and until the new work which is now in gestation finally appears, it is not easy for the student who is following the shifts of academic fashion to find a specific guide to this brief but eventful period. For that reason I have written this short guide, utilising a course which I have been teaching for the last four years. To some extent it is based upon the major works of twenty years ago, to some extent on the ongoing trickle of academic articles, which are often hard for the student to locate, and to some extent upon my own work, which is presently directed towards a new study of the duke of Northumberland. Inevitably I have had to assume a general familiarity with the structure of Tudor history, so although this is not a work of advanced scholarship, it is better to approach it by way of more general textbooks, such as John Guy's *Tudor England*, or my own *Politics and the Nation*.

David Loades

Bangor
September 1993

1

Henry VIII's will and the formation of the protectorate.

The fall of Thomas Cromwell in 1540 appeared to jeopardise the whole policy which Henry VIII had been pursuing since 1533, but the appearance was deceptive. However suspicious the king may have become of certain types of radical preacher, and of his minister's connections with them, he had no intention of reconsidering either his ecclesiastical supremacy or the administrative or jurisdictional changes which had stemmed from it . At the same time, fond as he was of humanist scholarship and reforming piety, he remained as averse as ever to doctrinal protestantism. Consequently the political agenda of the last seven years of his reign must not be seen in terms of factional conflict between catholics and protestants, but in terms of rivalry between conservatives and reformers within the parameters which Henry laid down. This was a situation which lacked both logic and clear cut factional structure. The Howard ascendancy, which followed the king's fifth marriage in July 1540 did not survive Catherine's fall at the end of 1541. Apart from the duke of Norfolk himself, the entire family was threatened with destruction early in 1542, and they survived at the expense of greatly diminished influence. That did not, however, spell the end of the conservative faction. The reformers recovered the initiative when Henry married Catherine Parr in the summer of 1543, but both Archbishop Cranmer and the queen herself remained vulnerable to the king's occasional moods of paranoia, which became worse as his health deteriorated. Everything depended upon Henry's increasingly unpredictable temperament, a situation vividly reflected in the third succession act of 1543. That statute unsurprisingly recognised Edward, the king's only surviving son as his immediate heir. But it then proceeded to exclude the legitimate offspring of both Henry's sisters in favour of his own daughters, Mary and Elizabeth, both of whom remained bastardised by previous statutes which were not repealed. Only if Edward, Mary and Elizabeth all died without offspring would the crown would pass to the descendants of his younger sister, Mary. The Scottish descendants of his elder sister, Margaret, were ignored[1].

Not only did this act clearly reflect the king's own idiosyncratic wishes, it also left the final determination of the succession in his own hands, empowering him to confirm or alter the order laid down by his last will and testament. In the event he was to confirm it unchanged, but it has been rightly said that the last four years were dominated by the situation created by this statute, and by the increasing certainty that, if the young Edward outlived his father, he would come to the throne as a minor - and probably one with a long nonage ahead of him. Edward had been born in 1537, and was therefore six when his future was confirmed in this manner. There had never been a whisper of doubt about his legitimacy in England; even the staunchest conservatives accepted it . However in catholic Europe he was regarded as a bastard, because his parent's marriage had been celebrated after the declaration of schism and while the realm was out of communion with Rome. To the strict catholic, therefore, Mary was her father's heir, irrespective of what any statute or will might say, and after her the crown should pass to her namesake, the infant queen of Scots. It was consequently of critical importance to Henry that he should succeed in bequeathing his power to a group of men who were prepared to uphold his own wishes, and with them the independence of his kingdom, The political struggles of the years 1543-1547 therefore have to be seen in terms of who was succeeding best in convincing their volatile master that they could be entrusted with these vital tasks. Henry was profoundly convinced that his ecclesiastical supremacy represented the will of God for England, and the security of his son's crown was intimately bound up with preserving it. Political success would therefore rest with those who could present the best demonstration of commitment to the same cause.

The fall of Cromwell had left the privy council dominated by his enemies particularly the dukes of Norfolk and Suffolk, Stephen Gardiner, the bishop of Winchester, and Sir Thomas Wriothesley. The privy chamber, on the other hand, continued to shelter a number of

Cromwell's reforming friends, who he had placed there to assist the promotion of his own cause. In the spring of 1540 they had not availed him, but they remained a potentially powerful source of influence. The critical event which realised this potentiality, and returned the initiative to the reformers was Henry's last marriage. Catherine Parr was not an irresponsible girl but a widow of 31, and for the first time in his life the king was looking for a companion rather than a bedfellow. The new queen was an intelligent and pious woman, deeply committed to the evangelical cause. Whether she had much direct influence upon Henry may be doubted, but she subtly altered the mental climate of the court, bringing the king's disparate family together in something approaching harmony, and drawing to Henry's attention good scholars like Richard Cox who shared her way of thinking. It was Henry, not Catherine, who appointed Cox and John Cheke to be young Edward's tutors, but in a different situation their names might well have remained unknown to him. By 1544 the emergence of another committed reformer, Sir Anthony Denny, to be principal gentleman of the privy chamber, the death of the duke of Suffolk, and the defeat of a conservative plot to get rid of Cranmer, had consolidated the reformers' ascendancy. This in turn attracted a stronger commitment from sympathetic but wary politicians such as the earl of Hertford and John Dudley, viscount Lisle. These men gained the king's approval by their efforts in Scotland, where war had been rumbling since 1542, and in making common cause with the reformers turned a court faction into a powerful political force, able to challenge the conservatives even within the council.

Even so the issue was not resolved. The conservative Wriothesley had become chancellor in 1544, and as late as 1546 a heresy hunt triggered by the arrest and examination of the radical Anne Askew, appeared to threaten the personal security of the queen. Whether this was actually a narrowly averted conservative coup, or another example of the king's penchant for making fools of his ministers, we cannot be sure, but in spite of the way the political tide had been setting over the previous three years, it was not until the autumn of 1546 that the power struggle was finally decided. Within a few weeks, between September and the end of November two apparently unrelated developments effectively destroyed the conservative position. According to his latest biographer the fall of Stephen Gardiner was brought about, not by his part in the abortive strike against Catherine Parr, but by a misunderstanding with the king over an exchange of lands[2]. The king was a sick and extremely bad tempered man by December 1546, so it is possible that the cause of the rupture was relatively trivial, but the effect was the bishop's total and deliberate exclusion from the body of executors who were to administer Henry's will, and in effect from the regency council. At almost exactly the same time, the earl of Surrey was arrested and charged with having treasonable designs upon the succession. He was rapidly joined in the Tower by his father, the duke of Norfolk, and brought to trial in January 1547. Surrey's offence was more one of indiscreet arrogance than of treasonable intent, but even in his very last days, just before he lapsed into unconsciousness, Henry's peers knew what they had to do and they were condemned. The earl was executed on the 19th January, but the duke, who had survived so many crisis, survived this one also, remaining in the Tower when the king died in the small hours of the 28th January.

Catherine was not with her husband in his last hours, perhaps because Henry could not bring himself to face the imminence of his dissolution. Cranmer, who was sent for, barely arrived in time. The man who was in control of the royal sickbed was Anthony Denny, and it was he along with John Gates and William Clerk, to whom the failing king had delegated the responsibility for stamping documents which he no longer had the energy or the co-ordination to sign. These documents included the final version of Henry's will, which was presented to him on the 27th January[3]. By the time this happened effective political power already lay in the hands of a triumvirate consisting of Edward Seymour, earl of Hertford, viscount Lisle, and Sir William Paget, the principal secretary. By establishing a firm alliance with Denny and Cranmer, Hertford and Lisle had finally defeated their rivals, and the astute Paget, a pragmatist who had his own place in the king's confidence, had moved rapidly to join them. Because it was stamped and not signed, doubts were later raised about the validity of Henry's will, but no one challenged it at the time, and there is no serious doubt that it represented the old king's last conscious intention. By the terms of that will, power was vested, during the minority of the young king "until he shalbe of the full age of eighteen yeares" in a body of sixteen named executors, who were also to form the regency council[4]. This body was authorised to order all the affairs of the realm, and "...also to do any Acte or Actes whatsoever that may tende to the honour and suretie of our said Souveraigne Lordes person, or to the advancement of his affaires..." The sixteen included a few prominent conservatives, notably Lord Wriothesley, the lord chancellor, Cuthbert Tunstall, bishop of Durham, and William Paulet, Lord St.John, but the erstwhile reforming faction enjoyed a clear majority, and that appears to have been Henry's way of ensuring that the problem of royal minority should not be allowed to prompt any thoughts on the subject of the royal supremacy.

The king's death was concealed for three days, not necessarily for any sinister purpose, but simply to enable everything to be put in place for a smooth succession. Mary could have raised a challenge to her half-brother, but there is no evidence that she ever had the slightest intention of doing so. Only the Emperor Charles V delayed his recognition of the new regime until he was sure there was not going to be any effective resistance. Edward was brought to London, and on the 31st January was proclaimed king under the title of Edward VI. The same day thirteen of the sixteen named executors met at the Tower and took order for the government according to their brief. Their most important decision was to appoint "somme special man" to act as head of the council, on the grounds that the "assured order and direction " of the king's affairs required an identifiable person to bear the main responsibility. This position they then articulated into two offices, protector of the realm and governor of the king's person, bestowing both upon the earl of Hertford, in consideration of his great experience of affairs, and also of the fact that he was the king's maternal uncle. It is often said that these decisions violated both the spirit and the letter of Henry's will, but such a course was no more than common sense in the circumstances. Nor is it a decisive argument to say that if he had intended such an arrangement he would have made it. It is most unlikely that Henry ever saw his will as a definitive document in that sense; no doubt if he had lived a few more days he would have made further modifications, so it is not reasonable to condemn either Hertford or the council for choosing such a course of action.

Whether their next move was equally justifiable, is, however, more open to dispute. Even before the old king was safely laid to rest at Windsor on 16 February, a clamour began for honours and rewards which it was alleged that he had intended to confer. In order to assess the validity of these claims, the council called on the testimony of the three men who had been closest to Henry in his last days, Anthony Denny, and William Herbert of the privy chamber, and Sir William Paget. Paget's was the testimony which really counted, because he seems to have conducted a number of negotiations, both with the king and with the potential recipients, both before and after Christmas. He testified to a long list of land grants, offices and titles, which he claimed had been frustrated by the king's death. There is no reason to doubt that such rewards had been discussed, but whether they had been firmly determined as he represented, may be doubted. Collectively they represented a very large disbursement, and although Henry had been intermittently generous to his servants, not even the 1525 largesse had been on this scale. On the 15th February the council, which of course included a number of the principal beneficiaries, accepted the whole list. Paget protected his own credit by awarding himself nothing, and one or two, for reasons which are now obscure, declined the proffered honours, but the majority were formalised in a hastily contrived ceremony on the 17th February[5]. The newly installed protector became the duke of Somerset, William Parr, earl of Essex became marquis of Northampton, John Dudley, viscount Lisle, earl of Warwick, and Lord Wriothesley earl of Southampton. Two days later the young king was solemnly escorted from the Tower to Westminster, where he was crowned with suitable rejoicing on Sunday, 20th February. His new and newly promoted, peers had all managed to find the appropriate regalia with remarkable speed; perhaps they had prepared it in advance.

So far, whatever tension may have existed below the surface, the new council had acted in public with unanimity and despatch. However, no sooner was the coronation completed than a rift appeared. On 18th February "resolving to give himself wholly to matters of state" Lord Chancellor Wriothesley put his functions in the court of chancery into commission to four civil lawyers. There was an immediate outcry from the common lawyers, who claimed that the chancellor had acted without proper warrant or authority, a view which was endorsed by the judges on the 28th February, when the council referred the matter to them. At a council meeting on 6th March Wriothesley defended his action vigorously, claiming that he was entitled to take such action *ex officio*, without a warrant. According to one source, he bore himself at that meeting with a high hand, claiming that his own office rested on a sounder base than that of the lord protector. If he was guilty of such provocation, he acted foolishly, but a certain doubt must be attached to the official story, because the lord chancellor was not only the leading conservative to have survived the collapse of 1546, he was also an abrasive and effective politician who was perfectly capable of challenging the protector's authority. It seems that he was guilty of rather a foolish misdemeanour, but it is one which could perfectly well have been rectified with little fuss if the will to do so had been present. In the event his error was used by his political enemies as a pretext to render him harmless. He was deprived of his office and sentenced to imprisonment and fine at the king's pleasure. He was soon released, his fine was remitted, and he later rejoined the council, but as a potential leader of dissent, his teeth had been effectively drawn.

In a slightly wider perspective, Wriothesley's fall can be seen as a step in the progressive strengthening of Somerset's position, a process which was advancing by other methods at the same time, and which was rendered urgently necessary by questions originating with the French and Imperial ambassadors. The councillors themselves may have been satisfied that they derived enough power from Henry VIII's will and from the statute of 1543, but the authority of statute was not understood outside England, and it was perfectly proper to point out that the authority of the dead king was worth nothing. Could the council, for example, conclude a binding treaty on Edward's behalf? On 1st March a commission was issued "for the settling of the Lord Protector and for choosing of the privy council". This had the effect of confirming the protector in office in the name of the new king, and of formally constituting the executors and assistant executors (twelve in number)[6] of the king's will into the Privy Council of Edward VI. The existing council was thus expanded to a more realistic size, and its authority placed on an internationally recognised foundation. A second commission dated 13th March confirmed these provisions, adding an express authority to negotiate on the king's behalf, and to move the great seal without further authority. On this occasion, however, the lord protector himself was given "full power and authority" to transact all business, and was not explicitly bound by the consent of the remainder of the council. Whether this should be seen as a logical extension of the position taken up on 31st January, or as a clever manoeuvre whereby Somerset outwitted his colleagues and gained a quasi-monarchical authority for himself, the effect was to transform the corporate style of government which Henry VIII seems to have intended into a full and personal regency exercised by the duke of Somerset. It was thus on 13th March, not on 31st January that the old king's will was abandoned, both in letter and in spirit.

2

The religious settlement; early moves towards protestantism.

The doctrines and practices of the English church in 1547 were those which had been defined by the Act of Six Articles eight years earlier. Sacramental teaching was orthodox in the catholic sense, with much emphasis on the mass in all its various late medieval forms. The sacramentarian denial of transubstantiation was a heresy which Henry particularly abhorred. The Lutheran teaching of justification *sola fide* was also banned, as was clerical marriage. On the other hand it was not only the repudiation of papal jurisdiction which separated England from the church universal. Not only had the monasteries been dissolved, but monks and nuns had also been allowed to repudiate their vows and return to the world. The doctrine of purgatory had been abandoned, pilgrimages prohibited and the great shrines, such as Glastonbury and Walsingham, destroyed. More positively vernacular scripture had been approved in the form of the Great Bible and although attempts had been made to restrict access to it when the conservatives had been in the ascendant, by 1545 the political success of the reforming party also meant that the Great Bible was open to anyone who could read. Cranmer had also prepared an English litany as early as 1544, which could be used with official approval, although in no sense imposed. In all probability a number of those leading reformers who were around the king in his last days had crossed the shadowy no-man's land between catholicism and protestantism, but Henry himself was not one of them, and extreme caution was therefore necessary. For all her dutiful submissiveness, it seems that the charges of heresy levelled against Queen Catherine Parr were justified. Her *Lamentation or Complaint of a sinner*, although not published until 1548, had been written in 1545 and it contained a number of unorthodox propositions[1]. Thomas Cranmer, although by his own account he continued to accept transubstantiation until 1548, had certainly embraced justification by faith alone, and was also secretly married, a fact which was perfectly well known to the king. Edward's tutors, Richard Cox, John Cheke and Jacques Belmain, are harder to assess, and there is no proof that they taught their young charge any protestant doctrine before his accession, but the rapid development of his conviction thereafter speaks for itself.

How aware Henry was of the religious climate around him in his last days must remain a matter of doubt. He may have been arrogant enough to believe that his own peculiar brand of orthodoxy was invincible, and that no one would dare touch it even after he was dead. On the other hand he may equally have been fully alert to the possibility of a protestant take over, and persuaded that the risk was necessary to protect the royal supremacy. Charles V appears to have believed that the English would take advantage of Henry's death to re-negotiate their relations with the papacy, and bring the schism to an end. But no one who knew Edward Seymour, or who understood the composition of the regency council, shared that conviction. Richard Hilles was more accurate when he described the Lord Protector as "a great enemy to the Pope of Rome". Nevertheless the signs of a new policy emerged only gradually. Not even Gardiner could find fault with Henry's funeral, nor with the coronation, in spite if the fact that it was shortened out of consideration for the king's "tender years". The first apple of discord, however, was cast before the end of February, when Cranmer sought a fresh commission for the exercise of his office. All offices held of the crown lapsed with the death of the monarch, but this practice had never before been applied to the episcopate. At the last demise of the crown, in 1509 all the bishops had theoretically held their offices from the pope, and conservatives such as Gardiner continued to believe that the bishops were ordinaries, whose authority derived from their consecration rather than from their appointments. Cranmer held the radical view that consecration, although desirable, was not strictly necessary, and that a bishop was merely an officer appointed to exercise spiritual jurisdiction on behalf of the king. The bishop of Winchester protested vigorously, but the council inevitably accepted the archbishop's advice, and for the first (and only) time in the history of the English church, its bishops were issued with new commissions at the beginning of the new reign.

The next bone of contention was the lenten sermons, particularly that preached by bishop Barlow of St. Davids, which called sternly for a thorough cleansing of a corrupt church. Gardiner pleaded with Paget, in whom he thought he saw a kindred spirit, to dissuade the protector from a course of "innovation". He was particularly alarmed by the iconoclastic tone of some of the official pronouncements of the new regime, fearing, rightly, that they would give encouragement to some of the wilder spirits who had been held in check by Henry's censorship. For whatever reason, Somerset relaxed control of the press. This may have been inadvertent - a mere inability to fill the old king's shoes - but it was more likely deliberate, and based upon a typically protestant conviction that the liberated truth would always triumph by its own force. Until the summer of 1547 conservative anxieties were stimulated more by the style of Somerset's ecclesiastical policy than by its content, but in July Cranmer issued a set of *Homilies*, and some of their worst fears were confirmed. The archbishop did not write all of these pieces himself, but he was the author of the most controversial, that on Justification, which set out clearly protestant teaching on the central doctrinal issue. Gardiner immediately joined battle. Such doctrine , he pointed out, was directly contrary to that taught by the *King's Book* of 1543, and authorised by the Act for the Advancement of True Learning in the same year, as well as by the Act of Six Articles. In other words it was illegal as well as being (in his opinion) erroneous. The bishop of Winchester's opposition, it should be stressed, was private and not public. Ostensibly he was concerned to uphold the authority of the royal supremacy, not to undermine it, but in a sense he was deceiving himself, because his real objective was not to defend the principle of the supremacy so much as the distinctive settlement which Henry VIII had created. In September he was summoned before the council, and refused to accept the royal Injunction which commanded the *Homilies* to be read. For this contumacy he was committed to the Fleet.

On 4th November the first parliament of the new reign convened, and immediately began to address various aspects of the religious situation. Both the Act of Six Articles and the Act for the Advancement of True Learning were repealed, withdrawing the legal force of the *King's Book*, and cutting the ground from under Gardiner's feet. It also became lawful for married men to be ordained, although a move to legalise the marriage of those already ordained failed. The statute of 1545 authorising the dissolution of chantries and colleges, which had

not been implemented and had lapsed with Henry's death, was revived
in a new and significant form. The original act had authorised the king
to take the property of these foundations on the grounds of his acute
financial necessity for the defence of the realm. This statute, however,
alluded explicitly to men's

> "...Ignorance of their very true and perfect salvation through
> the death of Jesus Christ, and...devising and fantasising
> vain opinions of purgatory and masses satisfactory to be
> done for them which be departed..."[2]

and went on to dissolve all intercessory foundations on the grounds of
this superstition. When the parliament was dissolved on the 27th
December there was no longer any statutory basis for doctrinal orthodoxy, but a clear pronouncement of the protestant position on justification, both in the *Homilies* and in the act for the dissolution of the
chantries. At the same time, both Cranmer and the protector were
aware of the extent to which this uncertainty was encouraging disorder. They did not need Gardiner to draw their attention to the prolifer-
ation of tracts, ballads and radical sermons denouncing every aspect of
the traditional faith. The mass was the commonest target for extremist
wrath, and consequently a potential flashpoint for physical conflict as
the conservative majority mobilised to defend one of the central practices of their faith. Such mobilisation was the last thing the council
wanted, and it was therefore moved to check radical provocation with
an act "against such as shall unreverently speak against the sacrament
of the body and blood of Christ". This statute did not specifically
defend the doctrine of transubstantiation, but it did describe the
sacrament as being of dominical institution, and worthy of reverence.
As such it was a purely disciplinary measure, and did nothing to
resolve the doctrinal uncertainties which were the basic cause of the
trouble. The council was endeavouring to maintain its authority
without revealing its policy, because it knew that policy would be
widely unpopular, and it was unsure of its ability to make it effective.
    The reformers' strategy in 1547 resembled that of Thomas Crom-
well in the early 1530s in that they deliberately made it very difficult
for law-abiding conservatives to find ground upon which to stand.
Gardiner was particularly thrown by this, because he was still genuinely committed to the royal supremacy, and after the first parliament
was reduced to arguing that it was unwise of the council, acting in the
king's name, to introduce innovations during the minority, the king

might have the authority to alter religion, he conceded, but if every new reign was to see a new settlement the church would lose all credibility and the pretensions of the papists would revive. The minority itself was not a problem;

> "A king's authority to govern his realm never wanteth, though he were in his cradle. His place is replenished by his council, as we have now my Lord Protector. And yet it is a difference in the judgment of the people, to direct and order things established, and to make the highest innovations."[3]

Consequently the council should leave Henry VIII's settlement untouched until Edward came of age. Gardiner was the most thoughtful and articulate opponent of the change, but he was not the only one. Bishop Edmund Bonner also refused to receive the injunctions, and was sent to the Fleet on the 18th September. The *Homilies* were again the main sticking point, but they were not the only one. Many conservatives were also worried by the requirement to set up a copy of the translation of Erasmus's *Paraphrases* alongside the English bible, and by the insistence that every cathedral was to support a free grammar school. This emphasis upon learning, which was also reflected in the requirement that every chapter should provide itself with a modest patristic library, was not in any specific sense protestant, and yet clearly bore the stamp of the reformers' priorities. In the late summer of 1547 the whole church was divided into six circuits, and commissioners were appointed to carry out a royal visitation of each circuit requiring, among other things, adherence to the injunctions[4]. This visitation was along the same lines as those carried out by Cromwell in 1536 and 1538. The commissioners were mostly laymen, and were chosen for their willingness to impose the council's policy. Apart from Gardiner and Bonner, the bishops accepted this visitation without demur, realising that there was no way in either law or logic that they could challenge the king's right to make it.

The articles of the visitation contained no doctrinal statements, but they did continue a campaign which had been launched in 1536 against what were significantly called "superstitious practices". The use of images, both in cathedrals and parish churches, was heavily discouraged on the grounds that they incited the credulous and simple minded to idolatry. The use of candles and torches was limited, and processions restricted. On the other hand sermons were required to be preached at least once a quarter, and every church was to provide itself with a "fair pulpit". The use of Cranmer's English litany was encouraged, and when there was no sermon the Lord's Prayer, the Creed and the Ten Commandments were to be recited in English. Every Sunday a chapter of the New Testament was to be read at matins, and a chapter of the Old at evensong. As they went around the commissioners also seem to have suggested various other ways in which worship might be simplified, over and above the requirements of the articles. By the end of 1547, in spite if the lack of doctrinal definition , no one can have been in much doubt that the church was about to undergo a process of change more far reaching, and more directly relevant to the ordinary worshipper than anything that had happened in the previous reign, with the possible exception of the destruction of the shrines. The convocations of the clergy, which met at the same time as parliament, are poorly recorded for this session, but there seems to have been no powerful groundswell of resentment against the changes. If anything, there was a desire to press on in the direction of a full English order of service, and a desire by the lower clergy to be directly represented in the main legislative assembly through membership of the house of commons.

Radical protestants were bitterly disappointed, both by the visitation and by what they saw as the slow and half-hearted progress of parliamentary reform. They frequently expressed this discontent, particularly to their Swiss friends, and those disciples of Bullinger who had already travelled to England, endorsed their lamentations wholeheartedly. However, given the weight of tradition which the council was trying to move, we should be surprised at its success, rather than its failure. Early in 1548 the desire was not so much to press on with the Godly reformation as to retain control of a volatile situation. Characteristically, on 16th January a long proclamation (Somerset's favourite means of communication) was issued upholding the traditional practice of fasting during lent. The king, it declared, was convinced that this should continue, not only for its spiritual benefits, but also for the encouragement which the large scale consumption of fish gave to the maritime community[5]. A few weeks later a further proclamation condemned private innovations in worship, and particularly in the celebration of the eucharist. Parliament had already authorised communion under both kinds, but this was clearly no more than an interim measure. Many protestants wished to abolish the mass entirely, while to the conservatives it became one of the fundamental features of their faith, which they were prepared to defend, in some cases at the risk of bloodshed. For the time being the old rite was to continue, and only the parliamentary modification was permitted. In due course an official order of public worship would be issued. Equally controversial was the question of images. Over the previous decade several attempts had been made to distinguish between those images which were "abused", that is offered the kind of worship that should be reserved for God alone, and those which were merely devotional aids - "poor men's books". The visitors of 1547 had discouraged all images, but they had not had the power to remove them. As a result the dispute between the iconoclasts and iconodules had continued to rage unabated, and in February 1548 the council concluded that order could only be restored by an executive decision. In the circumstances it was inevitable which way they would go.

> "...almost in no places of the realm is any sure quietness but where all the images be wholly taken away and pulled down"

declared the proclamation of 11th February. Henceforth all bishops were to proceed to the complete removal of images and pictures from all places of public worship.

This was the most important symbolic action which had so far been taken, and the implementation inevitably was patchy. Some London parishes had so far jumped the gun that the council had been making them replace images in the spring of 1547. Their compliance was now instantaneous. Many rural parishes on the other hand yielded to continuous pressure only after two or three years. The lives of many people were impoverished by this "stripping of the altars", especially of such as could not read the scriptures , and the disputes were not ended, as the council rather naively hoped[6]. Instead the focus of controversy returned to the mass. Having won on images, the radicals concentrated all their fire upon this "mystery of iniquity". Riots and unseemly brawls took place almost weekly during lent, and on the 24th April the council inhibited all preaching except by those specifically licensed by the king, the lord protector and the archbishop. Even this proved to be inadequate. Only a complete and fully authorised order of worship, which left no room for controversy or idiosyncratic interpretation could impose the desired uniformity upon a church that had become thoroughly confused and which could easily degenerate into anarchy. On 23rd September 1548 the council finally announced that such an order was about to appear: and until it did all preaching without exception was inhibited.

3

Agrarian and Trade Problems

The population of England and Wales in 1547 was around about three million, of whom some 85% lived in the countryside and earned their living by agriculture. A century earlier the population had stood at two and a half million, and had appeared to be falling. Three centuries earlier the population had been over five million, and was still rising. The Black Death in the middle of the fourteenth century had halved a population of six million in less than twenty years , and had remained endemic, which had resulted in a further slow fall until about 1450. Thereafter, for reasons which are still obscure, a recovery began, which accelerated steadily after 1500[1]. Both the fall and the recovery had major consequences for agrarian society, because a lot depended on the "fit" between the people and the land. In the late fourteenth and early fifteenth centuries there had been an acute labour shortage, but also a major decline in consumer demand. Marginal land, particularly in upland regions, went out of cultivation, and lord were forced to bargain away labour services. It was sometimes difficult to fin tenants, even on generous terms, and the steadily increasing price of wool tempted many major landholders, such as the great abbeys, to convert parts of there estate into sheep runs. The slack demand for tenancies meant that this process caused little tension, because if a sitting tenant did have to be moved to make way for the flock, an alternative holding could easily be found. However, with the recovery of population levels in the early sixteenth century, this ceased to be the case, but the profitability of wool continued to rise, and in consequence a conflict of interest between landlords and tenants began to appear. It was this conflict which became focussed into the issue over enclosures.

The great bulk of agricultural land was manorial, and manors were held (usually indirectly) of the king by military service. The manor was a legal rather than a topographical unit. One village might contain parcels of many manors, and a manor might be spread across several settlements, not necessarily contiguous. A manor derived its identity, not from a tidy boundary, but from its court, and the court was made up of all those who held land of the manor, and were known as the "homage". The court adjudicated all disputes concerning boundaries, land use, straying beasts etc, and determined the condition of tenures. It was held in the name of the lord, but usually presided over by his steward, and administered a corpus of traditional law known as the "custom of the manor"[2]. The land belonging to a manor was usually divided into three types, although there were local variations. First there were the demesne land, which was theoretically farmed directly by the lord; second there were the customary tenements held by the homage; and thirdly there was the common land in which all members of the community had defined rights according to their status. All customary tenures were theoretically unfree having originated in villein tenures, and could only be "pleaded", that is given legal security, in the manor court. The king's court took no cognisance of customary rights. By the early sixteenth century bondmen of condition, that is people who were unfree and could not personally plead in the king's courts, were relatively uncommon thanks to the relaxations which followed the Black Death, so that most customary tenures were held by men who were personally free, and this caused a good deal of confusion. By this time also there were a fair number of genuine freeholders; men who had obtained land by purchase or grant in full ownership and held directly of the king. There land was not part of any manor, and they were not bound by manorial custom because their tenures were pleaded in the king's courts. Much freehold land was actually held on lease, and those leases were also secured by the common law.

Because of these complexities, it was not easy for a lord to enclose manorial land. He could, of course, do what he wished with his own demesne, but if he wished to alter the status of tenurial land he could only do so either by consent or by unity of possession. If all the tenancies of a manor came into a lord's hands at he same time, so that there was no homage, then he could abolish the manor altogether, and create a seigneury, but that was extremely difficult to do. Enclosure by agreement was by no means uncommon, but it usually occurred when it was intended to keep the land under the plough[3]. There were distinct advantages to the tenant in having a consolidated farm "in severalty", rather than strips scattered through three large fields. But even in these cases there were problems; tenants would claim that the lord was taking more than his fair share of the best land, or a larger portion of the common than his share of the rights entitled him to. Enclosure by pasture, called by its critics "depopulating enclosure" was almost invariably controversial, and often resulted in attempts at fraud or coercion . A customary tenant, holding by copy of court roll, was legally secure and very difficult to shift, unless or until his tenure came up for renewal. The condition of renewal should have been determined by custom, but lords were increasingly (and justifiably) arguing that inflation was making the customary rates unrealistic, and insisting upon enhancement. As the manorial court was the lord's own court such pressure was hard to resist, because although it was possible to appeal against such a judgment to the king in chancery, that course was both difficult and expensive. Similarly the records of manorial courts could conveniently be lost, thus depriving all copyholders of their security. Again this was remediable, but not without time and money. Abuses of this kind were not common but they did occur, and caused a disproportionate outcry because of the increasing demand for holdings. More often landlords were acting strictly within the law because those dispossessed were either tenants at will or demesne tenants who could not, by definition, have any legal security[4]. Such consideration did not, however, pacify either those who felt aggrieved or those who took up cudgels on their behalf.

The so-called "commonwealth men" did not constitute a movement, nor were they an organised group. Some of them such as Hugh Latimer, were strong protestants; others, such as Thomas more or Thomas Starkey, remained loyal to the old faith. What they had in common was a passionate commitment to the Christian doctrine of the stewardship of wealth. It was the responsibility of the rich man to care for his poorer and less fortunate neighbour. Instead they claimed to see around them a conscienceless economic individualism. "It is mine own", they represented the landlords as saying, "and who shall warn me to do with mine own but as myself listeth?" Convinced, as Thomas More put it, that "sheep were eating up men", they launched a savage campaign of invective against the aristocracy and the mercantile community, describing them as

"Men without conscience. Men utterly void of God's fear...
Cormorants, greedy gulls; Yea, men that would eat up men
women and children..."[5]

In fact their economic diagnosis was well wide of the mark. Enclosure had slowed considerably over the previous thirty years, and the real impact of new dispossessions in the 1540s was minor, and geographically limited. However the myth was far more powerful and attractive than the truth, and when it was embraced by the Lord Protector early in 1548 became itself a political factor of great importance.

In his own eyes Somerset was doing no more than his plain duty, The Tudors had always accepted in principle that they should protect the weak against the strong and succour the widow and the orphan. Such action was a part of the burden of kingship, and in 1518 Wolsey, acting on the king's behalf, had established commissions to assess the scale of this particular problem, and provide redress. Those commissions had not established much, but they had sent out the right signals. Somerset believed what his learned and pious friends told him, and he also believed in his ability to succeed where Wolsey had failed. In May 1548 he removed the royal park at Hampton Court, and restored common rights to several villages on the royal estates. This gesture was followed up in the following month with a long proclamation, expressing the evils of excessive grazing, as seen by the commonwealth men, and promising effective action to see the "good old laws" enforced. Shortly after a commission was set up on the same lines as Wolsey's, to investigate the problems in the midlands; and the commission was headed by John Hales, one of the most militant commonwealth crusaders[6]. At first the protector's fellow councillors were willing to indulge his whim, and make conventional disapproving noises. But neither they, nor the other members of the ruling class, were prepared to take serious remedial action which was so directly contrary to their own interests. The real cause of social tension, as some of them realised, was not enclosure but the determination of landlords to secure economic rents for tenements which had been on log leases through a period which had seen prices rise by almost 200%. In the circumstances of the protectorate there was no way in which this legitimate end could be achieved, or even pursued without stoking the paranoid anger against greedy and irresponsible landlords, which was a natural emotion among the rural poor, and which the commonwealth men were doing there best to foster. The appearance of Hales' commission was followed by anti-gentry riots in the same area, and some of the protector's colleagues were quick to make the obvious connection.

The target of this rural anger was not the government, but those who were seen to be obstructing the governments good intentions, the local gentry. However, these men were also the indispensable agents of government, without whom no order could be maintained, and no policy implemented. Rural society was not, of course, simply composed of "peasants" and gentlemen. Each community had a complex hierarchy of wealth and status, from yeomen farmers and substantial craftsmen, such as millers and blacksmiths, through tenant farmers and landless labourers down to the cottagers who squatted on the common, and the vagabonds against whom every respectable mans hand was turned. An increase in this last element, real or imagined, heightened the general sense of insecurity, and in some places provided spare hands ripe for mischief. Although the gentlemen were the manorial lords and commissioners of the peace, the stability of rural communities depended largely upon the attitude of the "secondary leadership", the men of substance below the gentry level who filled such offices as parish and hundred constable or church warden. When, as was normally the case, they supported the magistrates and trouble was confined to the lower orders, it could be contained without difficulty. If, however, they became alienated, and became the leaders of discontent rather than its policemen, then trouble could easily escalate to a dangerous level. One of the most disturbing factors about commonwealth propaganda was that, by blaming the social malaise exclusively upon the gentleman " the great farmers and graziers", it tended to drive a wedge into rural society along this fault line. The consequences were to be seen very conspicuously in Norfolk in 1549.

The nature of an agrarian economy was to be vulnerable to disputes over tenure and changes of land use, just as it was vulnerable to the vagaries of the weather and periodic crop failures. But it was not usually vulnerable to rapid changes in the market, or fluctuations in the trade cycle. Most farming communities looked no further than the local market, but in some parts of England, the Cotswolds and East Anglia in particular, the much maligned sheep lead to another type of economic activity. Spinning and weaving had developed as rural crafts, partly because the raw material was on the spot, and partly to alleviate the problems of unemployment caused by the creation of sheep runs. In such areas rural prosperity was linked not so much to the weather as to the fortunes of England's domestic and overseas cloth trade. During the middle years of the fifteenth century, when agricultural tenants were benefiting from low rents and high security, both the cloth and wool trades were suffering from a severe slump. Exports were running at 57,000 cloths in the early 1440s, but that figure had dropped to 30,000 by 1460. By 1470 a steady recovery had begun which matched the growth of population , and that expansion continued throughout the early sixteenth century, until 1550, the peak year, some 150,000 cloths per annum were leaving the country. Much of the benefit stayed in the towns which controlled the trade, but some percolated down to the rural craftsmen to whom the work was "put out", and should be remembered amid the shrill clamour of the anti-enclosure lobby. There were also other rural industries whose impact upon particular communities was considerable. Iron smelting and gun founding in Sussex and the Weald of Kent, coal mining in Durham and Northumberland, salt panning in Cheshire, tin mining in Cornwall, and a number of others. The towns tried very hard to maintain control over manufacturing industry, and generally the government supported them. In 1536 the ropeworkers of Bridport in Dorset solicited and obtained a statute prohibiting the establishment of ropework outside the boundaries of the town, but some industries were rural in their nature, and in others the freer atmosphere of the countryside offered such clear advantages that no amount of legislation could succeed in checking the drift. The conventional wisdom of the time was that tighter quality controls and more supervision were the remedies for urban decline. As one writer put it

> "...every artificer dwelling out of all towns...should be limited
> to be under the correction of one good town or another, and
> they sell no wares but such as are first approved..." [7]

In seeking to follow such advice, as in accepting the priorities of the commonwealth men, the lord protector was actually defeating his declared objective, which was to protect the poor and contain the rise of vagabondage and crime.

In the 1540s the laments of urban decay were almost as vociferous as the protests against depopulating enclosures, and not very much more justified. Some towns had indeed declined relatively as well as absolutely in terms of population since the fourteenth century. Boston, Kings Lynn and Southampton had lost the bulk of there overseas trade to London. York and Lincoln were also seriously diminished. Bristol had shrunk by about a third, but still remained the third largest town in England. Most of the protests over depopulation and impoverishment were linked to requests for tax relief, and should not therefore be taken as objective assessments of the situation. In fact there were more towns with stable or increasing populations, but they were not drawing attention to the fact, and thereby inviting higher contributions. The most obvious example is London, the only true city in Britain, which had 40-50,000 people in 1450 and about 120,000 by 1550. London controlled almost 90% of the lucrative cloth trade, and was becoming a financial centre of European importance. Its wealth was a major factor in the finances of the crown, and the extreme conservatism of its mercantile establishment was about to be challenged by a rapid expansion of its geographical horizons. Norwich and Exeter were also doing extremely well, the former being the only town apart from London with more than 10,000 inhabitants. Some smaller towns, like Crediton, Reading and Rochester were also doing well, although overseas trade was becoming increasingly concentrated in the capital, several ports were doing well on a thriving coastwise trade, notably Newcastle-upon-Tyne which was growing rich on the increasing demand for sea-cole. The fishing industry had also expanded significantly, brining prosperity to many small harbours which could not hope to attract long distance commerce. This was partly because of a fortuitous migration of herring from the Baltic into the North Sea, but also because of the development of cod fishing on the Newfoundland Banks, which had been one of the benefits from the Atlantic voyages of the late fifteenth century. Early in Henry VIII reign as many as 180 boats had been making the lengthy voyage every year, and although that number had fallen substantially by 1547, there was still a lot of activity. Deep-sea fishing also provided the best possible training ground for master mariners, and that was one of the main reasons why the Council had sought to protect the lenten fast, at a time when so many traditional practices were under attack. There was no particular commercial crisis during the protectorate, and the harvests from 1546 to 1548 were generally good. Both these circumstances should have been conducive to tranquillity in the country side, but by 1548 it was clear that the situation across large parts of southern England was anything but tranquil, and was all set to get considerably worse.

4

Protector Somerset and the Scottish war

Henry VIII had deliberately provoked war against Scotland in 1542. He had recently signed a new agreement with the emperor, and was committed to a joint campaign against France in the summer of 1543. Remembering how James IV had served him in similar circumstances thirty years before, he determined upon a pre-emptive strike. His relations with James V had not been good for some time, because he had completely failed to persuade James to follow his lead against the pope, and the papacy had made much of the king of Scots, hoping to use him against his recalcitrant southern neighbour. In the summer of 1542 Henry began a diplomatic offensive, bombarding the Scots with demands for redress of alleged border grievances, and trying to insist that James came south to meet him, either in London or at York[1]. In return the Scots were conciliatory. They were not looking for a fight, and were prepared to offer reasonable redress, but they were not prepared to commit their king to enter England. Disconcerted, Henry found fault with the redress, and claimed that James was in the pocket of the French. At the end of September, acting on the king's direct orders, the duke of Norfolk launched a destructive week long raid into southern Scotland. James could hardly ignore such blatant provocation. He was a sick man and his authority could easily have been undermined. So he ordered the hasty assembly of 20,000 men, and launched them into the debatable land, north of Carlisle, as a means of retaliation. It soon transpired that he had walked into a trap. His ill-armed and untrained army was confronted at Solway Moss on the 23rd November by a smaller but much more professional English force, and put to flight after a battle that was little more than a skirmish. Casualties were light, but a large number of Scottish noblemen were taken prisoner, and three weeks later James V suddenly died.

His death probably had nothing to do with the battle, but it created a political crisis which played right into Henry's hands. The Scottish crown passed to James's infant daughter Mary, and the king of England immediately perceived an opportunity to establish his ascendancy over the northern kingdom on a long term basis. A marriage between Mary and his own five year old son Edward would lead eventually to a union of the crowns from which England would derive all the major benefits. The northern frontier would cease to exist, and England's superior wealth and population would make her the dominant partner in the union. The Scottish prisoners who had been brought to London after Solway Moss offered a means of effecting this policy, and they were all required to swear an oath to promote the marriage as a condition of their release. Early in 1543 they were allowed to return home, and Henry eagerly anticipated the signing of a treaty before he was bound to turn his attentions to France. He had, however, miscalculated in a rather naive manner. In January the earl of Arran had been appointed regent, and although he could not afford to defy the English, he had every incentive to play for time. Arran was not personally averse to closer ties with England, nor to measures for the reform of the church, but he was well aware that he was losing the patriotic high ground to the clerical party, lead by Cardinal David Beaton, which was also strongly pro-French. At the same time the so-called "assured" Lords, once they were out of Henry's reach, had little incentive to abide by their oaths. Eventually, on the 1st July Scottish envoys signed at Greenwich a treaty embodying the desired royal marriage, but it was soon evident that such undertakings were not worth the paper they were written on. In September 1543 the cardinal's party rose up in rebellion, and after a few days the regent defected to the rebels. In December the Scottish parliament solemnly repudiated all agreements with England and renewed the auld alliance. Henry had not only lost all the advantages of Solway Moss, he had also missed his summer campaign in France while trying to conclude what, from his point of view, was a side show.

What followed became known to the Scots as the "rough wooing". A new pro-English party was scraped together, led by the earl of Lennox, but the dominant tactic became the harrying of the Lowlands. In May 1544 Edinburgh and Leith were sacked by the Earl of Hertford, an exploit which coincided with Henry's last great expedition against France. By the end of the summer Boulogne had been taken, but a solution to the Scottish situation was no nearer. Unfortunately he had also fallen out with his ally the Emperor who had signed the treaty

of Crespy with Francis, and left the English to continue the war on
two fronts without support. Throughout the summer of 1545 Henry
strained every nerve to repel the threatened French invasion and to
mobilise diplomatic support in Europe. The war in Scotland degener-
ated into a constant series of small cross-border raids. Fortunately for
England the Scots were too weak to attempt any significant response,
even with French help, but the policy made absolutely no progress
towards its ostensible objective. Nor did Henry find any diplomatic
support; but he did manage to defeat the French fleet in the Solent and
frustrate the intended invasion. That seems to have persuaded Francis
that there was little point in continuing the struggle, and in June 1546
he signed the treaty of Cercamp, leaving Boulogne, for the time being
at least, in English hands. In the last six months of his life Henry was
at peace with France, and virtually bankrupt, but in the north, there
was unresolved stalemate. The Scottish government, now lead by the
queen mother, Mary of Guise, had successfully fended off the English
marriage at the cost of considerable physical damage, but had not
eliminated the pro-English party - now becoming increasingly associated with religious reform - nor escaped from the threat of renewed
hostilities. Henry was particularly galled and humiliated by his failure
in Scotland, and it is alleged that on his death bed he extracted a
promise from the earl of Hertford that his policy would be pursued to
a successful conclusion.

Whether he had given such an undertaking or not, as lord protector
Somerset quickly began to direct his attention to Scotland. The
combination of a French regent and a Francophile cardinal did not
please all Scotsmen, and in May 1546 a miscellaneous gang of assassins had broken into St. Andrew's castle and murdered the latter.
Occasionally supported by English warships, they were still holding
the castle in the spring of 1547 against a series of feeble campaigns by
the Scottish council. Meanwhile, English pressure on the border began
to build up again. Lords Wharton and Eure, the wardens of the West
and East marches, reinforced their garrisons, and stepped up the raid-
ing activity which was always the borderers' chief occupation and
amusement. Both submitted reports on the state of their fortifications,
and reported anxieties about the movements of French ships. In fact
there were almost no French troops in Scotland at this juncture, but
they were right to be concerned because at the end of June a fleet
under the veteran commander Leo Strozzi evaded the English naval
screen and bombarded St. Andrews castle into surrender. The tangles
of Scottish politics would always leave a few irreconcilables opposed

to whatever government was in power, but the English stock was low in July 1547, in spite of the military build up, which had already begun. Somerset probably intended another major invasion anyway, but the fall of St. Andrews left him with no option if he was to pursue a forward policy. By the end of August preparations had been completed, at an initial cost of over £30,000, and on the 5th September Somerset himself crossed the border north of Berwick at the head of an army of about 12,000 foot and 4000 horse. A powerful fleet under the command of Lord Clinton shadowed his advance along the coast. With no professional troops at his disposal, the earl of Arran called out the Scottish national array, and swiftly assembled some 20,000 foot and 1500 horse. However like the army that had invaded England in 1542, these men were neither well armed nor well trained, and the Scottish artillery was woefully inadequate. On 12th September the two armies came face to face at Pinkie Cleugh, as Arran endeavoured to contest the passage of the Esk, on the approaches to Edinburgh[2].

Unlike Solway Moss, Pinkie was a hard fought battle. Casualties were high particularly on the Scottish side, and Somerset was required to show some of his real quality as a soldier, but the outcome was the same. For the second time in less than a decade Scotland's main field army had been destroyed, but it remained to be seen whether Somerset had benefited from the earlier experience. Henry had been content with an unsecured diplomatic victory which turned out to be worthless. Somerset did not make that mistake. He was rightly unwilling to trust any party in Scotland to do his work for him, and set out to consolidate his military advantage in such a way as to enable him to resume coercive pressure whenever that should prove to be necessary. He lacked the resources to conquer Scotland, and judged that it would be too expensive to mount an army royal every time the regent needed her arm twisting. He therefore decided to set up a series of garrisoned fortresses to control strategic points and access. In the autumn of 1547 the country was virtually defenceless, and the establishment of these garrisons was easy: Inchcolm on the Firth of Forth, Broughty Crag on the Firth of Tay, Roxburgh in the eastern lowlands, and above all Haddington which controlled the centre of the net[3]. There were no major garrisons in the West March, only minor outposts, but Lord Wharton, operating out of Carlisle, was close enough to dominate the whole of Annandale. However, the intended control did not materialise. In spite of the division of the Scottish factions, the environment was generally hostile. Supplies could only be obtained by foraging, which was bitterly resented.   There were no armies to besiege such fortresses, but intermittent and unpredictable harassment sapped the morale of the garrisons, particularly during the hostile northern winter. The captains, such as Lord Grey and Sir Ambrose Dudley, were competent and conscientious, but communications were almost impossible and there was little or no strategic control, except that exercised by the council in London, which was too far off to respond to immediate needs. Bickerings and misunderstandings both amongst the garrisons and between the garrisons and Berwick, were therefore endemic[4].

The French had been completely wrong footed by the speed and success of Somerset's September campaign. He was scarcely in Scotland for two weeks, but by the time the main English force had withdrawn, it was already too late to do anything before the winter closed in. Henry II, who had succeeded his father Francis I in April 1547, was eager to score points off the English, but his main attention was focussed on Boulogne. Mary of Guise could be certain of a sympathetic hearing, but nothing would happen until the spring of 1548, and both sides settled down to make what use they could of the winter deadlock. Somerset's main initiative was propaganda. In February he published, both in Latin and in English, *An Epistle or Exhortation to Unitie and Peace*, in which he outlined in eloquent prose the benefits which would accrue to both sides from an Anglo-Scottish marriage. The names of England and Scotland would disappear, and be replaced by a single Britain; trade would be free, and Scotland would be left with her ancient laws and customs. This was Henry's policy, set out with genuine conviction. English agents in Scotland distributed many copies, and some, such as John Harrison, added treatises of their own; but they might as well have been talking to the mountains. The rough wooing had destroyed the credibility of all such visions, and the Scots spent the winter more profitably undermining the English garrisons. In January negotiations began for a marriage between the Scottish queen and the French dauphin, and French gold began to make itself felt in the alignment of the factions[5].

By March 1548, without any major campaigning, the English position had been seriously weakened. Supplying and reinforcing the garrisons was turning out to be difficult and enormously expensive. The more the garrison did to make its presence felt the harder they were pressed. Inchcolm had to be abandoned and the garrison at Broughty Crag lost control over the neighbouring town of Dundee. Whenever the English made a demonstration of strength, they found no serious opposition, but as soon as these forces were withdrawn the pressure was re-applied. It was scarcely a deliberate policy on the part of the regent, more a reflection of the climate of Scottish politics, but it was extraordinarily effective. Somerset's response was to concentrate his main strength at Haddington and Broughty, and to plan a new major expedition for later in the summer. This latter was, in a way, a confession of failure because the garrisons had been intended to make such major efforts unnecessary. Moreover, before any such plan could be implemented, disaster struck. On 12th June a powerful French fleet was sighted off Dunbar, and before the English could move to intercept, had entered the Firth of Forth and landed 6000 experienced French soldiers at Leith, complete with a formidable artillery train. This force was not large enough on its own to throw the English out of Scotland, but its coming significantly changed the balance of power. By the end of June the French commander, Montalembert, had conducted an assessment of the strategic position, and with significant Scottish support, moved directly to the siege of Haddington. The war then moved into a phase of equilibrium. Haddington was strong, and the garrison was at full strength, moreover Lord Grey was preparing to lead a strong relieving force from Berwick, but Lord Wharton suffered a serious reverse in the west march, and support for the English cause had virtually disappeared, except amongst the more militant protestants.

The most telling blow, however, was diplomatic rather than military. On 7th July the Scots and the French concluded the treaty of Haddington, which not only provided for full military co-operation, but also concluded that Queen Mary should marry the Dauphin Francis as soon as their ages should be convenient. In the meantime Mary was to live, and be educated in France. By the end of the month she had left her homeland, and was not to return for thirteen years. This move left Somerset's Scottish policy in ruins. The treaty of Greenwich was not only dead but definitely buried, and the logical course would have been for him to cut his losses, concentrating English strength on the defence of a border which now seemed likely to be hostile for many years. However, the protector was not motivated by logic, and may well have believed that the growing strength of protestantism in Scotland meant that the situation was not beyond redemption. In August 1548 he launched a strong force under the earl of Shrewsbury into the east march, which temporarily raised the siege of Haddington, but accomplished nothing else of note. In deciding to continue the war, Somerset may have been listening to his few remaining Scottish allies, or he may have been placing rather too much emphasis upon the anti-French riots which broke out in and around Edinburgh in the autumn of 1548. These caused considerable embarrassment to both governments, but were suppressed without undue difficulty. To justify his decision he abandoned the idealism of twelve months before, and reverted to the ancient English claim of suzerainty, thus casting doubt on the integrity of the whole policy which had been pursued since 1542 - or as the Scots would have said, revealing his true colours.

By the beginning of 1549 all the remaining garrisons were beleaguered, and only another major invasion could retrieve the situation. On 1st May the experienced Lord Grey was replaced as warden of the east march by the young and totally inexperienced Henry Manners, earl of Rutland. Grey had been clamouring to retire for some time, but the choice of Manners as his replacement is a mystery, unless it was felt that the prestige of his rank was needed, and that he would accept guidance from his experienced captains. In the event Rutland did reasonably well in containing the problems of his command. Another general levy was summoned for 20th May, but the intended expedition never took place. Although Somerset pressed on with his preparations in spite of the mounting evidence of disorder in southern England, eventually the much need troops had to be diverted to Devon and East Anglia. By then all the outposts in the west march, and several of the garrison fortresses in the east, such as Jedburgh and Home, had fallen to Franco-Scottish assaults[6]. By September the position of Haddington had become untenable, and it was evacuated. Although a handful of garrisons remained, by the time that he fell from power in October 1549, Somerset's Scottish policy had collapsed in total failure, at a cost to the English exchequer of over £580,000.

5

Protector Somerset and the Privy Council

The original intention of the protectorate had been to provide leadership for the regency council, and a single focus for the formal processes of government. In the official record of the 31st January 1547 it was stipulated that the office was being created

> "...with this special and expresse condicion, that he shall nat do any Acte but with thadvise and consent of the reste of the coexecutors in suche maner, ordre and fourme as is in the saide wille of our saide late Souveraigne Lorde...apoynted and prescribed."[1]

On the 3rd March, however, the main responsibility for the conduct of affairs was transferred to the lord protector, who, although still bound to consult the council was no longer constrained by its consent, and moreover was given specific authority to nominate such persons as he might choose to be privy councillors. On the 24th December 1547 these letters patent were confirmed in an even more permissive spirit. On that day ten councillors, that is the "moste part of the hole Nombre" of the original executors, relinquished the council's right to even advise on matters of policy. The fullness of power, which Somerset was accused in October 1549 of having abused, had therefore been given to him in due form by those very colleagues who accused him of the abuse. At the time of his fall it was said that he had broken an oath made in open council that he would "do nothing touching the state of thaffairs of his highness without thadvise and consent of the rest of the council". What was not said was that the oath had been taken between 31st January and 12th March 1547, and could therefore fairly have been said to have been superseded by the two subsequent patents. However, to establish that the protector was entitled to make important decisions himself, without taking advice does not necessarily mean that he was wise to do so. The history of Somerset's relations with the council is therefore more a question of his wisdom and political style than of his constitutional obligations.

A king took the advice of his councillors as and when he pleased. Their oaths were taken to him individually, and his alone was the responsibility for making all policy decisions. Part of Somerset's problem was that he tended to forget that he was not the king, and that although he might have the same responsibility for making decisions, he did not have the same immunity from criticism, because the counsellor's oaths were not sworn to him but to their young lord. It took some time for this discontent to develop, because every one was dealing tentatively with an unfamiliar situation. Until the end of May 1547 it appears that the council register contains a full and reasonably accurate account of the business transacted, allowing for the fact that many important and confidential matters would not have been minuted anyway[2]. The signatures of the councillors on each page attest to their actual presence at the place and time stated. After 1st June, however, the practice seems to have changed. Minutes were still kept, but the signatures become mere formal endorsements, sometimes added much later, and although it can be assumed that the business recorded was transacted, it was not necessarily on the days alleged, and not necessarily in the presence of any of the signatories. After 1st January 1548 signatures of any kind become rare, and it is probable that the council book was used as a formal record of business which was transacted in other places, and that council meetings in the proper sense virtually ceased. This conclusion is supported by the numerous memoranda and letters of advice which Somerset received from Sir William Paget, his old ally and confidant. Throughout 1548 Paget's communication assume that the protector is making all important decisions himself. There is scarcely a mention of the council, until a very revealing letter of 25th December, when criticisms were evidently building up in an audible and potentially dangerous way. Paget reminded Somerset that consulting the council was a useful way of finding out what other people felt about policies before they were decided upon, and thus anticipating adverse reactions. He was probably pointing out as tactfully as possible that the protector was getting out of touch with the political nation, something which not even a monarch could afford to do.

"...appoint us of the counsaile", he begged, "to attend upon

your grace and discharge us of forreyne offices in
particular to thintent we maye be thabler to assist your
grace for the over sight of the hole in generall..."[3]

Paget's advice was heeded up to a point. Council meetings did resume
although how regularly is not clear. They did not, however, transact
much in the way of business, because Paget continued to remind the
protector of important unresolved matters which would have been
automatically put on the agenda had a proper procedure been followed. Somerset's highly individual, not to say autocratic style did not
preclude consultation altogether; but like many kings, he tended to
talk only to those who agreed with him. Unwelcome advice tended to
be ignored. His critics later claimed that "he ordered the matters as
pleased himself refusing to here any mans reason but his own", which
would of course have been the unquestioned prerogative of the
monarch. Perhaps because it did not matter very much to him, Somerset's handling of the composition of the council tended to be conservative and low key. Henry's original regency council had included no
lord treasurer because the office was vacant at the time of his death,
but the lord chamberlain, normally a counsellor, was excluded, as was
one of the two principal secretaries. The chief officers of the
household were distinctly (and unusually) under represented. Within
the first weeks, before his patent of 3rd March, Somerset had brought
about the removal of the lord chancellor, and secured the admission of
his brother, Lord Thomas Seymour, who was also appointed lord
admiral. The office of Lord Treasurer he assumed himself. Over the
next fifteen months there were a number of changes, but they did not
adhere to any consistent pattern. Lord St. John held the great seal as
lord keeper from March to October, when Richard, Lord Rich became
chancellor. Rich had not been an original councillor. The earl of
Arundel, the lord chamberlain, Sir John Gage, the controller of the
Household, and Sir Thomas Cheney, the treasurer were added,
restoring normal household membership. Arundel and Gage were both
religious conservatives, and Gage was replaced as controller by Paget
in June 1547, losing his place on the council. Other additions were
William Parr, marquis of Northampton, Sir William Petre, the other
principal secretary, Sir Anthony Wingfield, the vice-chamberlain, and
Sir Thomas Smith, appointed to a third secretaryship in April 1548.
Apart from Wriothesley, two others were also dropped, Sir Thomas
Bromley and Nicholas Wotton, the latter because he was almost
permanently abroad on diplomatic missions. On this basis it

could certainly not be claimed that Somerset was packing the council. With the exception of Northampton all those appointed held offices which normally carried council membership. Northampton, Smith and Wingfield had protestant sympathies, but Arundel and Petre did not. In terms of membership the protector's dealings with the council were punctiliously correct; perhaps he took the view that it did not much matter who he was choosing to ignore.

In spite of his sympathy with the protector's policies, Northampton did not survive long as a councillor, being dropped after a major matrimonial scandal in January 1548. Sir Anthony Brown died in May, and Sir Edward Montague was excluded at some indeterminate point in the second half of 1548. With the council registers in such an unsatisfactory state during this period, it is not always easy to tell who was supposed to be attending. Two other names also disappear before the end of 1548; Sir Edward Wotton, whose office as treasurer of Calais probably kept him out of the country most of the time, and Cuthbert Tunstall, the aged and conservative bishop of Durham. Tunstall certainly opposed Somerset, both over religion and over Scotland, but there is no record of his having been officially excluded. During this period two new councillors were also added; Sir John Baker, a financial expert and Sir Ralph Sadler, a diplomat who had spent much time in Edinburgh. In January 1549 the earl of Southampton was quietly re-admitted, along with the earl of Shrewsbury, who was presumably being rewarded for his good services in Scotland. At the same time the lord admiral, Thomas Seymour, was expelled in dramatic circumstances. The protector's brother had been a difficult colleague from the start, not because he disagreed with official policy but because he was bitterly jealous. A man of considerable charm, his ambitions far outran his abilities. He believed that he should have been made governor of the king's person. A barony and the office of lord admiral were no consolation , and he embarked upon a clumsy and ill-concealed campaign to undermine the potector's authority. In July 1547 he secretly married the queen dowager, Catherine Parr, a match which his brother strongly opposed, but which Seymour had succeeded in persuading the young king to bless. In the autumn he excused himself from commanding the fleet against Scotland, and his place was taken by Lord Clinton. During 1548 he was suspected of colluding with some of the pirates whose activities he was supposed to suppress, and his corrosive relations with Somerset deteriorated still further. Finally in September 1548 Catherine died in childbirth, and Seymour began an even riskier venture, aimed at capturing the hand of princess Elizabeth.

This *coup* he planned to achieve using the same means that he had used to secure his previous marriage, the personal endorsement of the king. Edward was eleven by this time; old enough to feel his own importance, and to resent the tutelage to which his minority confined him. He was particularly resentful of the tight financial control imposed by Sir Michael Stanhope, Somerset's choice as principal gentleman of the privy chamber. Seymour recruited the services of John Fowler, one of the grooms, and began to feed Edward small sums of money for his personal pleasure. Acting sometimes on information received from Fowler, he began to lurk about the privy chamber uninvited apparently hoping to secure unsupervised access to the king. He was even incautious enough to observe on one visit that security was so slight that the king could easily be abducted[4]. By December 1548 his actions and words were becoming so reckless that they could not be ignored. He publicly opposed the granting of his brother's new patent, and talked about getting the protectorate annulled by parliament. It was also rumoured that he was collecting a substantial armoury at Sudeley Castle, and some form of action against him became inevitable. At the beginning of January 1549 Sir William Sharrington, the vice-treasurer of the Bristol mint, was arrested on charges of illegally diverting bullion, and an investigation revealed that most of the profit from this abuse had been channelled to Seymour to finance his conspiracy. On 17th January he was arrested, and an extensive enquiry into his activities commenced. What emerged was evidence of extensive subversion and abuse of office, but not necessarily amounting to treason. The protector was caught in a very difficult situation, because if he failed to act effectively he would be accused of favouring his kindred, while if he allowed his brother to be put on trial he could end up being charged with fratricide. Eventually he decided to proceed by act of attainder, probably to distance himself as much as possible from the whole distressing business. Seymour was condemned at the end of March 1549 and executed almost immediately. In spite of all precautions this decision rebounded upon Somerset, and added to the increasing difficulties from which he was suffering as the year advanced[5].

Before his fall in October the protector made a few further amendments to the composition of the council but again several of them are hard to fix in terms of date. Having sorted out his marriage, the marquis of Northampton re-joined some time before July. Sir William Herbert and Lord Wentworth were also recruited and Sir

Anthony Denny died during September. As Professor Hoak has pointed out, Somerset changed the composition of the council by about 30% during his two and a half years in power, but seems to have had nothing that could be construed as a policy, even in the early days when he was making orthodox use of its services. Formally the council related to the protector in the same way as royal council normally related to the king, but in reality it became merely a facade . This was not so much because Somerset was making all the decisions himself as because he was using alternative methods of control and consultation; the privy chamber to control the court and his own personal council for advice. Change in the privy chamber was slow, perhaps because at first he did not appreciate its potentiality. When the king was a child the old hub of the court seemed to have lost its significance. Apart from the addition of the king's tutors and the introduction of his brother in law, Sir Michael Stanhope, Somerset made few changes before the autumn of 1547. He did take steps to secure control of the kings privy coffers, but apart from that Denny retained control of what appeared to be a political backwater. However in August 1547 preparations for the Scottish war took a number of officers away from the household, and this led to significant reorganisation. Stanhope replaced Denny as chief gentleman, and took over the administration of the privy coffers; and members of Somerset's own household were moved in to take up the vacant offices. By the end of 1548 Stanhope had become, in fact although not in name, Governor of the king's person. With the withdrawal of the Earl of Arundel from the court he also became *de facto* lord chamberlain. The point of all this, of course, was that the king was beginning to grow up, and it was vital for Somerset's future security that he should grow up surrounded by the protector's servants and friends.

Unfortunately for him, Somerset was not particularly well served in this respect. Stanhope's regime was austere and unfriendly, providing an opening for Lord Seymour's blandishments and alienating the affections of the young king. The protector referred to himself in public as the king's "entirely beloved uncle", but there is good reason to believe that Edward did not see him in that light. John Cheke was a more congenial soul, and equally committed to Somerset's interests, but he was only one of the king's tutors and it is difficult to assess his influence. Although he perceived its importance, the protector did not devote enough personal attention to either the king or the court, and when he was seriously challenged the formal ascendancy which he established there turned out to be extremely vulnerable. The protector's private council is harder to assess. Apart from Stanhope the only member to obtain office was Sir Thomas Smith, who became third secretary in 1549. The others who can be clearly identified were William Cecil, John Thynne, Richard Whalley and Edward Wolf. Cecil and Thynne were both men of ability, but none were men of substance, who could realistically replace the privy council as a source of political wisdom. When it came to the point, thanks largely to his own manner of conducting himself, Somerset had only servants and agents rather than friends. Estranged from his former allies, Dudley and Paget, only Archbishop Cranmer was willing eventually to protect him from the consequences of his own folly.

It has been rightly said that the protector's main weakness was his temperament[6]. In securing power he showed energy and good political judgment, but in wielding it he was arrogant, abrasive and insensitive. Nowhere is this more apparent then in his dealings with the council. The council granted him his office in January 1547, and extended his powers both in March and December, and yet he persistently ignored the fact that he needed their support. He may or may not have needed their advice, but he certainly needed their consent. Even Henry VIII needed the consent, not only of his council but also of his parliament, to give force to some of his more controversial decisions. The council did not only exist to advise, it was an executive instrument, and if properly selected it also spoke, in a manner for the political nation. Somerset's selection policy was sound enough, but he did not want his councillors to tell him what he did not want to hear - that some of his policies were mistaken, and some were unenforcable. "Maugre the Devil self love and private profit, it shall go forward..." he said of one of his pet ideas, and that might almost stand as his political epitaph. Liberal in the modern sense Somerset certainly was not, and whether he was an idealist is controversial, but because he lacked that instinctive grasp of the possible which is essential in all effective leaders, most of his policies failed. In the summer of 1549 there were others who were prepared to profit from his mistakes.

6

The Foreign policy of the Protectorate

At the beginning of 1547 England was not well provided with friends. Only with Scotland was there open war, but the peace with France was uneasy. The French were concerned about English aggression in the north, and unreconciled to the loss of Boulogne. This relationship became more tense after the accession of Henry II in April, because he was not committed to his father's treaty, and hesitated before ratifying "the amity" which officially existed between the countries. The Emperor did not at first even return the greetings which were sent to him in the name of the new king, not willing to recognise a regime of which he did not approve until it was clear that nothing better was on offer. No such greetings were sent to the pope, and he was therefore the first to realise that the new English government intended to carry on where the old one had left off. Paget had already presented the council with a succinct and realistic appraisal of the international situation some months before Henry's death, suggesting that the best remedy for the potential hostility of France lay in the delicate course of trying to maintain good relations with both the Emperor and the German protestants[1]. Venice might also constitute a useful longstop, especially as the hostility of Rome could be taken for granted. Unsurprisingly, given Paget's influence in the early months of the reign, this course was followed. The German protestants, however, quickly turned out to be a broken reed. Already at war with the Emperor in the winter of 1546-7, the Schmalkaldic League was destroyed in the battle of Muhlburg in April, and although this did not go anywhere near destroying Lutheranism within the Empire, it meant that the surviving princes and cities kept a very low profile for several years, and were not interested in provocative foreign alliances. Charles, on the other hand, far from being triumphant, knew perfectly well that he needed a period of peace to consolidate his victory. His first priority was the security of his own dominions, and the religious settlement which he endeavoured to impose, the Interim, needed time and patient diplomacy if it was to be accepted. The last thing he needed was the triumphalism of Pope Paul III, urging him to trample on the serpent's head, and to seize the golden opportunity offered by Henry's death to restore the heretical realm of England to the fold.

Paul denounced the Interim, and Charles informed the papal nuncio that he never again wished to have the pope as an ally. Consequently the Emperor's instinctive hostility to the new regime in England was modified by political realism and his own priorities. The situation was also eased from the English point of view by Paul's attempt in March 1547 to move the council of Trent to Bologna. This was ostensibly because of an outbreak of the plague in the northern city, but Charles suspected an attempt to impose stronger papal control, and refused to allow the Imperial bishops to move. As a result the council was suspended soon after, and the threat of concerted catholic action against the dissident states receded even further. Somerset was well served by his resident ambassadors with the Emperor, Thomas Thirlby and Sir Philip Hoby, who were both intelligent and tactful in what was often a difficult position. The Imperial ambassador in England, Francois Van der Delft, was almost certainly right when he reported in 1549 that friendship with the Emperor was the cornerstone of English policy. However the difficulties did not go away. Charles soon accepted that his cousin and protege, princess Mary, was not going to make a bid for the crown in 1547, but he continued to regard himself as responsible for her spiritual welfare, and when she came under pressure to accept the book of common prayer in 1549, Van der Delft was quick to leap to her defence:

> "He (the protector) might well suppose, I said, That your Majesty and the king of the Romans would be displeased if she was either openly or indirectly pressed to change her religion; for as I told him before I knew well that even if she were wholly inclined to change, your Majesty would look for means of preventing her..."[2]

Somerset was prepared to give private undertakings, but not to issue a formal dispensation[3]. He was constrained to accept both the insult and this blatant interference in the domestic affairs of the realm in the interests of the much needed alliance. His restraint was justified, but not generously rewarded. Charles was willing to abide by the treaty he had signed with Henry VIII in 1543, but not to enter into any new undertakings. This meant that he would be bound to come to Eng land's assistance if the French attempted to invade, or if they attacked Calais, but not if they confined themselves to attempts to recover Boulogne. Over two years of persistent effort failed to persuade him to change his mind on this point, and so the "new conquest" remained unprotected by any Imperial guarantee.

Charles was not looking for a confrontation with Henry, any more than he was looking for a conflict with England. The strategic duchy of Milan had reverted to his control on the death of Charles of Orleans in 1545, and he knew perfectly well that Henry would seize upon the smallest pretext in an endeavour to regain control. It was partly to give the French no excuse to resume hostilities that he refrained from offering the English any safeguard for Boulogne. Henry was not slow to read these signs. However anxious he may have been to secure Milan, he knew that he could only do so at the cost of a hugely expensive war, which his exchequer could not sustain. Moreover with the German protestants in disarray and useless as allies, the time was not opportune. England, on the other hand, appeared weak, and once it became clear that the Emperor would stand aside, the recovery of Boulogne looked increasingly feasible. Lord Grey, in command there, had expected to be attacked as soon as the news of Henry's death was confirmed, but his reaction was premature. Francis had only been concerned to negotiate exact limits to the Boulogne "pale", and that negotiation was nearing completion when he died. As dauphin the new king had been notorious for his anglophobia, and within a week of his accession the English ambassador in Paris had sent in a perceptive and ominous appraisal of his likely policies[4]. Nicholas Wotton was probably the ablest diplomat to serve Edward abroad, but he confessed himself to be baffled by the new situation. Virtually all the men he had been accustomed to dealing with over the past three years had been swept from office. In spite of a hopeful plea for recall, Somerset decided to keep Wotton at his post, and he was right to do so. Henry, Wotton warned, was militarily ambitious and was dominated by two forces, neither of them known for their moderation, the duke of Guise and his notorious mistress, Diane de Poitiers. Both Boulogne and Scotland were high on his agenda.

Somerset was not always very good at acting on advice from abroad, or even paying due attention to foreign affairs. He had forgotten to inform the English resident in Venice of the king's accession for over five months. However his response to Wotton's despatch was prompt and purposeful. This was partly because the warning about Scotland suited his own priorities, and his first reaction was a letter to the north warning the march wardens to prepare against any raids which the Scots might launch in support of their allies. The fortification of Boulogne was resumed, although this meant sacrificing the treaty that had just been negotiated. Henry, it was assumed, would not in any case have ratified it . A immediate attack on Calais was also feared, and contingency plans were made to pull back the outlying garrisons. At the same time Lord Cobham at Guisnes, was instructed to refrain from any unneccessary provocation. Nevertheless rumour and bluff were more in evidence than action as the summer of 1547 advanced. Somerset justified his intention to move against Scotland in conversation with the Imperial ambassador, not on account of its failure to honour the treaty of Greenwich, but in order to pre-empt an expected French takeover. Imperial sources were also reporting that 4000 French troops had been sent to Scotland at the end of June. Both were exaggerating French aggressiveness for their own purposes, and when Somerset did march north in September he found no significant French presence. It was several months before Henry was in a position to respond. Consequently in the autumn of 1547 Anglo-French relations took a fairly low place on the agenda. Apart from Scotland Paget, acting on the protector's behalf, was mainly preoccupied with a rumbling controversy with the regent of the Netherlands. Mary of Hungary was a powerful woman, and the Emperor's deteriorating health meant that she often had an important voice in Imperial policy[5]. In 1547 she had taken up cudgels on behalf of a number of Flemish merchants who had grievances against the English government. Paget, however, was under pressure from English commercial interests not to concede too much, as they had their own agenda of grievances. Fortunately Paget's relations with the regent were good, and the dispute was substantially resolved without causing any further damage to Anglo-Imperial relations. Such wrangles were endemic because of the importance of the London/Antwerp trade to both parties, and the English government was vulnerable to both sides because of its dependence upon the financial services of the city of London.

Somerset's victory at Pinkie had surprised the French considerably. England was stronger than Henry had supposed, and the question of Boulogne therefore required more thought and preparation than he suspected. He was also mistrustful of the Emperor's apparent inactivity. If he found himself committed to a hard campaign in the north, as opposed to a lightning strike could he trust Charles not to take advantage of his preoccupation? On the other hand Scottish resilience and the forceful pleas of Mary of Guise meant that he could not only find considerable leverage in the north, but he had the perfect justification for doing so. In February and March 1548 he began to mobilise. Wotton reported evident preparation for war, and troop musters which might be intended for Scotland, Boulogne and Calais. There were rumours that Gaspard de Coligny had intelligence contacts within the Boulogne garrison, and the commander on the spot became nervous and despondent. In May Sir John Bridges reported that a powerful French force was encamped only a short distance away, and that his outer defence works were in no state to resist serious assault. Somerset took all these representations with a pinch of salt. He was convinced, as he told Van der Delft, that the main French effort that summer would be in Scotland, and that any attack on Boulogne would be no more than a diversion. At the same time he asked for permission to recruit 2000 German mercenaries. The Emperor refused, on the grounds of his "amity" with the king of France, but secret instructions were issued not to impede the English agents, and the men were raised. They were to be important in 1549, but not in the way that the Emperor had envisaged. As it happened, the protector was correct in his estimate of the military situation, but this did not enable him to confront it effectively, there was no serious attack on Boulogne, and he was able to commit his main military force to the north, but this did not enable him to defeat the French in Scotland.

In spite of his success in the treaty of Haddington, Henry was by no means happy with his progress at the beginning of 1549. He was no nearer to obtaining Boulogne, and the Scottish involvement was proving unexpectedly expensive. The scandal surrounding the fall of the protector's brother appeared to offer at least a prospect of advantage. De Selve, his ambassador in London was instructed to investigate. Did Lord Seymour have any significant support? Was there any possibility of making capital out of a factional conflict within the English council? When Seymour's execution failed to produce any measurable reaction, Henry considered cancelling all further support for Scotland, and signing a truce over Boulogne. This despondent mood passed, however, as it became clear that the protector was in increasing difficulties. Having seriously underestimated English strength in 1547, the king was now in danger of making the opposite mistake. Paget had already urged Somerset to abandon the Bill of Uniformity going through parliament in January, on the grounds that it would stir up uneccessary contention at a time when the need above all was for unity in the face of foreign threats. Such a course would also have the additional advantage of conciliating the Emperor, whose friendship had never been more necessary. There were also ominous rumblings of social discontent in Suffolk, Norfolk, Kent, Wiltshire, and many other southern and midland shires[6]. The gentry and aristocracy would soon be urgently needed at home to preserve order; so it would be best to abandon the parliament altogether as soon as it had voted supply, and concentrate on building up good relations with the Habsburgs. Somerset agreed that such a relationship was necessary, but was not disposed to make the sacrifices that Paget deemed necessary. The Uniformity Bill duly became an act, replacing the traditional mass with a new order of service from Whitsun, and parliament was not prorogued until 14th March.

Somerset was probably right in calculating that the Act of Uniformity would not make much difference to the Emperor's appreciation of the international situation, but he seriously underestimated the threat of civil disorder. Had Henry not also been rethinking his options the crisis might have arrived sooner. As it was the protector was given three months to dig himself out of trouble. He failed for a variety of reasons. In the first place Charles resisted all blandishments when it came to including Boulogne in the Anglo-Imperial treaty; and secondly Somerset remained so wedded to defending his interests in Scotland that he allowed disturbances in East Anglia and the south west to get out of hand. By July it had become clear that order could only be restored by abandoning all ambitions in Scotland, and moving powerful forces of mercenaries to assist Lord Russell in Devon and the earl of Warwick in Norfolk. By delaying so long the protector made his position appear to be even worse than it really was. The borders appeared to be denuded of troops, but that was not in fact the case, and different tactics might have left the English position in Scotland with at least a shred of credibility. At the same time rebellion sent Henry the signal he had been looking for. The English government was now in such deep trouble that the re-conquest of Boulogne would be a mere formality. On the 8th August he declared war.

Coligny had probed the defences of Boulogne several times earlier in the year, in actions which were officially disowned but privately encouraged. He had suffered a number of casualties and had discovered no exploitable weakness, but when the declaration of war permitted a more robust approach, he soon began to make progress. The English garrisons were at full strength, but the German mercenaries soon proved to be unreliable. Softened up with French money a large number of them surrendered on demand, leaving three of the outer defences, Ambleteuse, Newhaven and Blackness untenable. They had all fallen by the end of August. Sir Henry Palmer then withdrew the garrison of Bolemberg into the main fortress, leaving the whole of the Pale in French hands. He was recalled and severely reprimanded, but the damage had been done. Nevertheless Boulogne itself held out. Coligny attempted to take the harbour, and failed, so that the garrison continued to be supplied from the sea. What had at first looked like being the quick campaign Henry had hoped for had, by the end of September turned into a regular siege. Plague broke out in the French camp, driving away the king, who had come in anticipation of a triumphant entry, and he again began to have second thoughts about proceeding. A long siege would not only be expensive, but it might also tempt the emperor to abandon his position of neutrality. However, before discretion could overcome his valour news arrived that Protector Somerset had fallen from power, and there was a reasonable prospect that England would be paralysed for some time by a domestic power struggle. The siege of Boulogne went on.

7

Printing and Publishing

Book production was primarily a commercial operation. The earliest printers had worked, like the scriveners before them, to commissions from particular patrons, but by 1500 it had become normal to publish speculatively, for stock. Books were produced in short runs of 200-500 copies and sold over the counter, either by the publishers themselves, or by a new type of middleman, the bookseller. The accounts of the Oxford bookseller John Dorne for 1520 give an interesting glimpse of the variety of works which were then on offer to an educated public, as well as some idea of the prices and level of demand. Apart from the very first, William Caxton, most of the early printers to work in England were French or Flemish, and in 1483 they were given statutory exemptions from the trading restrictions which normally prevented foreigners from setting up their businesses in English towns. Apart from intermittent operations in Oxford and Cambridge, and the occasional appearance of individual printers elsewhere, English publication was concentrated in London. By the 1530s the native printers were sufficiently numerous, and sufficiently well organised, to begin to cut back on the privileges of the foreign masters, and in 1534 the statute of 1483 was repealed. Before that time the controversies surrounding the printers had been almost entirely commercial, but thereafter the appearance of Lutheran polemic and the passions aroused by the king's Great Matter added an entirely new dimension to the trade. Before 1520 the majority of books printed in England fell into a few broad categories. There were technical treatises - "how to do it" books - works of piety and edification, tales and romances, and liturgical books. Demand for the latter was very heavy but before 1534 the great majority were imported, partly because there were not enough printers in England, and partly because the workmanship of Antwerp or Paris was alleged to be superior[1].

The first use of printing for what might be described as a propaganda purpose was the issuing of Henry VIII's *Assertio Septem*

Sacramentorum in 1521 by Richard Pynson. Nevertheless by 1525 the ecclesiastical authorities were becoming nervous. Germany was by that time awash with printed pamphlets and short tracts, known as *flugschriften*, mostly attacking the church and promoting the ideas of Martin Luther. These ephemera were essentially directed at a German readership, and they made no impact in England, but some copies of Luther's more substantial works were imported, and the idea could easily have been infectious. In 1524 bishop Cuthbert Tunstall of London was sufficiently concerned to summon all the printers and booksellers in London and deliver a solemn warning against dealing in heretical books. He then imposed his own licensing system to control both imports and home products. For the time being the London printers do not seem to have been interested in this hazardous trade; presumably they judged that the demand was too small to justify the risk. However the situation began to change with the appearance of William Tyndale's English translation of the New Testament. This was published at Worms in 1526, and imported in large quantities. It soon became a best seller, and was followed over the next few years by a number of protestant polemical works in English by George Joye, John Frith, William Barlow, and a number of others. By 1530 the English were clearly acquiring a taste for controversial literature, and the government stepped in to support the church. A proclamation in June of that year set up the first index of prohibited books, and placed control in the hands of the council[2]. At first the problem was largely confined to imports from abroad, and under Thomas More's chancellorship several traffickers were caught and executed.

After More's resignation in 1532, however, the atmosphere began to change. Heretical works were still prohibited, but catholic polemic attacking the king's divorce now joined them on the index, and vernacular scripture was no longer frowned upon. Between 1535 and 1541 fourteen editions of all or part of the bible in English came off the London presses, and under Thomas Cromwell's protection theologically suspect works by Tyndale and Joye were openly printed and allowed to circulate. Cromwell's fall was followed by a reaction. The English bible was never withdrawn, but the production of new editions fell off dramatically. Strong protestants like John Hooper and John Bale withdrew to Germany, and such books as *The Image of Both Churches* were produced in Antwerp. As Henry's reign drew to a close control relaxed a little, and a work by George Joye attacking Gardiner was one of the surprising pieces to find its way onto the open market. Henry had, of course, a positive use for the press, and much of his own propaganda was published, particularly after 1535. A royal printer was appointed to be the principal agent for this material, and a system of royal licences or patents was also established to promote work which the king believed to be beneficial. The possession of such a patent was a lucrative privilege, and also breached the control which the London stationers' company was beginning to establish over the industry[3]. By 1547 the council had already noticed that the issue or withdrawal of patents was a useful way of keeping the stationers' company in line. The patentees were used particularly for the production of large quantities of primers and service books, while articles and injunctions for royal visitations and such manuals of orthodoxy as *The King's Book* of 1543 were issued by the king's printer.

The advent of the protectorate in 1547 did not bring any immediate change to the law, but it transformed the climate in which it was administered. Works of a specifically protestant character, such as Heinrich Bullinger's *Two Epistles* and John Calvin's *A Faythful and most Godly Treatise* began to appear in ever increasing numbers, while Richard Smith was compelled to recant "popish" doctrine at Paul's cross in May 1547, and to burn copies of his *Defence of the Blessed Mass*, which had been published in the previous year. New A.B.C.s replaced the old primers and fifteen new editions of the English bible appeared over the space of five years. There is no doubt that, given the chance, the reformers were much more prolific authors than their opponents. In 1539-40, the last year of Cromwell's ascendancy, 125 titles had been published in London, while in 1540-41 the total had fallen to 42, the difference being almost entirely accounted for by the disappearance of religious works of a reforming nature. At the beginning of Edward VI's reign a similar thing happened. In 1546-7 about 100 titles appeared; in 1548-9 this had shot up to 225, and the number of presses in operation had risen from 25 to 39[4]. This was partly because Londoners who were free of other companies were seeking to take advantage of the buoyant market, and partly because the Godly in the city were willing to welcome refugee craftsmen from the continent, temporarily overcoming their natural exclusiveness. The Dutch printers Stephen Mierdman and Giles Van der Erve, who had been publishing English protestant works for some time in the Netherlands, moved their base of operations to London. The peak of this brotherly euphoria had passed by 1550, when traditional suspicions began to reassert themselves and the market began to show signs of saturation. In spite of the continuing advance of protestantism the number of titles began to fall back, and in 1552 had returned approximately to the level of 1547.

This did not necessarily mean that the trade had become less profitable, and significantly the number of presses in operation hardly went down at all. The excitement of polemical freedom had, however, partly given way to the bread and butter business of providing for a new establishment. Thousands of copies of Cranmer's *Homilies* and of the English order of communion, issued in 1548, were printed and sold although the latter had been superseded in a year by the first *Book of Common Prayer*. At least 20,000 copies of the latter were issued, and that was in turn superseded in 1552. There was no longer any import trade in liturgical works, the whole rich variety of missals, breviaries, psalters, primers, manuals and processionals having been consigned to the bonfire. All this spelled good profits to the London printers, and it is not surprising that they continued to take on more workmen. The reformation, however, did not advance swiftly enough for some of its more ardent protagonists, and from the beginning of the reign there was a fringe of radical polemic which did not meet with official approval. Most of this was published clandestinely, with bogus, and even joking colophons such as "H. Lufte, Wittenburg" or "Hans Hitprick". Some of the printers responsible were probably established craftsmen, such as John Day and William Sheres, who were known to have radical sympathies; others may well have been pirates, operating with borrowed or stolen type. In spite of this annoyance, the protector made little effort to catch or punish those responsible, although some of them may have been proceeded against under the statute against revilers of the sacrament. The encouraging atmosphere of these years also prompted a revival of out of London publishing, something which more rigorous regimes discouraged because it was harder to control. In addition to Oxford and Cambridge, short lived presses also appeared in Canterbury, and at Ipswich where John Oswen printed scurrilous anti-catholic tracts such as John Ramsey's *Plaster for a galled horse* without incurring any penalties. A second printer, Anthony Skolker also operated at Ipswich, which was one of the most important protestant centres outside London. Skolker specialised particularly in the publication of translations, and he and Oswen between them produced some thirteen or fourteen English versions of works by Calvin, Melanchthon, Oecolampadius, and others. It must be remembered that at this stage protestantism was still largely imported. Under Cromwell's protection there had been some attempt to give the new doctrines an English face by permitting the publication of old Lollard works such as *The Lantern of Lyght* (1535). Less dangerously reforming propagandists also pointed out that their criticisms of the clergy were by no means unprecedented. The author of *A proper dyaloge betwene a getillman and a husbandman* wrote

> "For here agaynst the clergye can not bercke
> Sayenge as they do / thys is anew werke
> Of heretykes contryved lately
> And by this treatyse it apperyth playne
> That before oure dayes men dyd compleyne
> Agaynst clerckes ambycyon so stately."[5]

At a later date English reforming writers such as John Bale and John Foxe were to argue that the overthrow of antichrist, which they celebrated in their own day, had begun in the fourteenth century with John Wycliffe and his Lollard followers, "...who begat Hus, who begat Luther, who begat truth". Several Lollard works had also been printed abroad in the fifteen thirties and forties, but it was not until the later part of Mary's reign that protestantism really began to acquire an English identity. Ironically, that was less through an effort of their own than because catholicism, in a persecuting and intolerant mode, began to be associated with the interference of foreigners in the shape of King Philip and his advisers[6]. Throughout Edward's reign "Englishness" in religion continued to be represented by the peculiar compromise which Henry VIII had created. For serious theology, as distinct from polemic or liturgy, the English reformers looked to the continent, and translations made up a major part of the pastoral and didactic material which came off the English presses during this period.

Not only were several of the more productive printers foreigners, but protestant refugees from all over Europe sought asylum in England from the mounting pressure of the counter-reformation. Some of these were distinguished theologians, such as Martin Bucer and Peter Martyr Vermigli, uprooted by Charles V's Interim, who came by special invitation of archbishop Cranmer. Cranmer wished to call a council of leading protestants to co-ordinate strategy against a catholic church which was fighting back strongly after its early reversals. He also wished to obtain their advice and assistance in the creation of his new ecclesiastical establishment in England. Both Philip Melanchthon, Luther's heir and Heinrich Bullinger, Zwingli's successor at Zurich were invited, but neither came. Bullinger had no incentive to leave his home, and was well represented in England by disciples such as John and Conrad ab Ulmis. Melanchthon, on the other hand, was under heavy pressure from rivals within his own church, and did not feel that he should leave Germany. Cranmer had even had his expenses approved by the council before he finally decided to refuse. Bucer, Martyr, and a few lesser colleagues did not constitute the council which Cranmer wanted, but they were a considerable help to him, particularly in his liturgical projects[7]. They did not, however, make the new church appear any more English to the xenophobic islanders. Bucer and Martyr were absorbed fairly easily into the cosmopolitan world of the universities, but most of the ordinary refugees tended to settle in communities defined by their crafts and places of origin. Somerset deliberately settled a group of Flemish weavers in the dissolved abbey at Glastonbury, but the majority lacked specific English patrons, and went where the opportunities seemed to be most promising. Some settled in Norwich, some in Canterbury, and some in Southampton, but the largest number ended up in London. Both the crown and the city government were sympathetic to their plight, and they were allowed to settle in a number of the "liberties" which had been left by the dissolution of religious houses, taking over the disused churches for their own worship. So eventually there were French, Walloon and Dutch congregations, each with their own ministers, and following their own reformed rites[8]. The English prayer books were translated into the appropriate languages in the hope that these congregations could be persuaded to use the English rite, but none of them did so. Bishop Nicholas Ridley of London deplored this as a potential source of disorder and confusion , but neither Somerset nor the regime which followed him found it politically expedient to listen to such representations . There were small numbers of other nationalities, particularly Italians and Spaniards, who had their own churches, but who did not enjoy the same privileges.

The latter part of the reign saw a move back toward censorship and control. The government became more, rather than less protestant, but the council had become disillusioned with Somerset's policy of *laissez faire*, and after his fall attempted to tighten up discipline in a number of ways. Licensing had been placed in the hands of a council commission in 1549, and in 1550 a proclamation denounced offenders for failing to show suitable gratitude for the king's "Godly proceedings".

"...having caused God's word to be truly and sincerely taught and preached, and a godly order for the

administration of the sacraments", the young king was"...most
sorry, and earnestly from the bottom of his heart doth
lament...to hear and see so many of his subjects to abuse
daily by their vicious living and corrupt conversations that
most precious jewel the word of God."[9]

Statutory penalties which had remained unused again began to be
enforced. In 1552 John Lowton, the author of a "seditious ballet" was
put on the pillory, while printers were interrogated and had their stock
confiscated. It was still a mild regime by comparison with that of
Cromwell, or the latter days of Henry's reign but by 1552 the council
was sensitive to criticism, both religious and political, in a way that
the protector had not been, and it could be said that he had paid the
price for his unconventional attitude. The "commonwealth men",
unnerved by the effect that their moralistic denunciations had had
upon the volatile social situation in 1548-9, drew back and imposed
restraints upon themselves. Meanwhile, in order to place this relatively indulgent period in perspective, it should be noticed that a number
of catholic authors had gone into exile in their search of freedom to
criticise the "young Josias" and his mentors - Richard Smith, Maurice
Chauncey and William Rastell most notably, and at least one London
printer had gone with them for the same reason. Robert Caly settled in
Rouen and published a number of works of anti-protestant polemic
before the tide turned and he was able to return to England on the
accession of Mary.

8

The Prayer book of 1549

Two measures of exceptional importance for the progress of the English reformation were legislated in the second session of Edward's first parliament. The first was an act removing all positive laws against the marriage of priests. The celibacy of the clergy had never been a primitive practice, but had been introduced by the reformers of the eleventh and twelfth centuries in an attempt to reduce the worldly preoccupations of the secular priesthood. Marriage or co-habitation had always been forbidden to regulars of both sexes. The reformers of the sixteenth century argued that the original intention of their predecessors had not been fulfilled. They did not, for the most part deny that chastity was the preferable state of life, but marriage was not forbidden by scriptures , and in practice the rule of celibacy was evaded and ignored in a way which positively encouraged abuse and hypocrisy. It was, they argued, preferable for a man who did not have the gift of continence to take a wife and accept an honest responsibility for his children, than to be reduced to shifts and expedients which discredited him, and left both his partner and his offspring without any legal status or protection. The matter was fiercely argued on both sides, but the lower clergy had already declared in favour of marriage, and parliamentary opposition was confined to the more conservative bishops and a handful of lay peers. The bill passed comfortably in both houses, and was implemented at once. By the end of the reign nearly half the bishops and about a quarter of the lower clergy availed themselves of its provisions. The proportion of the latter varied greatly from one diocese to another, and was not always associated with protestant convictions. Even in remote and conservative sees like Carlisle and Bangor a significant number of clergy were found to be married when Mary's visitors sought to reimpose the former canon law[1]. In the long term after its revival by Elizabeth, clerical marriage was to produce social benefits of no small importance, providing

English society with generations of leaders in all walks of life.

The second measure was the act providing for uniformity of services throughout the English church. This was a far more original and revolutionary measure than might at first appear, because there had never been any tradition of uniformity in the western church. The basic rites were universal, but they took a multitude of different forms, varying from diocese to diocese, and even parish to parish. In England and Wales there were five rites; Bangor, Lincoln, Hereford, York and Sarum, or Salisbury. Of these the Sarum Use was by far the most common, but there was no requirement to use it in either province. With the establishment of the royal supremacy the term *Ecclesia Anglicana* had taken on a new meaning. Previously it had been a loose term, simply meaning "that part of the church which happens to be located in England". After 1534 it meant "the church under the jurisdiction of the king of England". This meant that uniformity on a national, as opposed to provincial, basis became possible for the first time. However, during Henry's lifetime nothing had been done to bring this about. Meanwhile in other parts of Europe reformers, both catholic and protestant, were creating new rites. The best known catholic effort had been that of Cardinal Quignon in 1536, which had been designed to meet some of the criticisms which had been levelled at the increasing luxuriance of the existing uses. It had stripped away two thirds of the accretion of saints days, and introduced an important scriptural lexionary. For those reasons it was seen in some quarters as making concessions to the protestants, and although it went through scores of editions, it was never officially recognised, and was rejected by the council of Trent. Consequently, instead of increasing uniformity, it increased diversity.

Luther had written a number of liturgical pieces, but there was no single order for Lutheran churches as a whole. Initially each city had devised its own rite, and that tradition was continued after the evangelical movement began to capture princely jurisdictions as well. Neither Luther nor Melanchthon ever seem to have thought that uniformity was important, but that may possibly have been because they knew that they had no means of imposing it. Liturgy could also be designed to lead belief rather than to follow it, and an example of this can be found in the *Kirchen Ordnung* of Herman Von Wied. A somewhat eclectic convert to protestantism, the archbishop of Cologne had attempted in 1542 to bring together elements of Lutheran and Zwinglian teaching into a single rite. This interesting experiment was more read and discussed than it was used, but a number of distinguished scholars had advised on its composition, including Bucer, Melanch-thon and Osiander. Cranmer knew all these rites, as well as many of those of the early church, and had long been a convinced believer in the virtues of a vernacular liturgy. As early as 1543 he had started work upon a draft order, based partly upon Quignon and partly upon the Sarum Use, and in 1545 he had produced a revised draft[2]. The king knew of this work, and encouraged it, but never gave it official approval. In this as in so many other respects, Henry seems to have kept his reforming ideas and his conservative instincts in unresolved tension. Consequently when the atmosphere became favourable for change in 1547, the archbishop was hardly starting from scratch. Nevertheless he decided to proceed slowly and deliberately, and made no attempt to rush out the drafts which he already had. His first innovation arose from the statute of 1547 which permitted communion in both kinds. This required a small modification to the ritual of the mass, and Cranmer seized the opportunity to issue an English *Order of Communion* in March 1548. This had virtually no doctrinal significance, and although disliked by many conservatives who objected to change *per se*, it encountered very little resistance.

At this stage the liturgy was not in the front line of doctrinal conflict. Much more important was the council's assault on traditional practices. Each successive festival during 1548 saw edicts prohibiting the time honoured customs; no candles at Candlemas, no ashes on Ash Wednesday, no palms on Palm Sunday, no creeping to the cross on Good Friday. All these changes caused anger and distress, and in many places where there was no effective means of coercion, they were simply ignored[3]. They were also very negative, taking away familiar ceremonies which had conveyed comfort and reassurance, and putting nothing in their place. In theory ceremonies were supposed to be replaced with edifying sermons, but in practice there were seldom preachers to deliver such sermons, and when there were they were usually left talking to those who were already converted. While this was happening, Cranmer also issued a doctrinal questionnaire to his episcopal colleagues, concentrating particularly upon the mass and upon the intercessory prayer. The replies revealed what he must have known already, that the bishops were divided right down the middle, with a slight majority on the conservative side[4]. The new liturgy which was occupying his thoughts would have to be carefully framed. There was already so much anxiety about radical change that the simple protestant rite which he would probably have favoured might well have provoked a confrontation. At the same time none of the conservative bishops was anxious to defy the king's authority, and there was a strong argument for giving them something which at least reasonably flexible consciences could stomach.

The archbishop probably laid a draft of his new order before a conference of bishops and theologians at Chertsey Abbey at the end of September. It was discussed both there and subsequently at Windsor, where there seems to have been consensus but no complete agreement. The identity of those attending these discussions can be inferred, up to a point but not known with certainty. What does seem to be clear is that Cranmer did not attempt to give himself an easy ride by consulting only those who agreed with him. There was some sharp dissent, although most of the conservatives ended by accepting his proposals. The agreed draft was then submitted to all the bishops during October by which time the bill of uniformity was already being prepared. There is no evidence that the proposed book was ever submitted to convocation, but since the records of that session have been destroyed, the point cannot be proved either way. The king later seems to have believed that convocation had approved it, but he may have been misled. The bill was introduced into the house of commons on 19th December, where it had an easy passage. A few days later, however, there was reported to be "great sticking" in the house of lords over the mass, and it seems clear that a small minority of the conservative bishops were digging their heels in. The bill passed eventually with only minor amendments, and the final draft of the Prayer Book was appended as an annex. It was described as one convenient form of worship to put an end to the divisions and "unquietness", devised by Godly and learned men from the scripture and the practice of the primitive church. In fact the bulk of it was an elegant translation of the Sarum Use. The new order was to come into use on the feast of Pentecost coming (1549), and thereafter any minister refusing to use it, or using any other order was to be subject to graded punishments, culminating in life imprisonment for the third offence. Any person preaching against the prayer book, or denouncing it in any other way, was also to be punished. Every parish was to provide itself with at least one copy at its own cost before the date of implementation, but no penalties were proscribed for those laymen who might choose to evade their obligation by simply absenting themselves from their parish churches.

The debate in the house of lords focussed mainly on the nature of the divine presence in the eucharist. On this central issue the actual wording of the prayer book rite was vague, but the explicit removal of the elevation of the host after consecration, which had been central to the visual impact of the mass, implied a denial of transubstantiation which the more extreme conservatives, such as Tunstall, found unacceptable. At this stage Somerset was more concerned to obtain agreement than he was to insist upon a protestant definition, so although some strongly protestant statements were made in the debate, they were not insisted upon. By far the most revolutionary aspect of the order from the viewpoint of the majority of the communicants was not its doctrine but its language, and that was not really controversial among the bishops. Conservatives preferred Latin because they believed that the central rite of consecration contained a mystery which the profane could not, in any case, understand, but even Gardiner did not believe that language was of doctrinal significance. The main point of the Prayer Book, in any case was not to make doctrinal statements, but as Cranmer said in his preface, to provide for an orderly reading of the scripture throughout the year, and to increase the unity of the realm by removing the diversity which had hitherto appertained between one diocese and another. In reality the Prayer Book said relatively little in protestant terms, which was why it was immediately attacked by the disappointed disciples of Zwingli and Bullinger[5]. Most of its statements were by omission, not only of the elevation, but of the bulk of the calendar and almost all of the devotions to the saints which had made up such a large part of traditional piety. Purgatory had already gone in the *King's Book* of 1543, but the office of the dead was now further diluted, and intercession reduced to a minimum. For those who had traditionally looked to the office of the church to fortify them through a deathbed struggle, there was little comfort now to be had. The assumption of election, which was axiomatic in a truly protestant rite of passage, did not appear either, leaving the compromise unsatisfying from everyone's point of view, in spite of the beauty of the liturgical language.

The trouble with the Prayer Book was not so much that it was written by a committee as that it was a deliberate compromise. It represented as much of Cranmer's mature theological position as he thought he could impose. When it was presented to Bishop Gardiner in prison, he declared it to be acceptable. The violent reaction to its introduction at Sampford Courtenay, which triggered of the south western rebellion, was very far from typical. Most conservative clergy accepted the letter rather than the spirit of the change. They used the communion service but ignored the rubric instructing them to read it audibly, so the congregation could not tell what language was being used. They omitted the elevation, but replaced it with some other gesture of similar significance which was not explicitly forbidden. As John Hooper wrote indignantly to Bullinger,

> "The public celebration of the Lord's supper is very far from the order and institution of our lord. Although it is administered in both kinds, yet in some places the supper is celebrated three times a day. Where they used heretofor to celebrate the mass of the apostles, they now have the communion of the apostles; where they had the mass of the blessed virgin, they now have the communion which they call the communion of the virgin..."

Vestments and candles were retained, and the English psalms were chanted to sound as much like the Latin as possible. "God knows to what perils and anxieties we are exposed by reason of men of this kind", he continued. The point of the new eucharist was that it was supposed to be a communion of the people, not a private sacrifice offered by the priest. The reference in the prayer of consecration to Christ's "one oblation of himself once offered" was an explicit departure from the doctrine of sacrifice, but it could easily be glossed over and obscured if access to the communion was restricted. By imposing the qualification for admission in rigorous and legalistic fashion it was not difficult to reduce the communicants to a token number, thereby preserving the spirit of the mass and obeying the letter of the law at the same time. By the time that he wrote this letter, Hooper was satisfied that Cranmer's ideas on the eucharist were substantially the same as his own. So the question of further revision was not one of doctrinal disagreement but of political strategy.

In spite of the criticisms which were levelled at it, in one respect the Prayer Book was a great success, because its reception demonstrated that there was no powerful political faction in England which was prepared to defy the king's authority in defence of the Henrician settlement. The south western rebellion was a peasant revolt lead by minor clergy; the type of disturbance that was guaranteed to rally the aristocracy behind the government. The same was true in Oxford shire, where similar elements were engaged. Princess Mary's principled resistance was potentially more serious, but in spite of her popularity she could not command a following on this issue, and had in any case no intention of leading an open resistance to her brother's council. As a result, once the political crisis of October 1549 was resolved,

Cranmer was able to discover the courage of his convictions, and in March 1550 he followed up his Prayer Book with a reformed ordinal. Although this was based on the Sarum pontifical, it restricted the orders conferred to three - bishop, priest and deacon - in accordance with standard protestant use. The traditional form of the laying on of hands was preserved, and the delivery of "instruments" to bishops and deacons remained unchanged - a pastoral staff to the former and a New Testament to the latter. However the new priest now received a bible in addition to the paten and chalice, and his revised charge ran "take thou authority to preach the word of God, and to minister the Holy sacraments in this congregation". The old charge had been to "...offer sacrifice and celebrate mass for both the living and the dead", so the reformed ordinal made explicit changes in the priestly function which had been implicit in the Prayer Book, and completed the first phase of the protestant revolution. By the time that had happened it had become clear that the first liturgy was no more than an interim measure. With the earl of Warwick in political control and firmly committed to further reformation, it could only be a matter of time before a less equivocal rite was authorised.

9

The risings of 1548-9.

Whatever else may be said about the troubled summer of 1549, it cannot be claimed that it was thunder out of a clear sky. Not only had there been vociferous complaints in sermons and in pamphlets about "unnatural lords..step lords" and their avaricious ways, there had also been a considerable number of uncoordinated protests and agrarian riots in the summer of 1548. Disturbances were reported to the council from Kent, Leicestershire and Warwickshire, all of which were contained by the local gentry, and from Cornwall, where a more serious uprising required the intervention of professional troops. In Cornwall the problem was not so much agrarian as religious and personal. Cornish conservatism had an aggressive tinge which was not normal elsewhere, and may well have been linked to a strong sense of cultural separatism. William Body, the archdeacon, was an abrasive and intemperate man, who represented the unacceptable face of the reformation. The council had been warned as early as December 1547 that he was a troublemaker, and in April 1548 a mob attacked his house at Helston and lynched him. The leaders, who seem to have been clergy and respectable householders, had then issued a statement denouncing Body and all other adherents of the "new ways", and demanding a moratorium on all change until the king attained his twenty fourth year. The local justices were then confronted with an angry crowd which they estimated at 3000. They informed the council, and hastened to summon assistance. Gentry from the surrounding area with their retainers and a small number of garrison troops from Devon were on the scene within a few days. The rioters seem to have had little sense of purpose or direction beyond venting their anger, and had descended to looting. They were quickly dispersed and the ringleaders arrested. About a dozen were subsequently tried and executed. With hindsight it is easy to say that the council should have taken more warning by these"stirs" than they did, but at the same time the message seemed to be that the local resources would be adequate to cope with any problems which might arise. Probably the protector himself, with his eyes still firmly fixed on Scotland, was responsible for this misguided optimism. Somerset also did not want to see this kind of trouble for another reason. He had been sending out vigorous signals since the summer of 1547 that popular agrarian grievances were understood and would be remedied. He did not wish to admit to himself that he did not have the power to deliver on his promises. "It boots not how many laws are made" grumbled one protester, "for men to see how few or none put in execution". Those same noblemen and gentlemen who were making statutes under the protector's watchful eye in parliament were omitting to enforce them when they returned home to their estates. As some were later to point out, even Somerset himself was not entirely innocent on that score[1]. The protector's policy, therefore, however traditional it might have been , lacked credibility, which was why the appearance of enclosure commissioners tended to provoke riots rather than to appease them. It may well be that other councillors , notably the earl of Warwick, were more realistic in their assessment of the situation , but they failed to get their message through to a man who was increasingly isolated and self-absorbed. However, hindsight may again mislead us, because 1549 has gone down in history as a year of unprecedented disorder and social disruption, and there tends to be an assumption that the realm was on the brink of dissolution. In fact this was very far from the case. The risings were fuelled by anger and frustration, not by any positive political purpose. There were no leaders of consequence, and the aristocracy did not divide against itself, as it was to do with fatal consequences in the civil war of the following century.

The king's *Chronicle* gives a succinct but fair impression of what happened in May and June;

> "The people began to rise in Wiltshire, where Sir William Herbert did put them down, overun and slay them. Then they rose in Sussex, Hampshire, Kent, Gloucestershire, Suffolk, Warwickshire, Essex, Hertfordshire, a piece of Leicestershire, Worcestershire and Rutlandshire, where by fair persuasions, partly of honest men among themselves and partly by gentle men they were often appeased..."[2]

Wiltshire and Sussex provide two good examples of aristocratic response to these "stirs". In the former a mob made the mistake of attacking Herbert's park. He was ready for them with a force of his own retainers, and put them to flight with a number of casualties. Thereafter the county remained in "a quavering calm" as Lord St. John reported. In Sussex the earl of Arundel summoned the chief malcontents and a number of justices to Arundel castle, and there, partly by skill and partly by the weight of his prestige, negotiated a local settlement which forestalled violence. Only in three of the innumerable counties to be affected did the situation get out of local control. One of these was Oxfordshire, where the local gentry, intimidated by the number and purposefulness of the protesters, failed to co-ordinate their responses and were able to do little more than protect their own homes[3]. The situation was redeemed by Lord Grey of Wilton, who was on his way to the even more serious disorders in Devon. The council allowed his force of some fifteen hundred horse and foot to be temporarily diverted from their main task, and the rebels, with more courage than good sense, concentrated to resist them. They were defeated in a series of fierce skirmishes, "...some slain, some taken and some hanged" as the king laconically recorded it. The appearance of Grey's men had restored the courage of the local gentry, and they were more than adequate to the task of mopping up and bringing the offenders to trial. Grey was markedly brutal in his methods, and several of those taken in arms were executed by martial law, including two or three priests who were hanged in their vestments from the steeples of their own churches *pour encourager les autres*.

Oxfordshire could hardly be described as a serious military campaign, but the other two counties which surpassed local efforts at containment became altogether more difficult problems, and it is for them that the year is chiefly remembered. Significantly both Devon and Norfolk had recently lost their most powerful resident nobility. The Courtney earls of Devon had been destroyed by Cromwell in the so-called "Exeter conspiracy" of 1538, and the Howard dukes of Norfolk had fallen as recently as 1546, victims of the last court *coup* of Henry VIII's reign. Whether either the marquis of Exeter or the duke of Norfolk could have performed the service that the earl of Arundel performed in Sussex can never be known, but it is clear that nobody else in those counties had the prestige to try. Elsewhere conservative peers, such as the earl of Shrewsbury and the earl of Derby, who had no particular sympathy with the direction of government policy, nevertheless succeeded in containing expressions of discontent which would have threatened their own position even more directly

than they threatened the council. Although popular religious conservatism undoubtedly played a part in stimulating many of these disorders,
they were (and were seen to be) predominantly social and economic in
their inspiration. Unlike the Pilgrimage of Grace, they attracted very
little covert aristocratic sympathy, let alone leadership, and consequently presented proportionately little danger to the fabric of the
state.

Only in Cornwall does this generalisation partly break down. The
county was relatively poor, and enclosure was not an issue. The riots
which broke out in Bodmin in the early summer were fuelled by a
variety of grievances against the advance of the reformation, and
began before the compulsory introduction of the Prayer Book. This
was not a *jacquerie*, but involved many of the most substantial citizens, including the mayor, and several middling and minor gentry
from the surrounding countryside, notably Humphrey Arundel of
Heland, whose maternal grandfather had been one of the chief leaders
of the great "stir" of 1497. The sheriff, John Milton, professed himself
unable to act, perhaps because events were moving too fast, or perhaps because he did not feel as though he could trust his colleagues.
Encouraged by his inactivity, and fired by distant memories of '97, the
dissidents decided to march on London, and set off bearing the banner
of the five wounds, a symbol which made any specific list of grievances unnecessary. At the same time a second group from Bodmin
moved south towards Plymouth, capturing Sir Richard Grenville who
had endeavoured to negotiate with them on the way. In Cornwall at
least there were strong echoes of the Pilgrimage of Grace. However,
before the projected march could get very far, the rebels were absorbed into a larger, and rather different demonstration that was building up in Devon. This also started off as a religious protest, when the
villagers of Sampford Courtenay refused to allow their vicar to use the
new order of service on 9th June. However, unlike Bodmin, this gesture quickly turned violent when a gentleman who ventured to try and
disperse the crowd was murdered. For some reason which is not entirely clear, animus against the gentry seems to have been stronger in
Devon than almost anywhere else in England. According to one
account, news of the events at Sampford Courtenay were greeted with
spontaneous outbursts of enthusiasm all over the county[4]. So rapidly
did the disorder spread that the forces of law and order were almost
literally swept away. The total number of insurgents may not have
been great as a proportion of the total population, but they were
energetic, and were quickly joined by vagabonds and other fringe

members of the community who had little to lose.

The gentry therefore failed as completely in Devon as they had done in Cornwall, but for very different reasons. In the latter county there was, or appeared to be, considerable sympathy for the insurgents on the part of their natural leaders. In Devon, on the other hand, many of the gentlemen who were so disliked were absentees, outsiders who had bought the land of dissolved religious houses, and seldom or never appeared. At the same time a number of the old gentle families, such as the Pollards and the Carews, were moving firmly towards protestantism, and thereby alienating their natural support. Sir Peter Carew, the head of the most powerful gentry family, had married outside the county, and was away on his wife's estate in Lincolnshire when the trouble started. Lord John Russell had received most of the forfeited Courtenay and Pole lands after 1538, and had briefly been president of the shadowy council in the west[5] but he did not normally live in the county, and had no significant following. By the time that the news of these disturbing developments reached the council in London the Devon and Cornwall insurrections had merged, and it was the clergy rather than a handful of Cornish gentlemen who were providing the main leadership. This fact was clearly reflected in the articles which the rebels then produced. Virtually every demand was for a return to traditional religious practices, and couched in such peremptory terms that Cranmer, who replied on the council's behalf was beside himself with fury[6]. Neither the matter nor the manner of this exchange left any room for negotiation, but Somerset never the less endeavoured at first to temporise. He may have believed that the rebels intransigent front was a bluff and they would accept reasonable terms if they were offered; or he may simply have been making the best of a bad job, having no real force to send. He summoned Sir Peter Carew from Lincolnshire and sent him down to Devon with instructions to pacify the insurgents by negotiation.

Carew did his best, although it is hard to believe that he had much confidence of success. He found Exeter full of fugitives, many of them gentry, and the countryside dominated by armed bands. He had enough men with him to avoid sharing the fate of Sir Richard Grenville, but he had no authority to make the concessions which were demanded, and the discussions were a waste of time. Direct violence was narrowly avoided when one of his men inadvertently set fire to a barn near Crediton in the course of a parley, and after several close escapes Carew returned to London to report the failure of his mission, leaving Exeter closely besieged. The protector was highly displeased, but had in fact taken the decision to use armed force, and Lord John Russell was despatched about the 24th June. Russell's instructions were highly ambiguous, apparently envisaging another round of negotiations before resorting to coercion. This may have been because of Somerset's lingering hope of avoiding bloodshed, or because he still could not give Russell enough men. Whatever the reason, it made for a very slow and hesitant campaign. Russell was a cautious and not very effective soldier, and it was not until he was joined by Lord Grey and Sir William Herbert on about 24th July that he was finally convinced that he had sufficient power to act. The story of his numerous hesitations make the council's mounting impatience entirely understandable, but Russell avoided the danger of any military setback, no matter how small, and the vigorous and efficient defence of Exeter relieved him of any urgent need to rush to its relief. His well armed force of about 4000 men, nearly half of them seasoned professionals, did not leave the issue long in doubt. The rebels fought with great determination and reasonable discipline, but they were defeated in a series of engagements and suffered heavy casualties. Between the 3rd and 7th August the siege of Exeter was raised, and the last rebel force was defeated at Launceston. It had been a messy and brutal campaign, and by the time that Russell had finished imposing martial law upon the survivors, some 4000 men had died, either on the battle field or the scaffold. For the protector this was a double disaster, because he had first failed to prevent full scale rebellion, and then failed to exercise moderation in its suppression. In fact he had been unable to control the situation at any stage, and lost credibility both with a chastened aristocracy, and with a commonalty which was both cowed and resentful.

Everything about the Norfolk rebellion was different, except the outcome. There was little emphasis upon religion, and clergy were not prominent among the leaders. Enclosure, on the other hand, was an issue, particularly the enclosure of common land which adversely affected the interests of those small freeholders who were particularly numerous in Norfolk. The insurgents symbolised one of their chief grievances when they killed and ate large numbers of sheep at their camp on Mousehold Heath. There was a background of social tension in East Anglia going back several decades. An anti-gentry riot had broken out at Griston in 1540, and another near Kings Lynn in 1548, but both had been contained by the local magistrates. On the other hand the actual events that lead to the major outbreak of 1549 were trivial, almost ridiculous, and would have passed unnoticed if the whole countryside had not been like dry tinder waiting for a match. Some drunken revelry at Wymondham, and a feud between the neighbouring yeoman families of Kett and Flowerdew resulted in some fences being destroyed at Hethersett on 6th and 7th July. There the matter might have ended if Robert Kett, for some reason which has never been satisfactorily explained, had not then set himself at the head of a small mob which had gathered, and urged them on to greater things. Kett was a man of old and substantial family, on the fringes of the minor gentry. He may have been motivated by the exclusiveness of those above him on the social scale, or he may have had a genuine attack of conscience for the enclosure for which he had himself been responsible. For whatever reason he and his followers set about the systematic destruction of fences in the Wymondham and Heathersett area. The news spread with great speed, and similar mobs appeared all over East Anglia in the second half of July, with the same programme.

The "camping movement" as it was called largely abstained from personal violence, although a few gentlemen were imprisoned, and can be more accurately be described as a demonstration rather than a rebellion[7]. Having vented their anger, in most places the demonstrators were persuaded to disperse after a few weeks in return for indemnity and renewed assurances. That, however, did not apply to Kett's main camp, which he set up on Mousehold Heath outside Norwich. Similar terms were offered to Kett on the 21st July, but he rejected them, and the next day his men successfully infiltrated the city, which fell into his hands. Although many of the citizens of Exeter had sympathised with the rebels at their gates, the city had held out resolutely, but Norwich offered no significant resistance. This may partly have been because discipline in the rebel army was good, and there was no fear of sack or plunder. Kett had considerable powers of organisation, and knew what he wanted, but he had no idea of how to achieve his objectives, except to sit tight and wait for a reasonable offer. Given the nature of his support time was not on his side, but there was no question of a march on London, and he was obviously very anxious to emphasise that his movement was directed against the local gentry, not against the king or council. Unfortunately for him, that was a distinction that the protector could not afford to recognise. Reluctant though Somerset may have been and stretched as his resources undoubtedly were, he was compelled eventually to resort to force. The marquis of Northampton with about 2000 men moved into Norfolk, and reached Norwich on 30th July. The result was the kind of fiasco which Russell had been so careful to avoid. Kett's men were numerous, and far more resolute than their mild demeanour may have suggested. After a fierce engagement, Northampton (who was no soldier) was driven off with the loss of over 100 men.

By this time, Kett was caught in an inexorable trap. His victory was useless, because it brought him no nearer to achieving his aims, and merely ensured that the next army to come against him would be stronger, and determined to destroy him. On the 10th August the earl of Warwick was put in command of the operation, and on the 15th all the gentry of East Anglia were commanded to join him in arms. On 23rd August Warwick reached Norwich with about 6000 foot and 1500 horse, including 1400 mercenaries. At the eleventh hour, and realising the weakness of his position in the face of such an army, Kett attempted to negotiate. Warwick appeared to be willing, but his own men, probably fearing betrayal, frustrated him, and he lost control of the situation. On the 24th Warwick recovered control of Norwich, and two days later the rebel army on Mousehold, having lost all semblance of discipline, was slaughtered in a pitch battle. Unlike Russell, Warwick was restrained in the penalties which he exacted. Apart from the leaders the loss of life off the battlefield was light, and by the end of September order was fully restored. Nevertheless the grievances which had given rise to the "camping movement" did not go away, and the authorities continued to fear a recurrence for many years. The principal beneficiary was Warwick himself, who now had an army, and the prestige of victory to use for the other political purposes which he had in mind.

10

The Coup Of October 1549

There are two views of the actions that brought down the duke of Somerset and ended the protectorate. One is that it was the culmination of a deep laid plot by the earl of Warwick, the roots of which went back to the days of Henry VIII. According to this version, Warwick had become jealous of his colleague's more highly rated successes. Recognising the strength of Seymour's position in February 1547, he had not only acquiesced in the establishment of the protectorate, but even feigned enthusiasm for it. However, as soon as the opportunity arose he made use of the foolish ambitions of Lord Thomas Seymour to sow discord between the brothers, calculating that whatever the outcome the protector's position would be weakened. Seymour's execution in March 1549, and the repercussions from it, had fully justified his expectation, and by the summer of the same year he judged that the time was right to strike. He began to complain vigorously but secretly to his colleagues about the protector's arbitrary and secretive ways, and inveigled a group of religious conservatives, led by the disgruntled Wriothesley, into a plot, cynically deceiving them into believing that he favoured the return of the Henrician religious settlement. When the plot had succeeded, he jettisoned his allies and seized power for himself, entering into an opportunistic alliance with the more extreme protestants in order to protect himself from conservative revenge. The alternative view is that the true originators of the *coup* were the conservative peers, and that their principal objective was to halt the protector's advance towards protestantism. According to this thesis the plot was an opportunistic one, which only came into existence when Somerset's failures in the summer of 1549 had made him vulnerable. Warwick joined the plotters on their initiative because he was a powerful man and a skilled soldier, and he accepted their invitation because he had become convinced of the protector's incompetence rather than for any ideological reason.

There is no significant evidence to support the idea of a secret antagonism between Seymour and Dudley before 1547. If anything the evidence from behind the scenes supports the ostensible accord and alliance which they presented to their conservative opponents. There were contemporaries who believed that Warwick engineered the fall of Thomas Seymour, but they did not actually say so until after 1549, and there is a natural suspicion of hindsight about their opinions. Warwick himself claimed that he tried to protect Seymour from the consequences of his own folly, and that is just as plausible an interpretation of the surviving direct evidence. Warwick kept up a normal and civil correspondence with the protector, and equally importantly with his aides John Thynne and William Cecil, until about the middle of August 1549 when the letters abruptly cease. There may be another explanation, but this probably indicates the point at which the earl became convinced that his former friend and colleague would have to go, a decision which coincided with, and may well have been influenced by, his campaign against the rebels in Norfolk. Whether he joined an existing conservative plot, or was himself the instigator of the subsequent moves is not clear. It may well be that several people had the same idea at about the same time. The Imperial ambassador believed in September that the earl of Arundel was the prime mover and that his motive was to "restore religion"[1]. Van der Delft saw English affairs through tinted spectacles, but he may have been right in this case, because it seems that the princess Mary was approached at about the same time to accept the regency for her brother. Both Arundel and Warwick are mentioned as having been among those who made the approach, but Mary disclaimed all interest, and her attitude was probably critical in determining the subsequent course of events. Instead of having a positive focus in the creation of a regime which would certainly have turned back the reformation, the conspirators aim now became chiefly negative - the removal of Somerset - and the policy of any future government became indeterminate.

By the beginning of September there was a broad agreement among the majority of the council that the protectorate in its existing form would have to end, although some were probably in favour of attempting to persuade Somerset to modify his attitudes before making any move against him. Meanwhile it was business as usual. Warwick was suspiciously slow about disbanding the troops which he had brought back from Norfolk, but the excuse that the security situation around London was still fragile must have seemed reasonable enough. After all the citizens had been commanded to muster in

armour and to lay artillery on the city wall not long before. Somerset
went on conducting the affairs of state in an apparent atmosphere of
normality until about the 3rd October, but by that time both he and his
opponents knew that a crisis was imminent. Warwick was not the only
councillor to move troops into the vicinity of the capital, and about a
dozen members were meeting regularly in houses about the city,
Arundel, Warwick and Southampton were being particularly conspicuous[2]. Somerset had about 500 of his own men within call, but
nowhere near enough to out face the "London lords" if it came to a
showdown. He had already summoned Russell and Herbert to return
from the west "for matters of importance", but he knew that he could
not necessarily count on their support[3]. On the 5th October he played
the only card that he had left, and issued a proclamation declaring that
the king was in danger from traitorous conspirators. All loyal subjects
were to muster at once at Hampton Court for the king's protection -
and of course, that of his "entirely beloved uncle". The only person of
importance to respond to this summons was Archbishop Cranmer,
who arrived the next day with sixty men. The fact that Cranmer was
no party to the conspiracy was not only a reflection of his known
friendship to Somerset, but also of the conservative religious intentions of the conspirators. Paget, Petre and Smith were also with the
Protector at Hampton Court, but Paget was playing a deep game, and
neither Petre nor Smith were men of much substance[4].

According to one report 4000 "peasants" responded to the protector's call, but even if the figure is correct such unarmed and untrained
recruits would have been of little use. That same night, 6th October,
hasty attempts to fortify Hampton Court were abandoned, and Somerset withdrew to Windsor taking the king with him. Although Windsor
was much more defensible than Hampton Court, his position was
growing daily weaker. Not only had his proclamation given his
enemies a perfect opportunity to brand him a social revolutionary,
stirring up the commons against their natural lords, but his removal to
Windsor could also be represented as an attempt to kidnap the king
and hold him hostage. However, not all the problems were on one
side. It was all very well for the "London lords" to profess their loyalty and to denounce Somerset as a traitor, the fact remained that he was
with the king and they were not. If they used their overwhelming
military superiority to besiege or attack Windsor, they would be in
arms against their sovereign lord. Moreover it was not certain that the
protector's appeal would produce only unarmed peasants. The longer
the crisis continued, the more chance there was that his friends would

start to make some headway; surprise had been on their side, but time was not. On the 8th October both sides appealed for the backing of the city of London, Somerset's request being covered by a personal letter from Edward. The lord mayor stalled, and insisted on consulting the common council, but there was no evading the issue. The councillors were actually present in the city with their armed retainers; on the other hand the king's autograph summons could not be ignored. The citizens had reminded themselves of the troubles they had endured through becoming involved in a similar dispute in the reign of Henry III, and tried desperately to avoid taking sides.

> "...forasmuch as thys ayde is requyred of the kinges maistie, whose voyce we ought to hearken unto, for he is our high shepherd, rather than unto ye lordes; and yet I would not wish the lordes to be clerely shaken off, but that they with us and we with them may ioyne in sute and make our most humble peticion to the kinges maiestie, that it would please his highnesse to heere such complaynt against the government of the Lorde Protector as maye be iustly alleged and proved..."

For the moment the important thing was that they did not send 500 men to Windsor, and if a conflict should break out, it remained uncertain where the loyalties of this large and powerful community would lie[6].

By 9th October both sides were manoeuvring hard to secure the best possible negotiating position. Neither party wished to fight, Somerset because he did not have the means to do so, and the council because they were aware of the legal and moral ambiguities of their position. The protector sent out handbills denouncing "the painted eloquence...of crafty traitors", and the lords responded with a lengthy denunciation of his malpractices, accusing him of every kind of abuse, and of terrorising his young sovereign. In these exchanges it was the council which forced the pace, and they also took the initiative in commencing negotiations, using Sir Philip Hoby, recently returned from the Imperial court, as their agent. Hoby had to some extent the confidence of both sides, and was a good choice as mediator. For the next two days he shuttled backwards and forwards between London and Windsor, Bearing letters to and from the king, and between the lords and Cranmer and Paget, who were still with Somerset. There were rumours that the protector had replaced the king's servants with his own, and that he was planning to whisk Edward out of the country - although where they were supposed to be going was never mentioned. Whether these exchanges were really being conducted behind Somerset's back, or whether that was a fiction designed to facilitate the proceedings is not clear. Nor is it entirely clear how the negotiations were brought to a successful conclusion. The chronicler Richard Grafton, who was in London at the time but wrote his account some years later, gave the whole credit to Hoby:

> "And truely he did so wisely declare his message, and so gravely told his tale in the name of the Lordes, but therewithall so vehemently and so grievously against the Protector, who was also there present by the king, that in the end the Lorde Protector was commanded from the kinges presence and shortly was committed to ward..."[7]

this is clearly far too simple. If Edward was capable of resolving the whole tangle by straightforward command, why had he not done so before? Could a twelve year old boy, who had been moved around like a piece of expensive crockery, and was going to remain under tutelage for at least two more years, have suddenly asserted himself in such a dramatic fashion? Whether or not Somerset had replaced the king's servants, Windsor was certainly full of his men, and if a scene of the kind described was enacted, it must have been with his prior knowledge and agreement. In other words the protector had been persuaded to surrender on terms, but what those terms were, and who arranged them can only be deduced.

It was never in anyone's interest to claim the credit for this coup, partly because Somerset's fate continued to be a live political issue until 1552, and partly because it involved an understanding of which neither of the principal parties was subsequently very proud. On the 10th October Cranmer and Paget intimated to the council that Somerset would yield his office "on honourable terms", and the protector himself gave assurances that he would be bound by any terms which might be negotiated between two representatives of the council and two whom he would nominate himself. We do not know whether this offer was ever accepted, but if it was it would partly explain the known course of events. The London lords continued to speak as if they were demanding unconditional surrender, but they were probably no longer being completely frank with each other. Somerset had already addressed a private plea to Warwick, appealing to their long standing friendship, and although there is no record of the Earl's response, this letter may well provide the clue. The Protector was anxious to extricate himself from a very dangerous situation with his life, and as much honour as he could salvage. He was also genuinely concerned for the future of the church. At the same time Cranmer stood to lose everything that he had gained for the reformation if Somerset should be overthrown by a group of religious conservatives. However, since Mary had declined the Regency, the religious tone of any government which might take over from Somerset still had to be decided. Warwick also knew perfectly well that Edward's protestant-ism was not just a childish whim; two or three years more and it would be a settled conviction that would remain with him for the rest of his life. Moreover, for the same reason the king trusted and respect-ed the archbishop. If Warwick had any ambition to profit from the Protector's overthrow, these circumstances indicated a clear course of action. If the Earl could come to an understanding with Cranmer, promising the continuation of reform in return for political support, and making some undertaking for Somerset's personal safety, then the archbishop in turn would have a better chance of persuading the Protector to give up the unequal battle to maintain his position. At the same time this would hardly be a negotiation which could be carried on in the open, given Warwick's need to maintain a solid front with Arundel and Wriothesley until Somerset was safely disposed of.

There can be no certainty that this is what happened, but it would help explain why Hoby's final mission on the 10th October was so effortlessly successful. He reassured the protector that the councillors sought neither his life nor his property, but merely resolved to see the realm better administered for the king[8]. If Hoby's words had been privately endorsed by the earl of Warwick, then Somerset would have had much better cause to trust assurances which at first sight appear specious and insubstantial. Later the same day the protector's servants were dismissed from the court, and Sir Anthony Wingfield, the vice-chamberlain, accompanied by several gentlemen of the privy chamber, were sent to Windsor to reinforce the council's control. Two days later the whole body repaired to the court, where they knelt at the king's feet and received his solemn thanks for their services. What Edward thought privately about the events that he recorded so briefly in his journal we do not know, but if there had ever been any true affection between himself and his uncle, it had probably been ended by the frightening circumstances of their move from Hampton Court to Windsor. On the same day Sir Thomas Smith, Sir Michael Stan

hope, Sir John Thynne, Edward Wulf and William Grey, described as
"...the principle instrumentes and counsilors that he dyd use both at
this tyme and otherways also in the affayres of his yll gouvernement"
were sent to the Tower[9], If any danger still remained, it was from
those forces which Somerset had endeavoured to raise before his
surrender, and whose summons had not been countermanded. Letters
were therefore sent out, commanding any who had raised such forces
to return home, and ensuring that any troops which remained and were
not directly under their control - such as those still lead by Russell and
Herbert - were amenable to the council's orders. On the 14th October
the situation was sufficiently under control for Somerset himself to be
sent to the Tower, and the office of protector to be formally abolished.

Throughout this crisis the lords of the council, although they clearly represented a prevailing aristocratic disillusionment with the protector, nevertheless conducted themselves with a bombastic self right-
eousness which can easily deceive the casual observer. The had in fact
created the situation which they were so loudly deploring in October
1549, and although Somerset may have acted unwisely in a number of
ways, he had not in fact exceeded the powers that they had given him.
His fall was much lamented by those he had ostensibly been trying to
help, although his policies had brought them little benefit. The fact
that they continued to support him was not particularly relevant in the
autumn of 1549, but it was to become important again in 1551.
Meanwhile his fate, and the fate of the reformation which he had
brought about hung in the balance. It remained to be seen whether the
council would honour the public guarantees which Hoby had delivered on their behalf, and that was going to depend on who emerged as
primer inter pares in the new situation. In the circumstances a power
struggle was inevitable, and the imprisoned duke was not the only
man who looked to the outcome with fascinated attention. The protestant preachers feared the worst, and bishops Gardiner and Bonner
began to look forward to an early release. "The papists", wrote John
Hooper, "are hoping and earnestly struggling for their kingdom".

11

The Struggle for Power, October 1549 - January 1550.

With the abolition of the protectorate, the responsibility for government theoretically reverted to Henry's surviving executors. In practice, however, that responsibility was picked up by the council as it existed on the 14th October 1549, a council which had been augmented by the admission (or readmission) of three middle ranking conservatives on 6th October. It is hard to see the appointment of Sir Richard Southwell and Sir Edmund Peckham, or the reappearance of Nicholas Wotton, as anything more than a device to strengthen the hand of the conspirators against the protector. The death of Denny in September, and the exclusion of Smith and Somerset during the coup thus meant that the balance of the council had been tilted slightly but significantly in a conservative direction. There was at first no sign of a split along religious lines, and a report of the 17th October still described Warwick as being at one with his colleagues. However nothing was actually done to restore traditional worship, and the conservative bishops remained under restraint. As soon as Edward returned to Hampton court on 15th October, the privy chamber was reconstructed. Sir Michael Stanhope, already in prison, was removed from office. Six "lords of the council" and four knights were then appointed to be in regular attendance upon the king[1]. Henceforth the privy chamber and council were to be kept in line by a significant overlap of personnel, and access to the sovereign would be controlled by the same men who made the political decisions. The six lords were Northampton, Warwick, Arundel, Russell, St. John and Wentworth; the four knights Andrew Dudley, Edward Rogers, Thomas Darcy and Thomas Wroth. Of these ten at least five could be broadly described as friends or supporters of Warwick, but there is no indication that the appointments were the result either of a party conflict or a carefully contrived compromise.

If there was a conflict going on within the council in the second half of October, it was exceedingly well concealed, but the logic which had led to the creation of the protectorate two and a half years before had not gone away. There was still a good case for having an identifiable person at the head of the government, because Edward at thirteen was no more credible as a monarch than he had been at ten. It is possible that a fresh attempt was made to persuade Mary to accept the regency, and that this time Warwick was not a party to the offer. Perhaps he was seen to be too close to Cranmer, or perhaps he just displayed a suspicious lack of zeal when it came to promoting conservative moves, but by early November the earl was beginning to feel vulnerable and in need of support within the council. It was at this point that his alliance with the archbishop began to pay dividends, because when the king wanted personal advice or support, he sent for Cranmer. It may have been by this means that the appointment of Sir Thomas Arundel to the council was blocked in early November. There was a known intention to promote Paget to the peerage, which would have disqualified him from his existing office as controller of the household, and Arundel was the conservative choice to follow him[2]. Warwick, however, was particularly suspicious of Arundel, who had recently tried to enter the service of the princess Mary, and managed to secure the appointment of Thomas Goodrich, the protestant bishop of Ely, to the council instead. With hindsight this appointment can be seen as a turning point. As late as 7th November Van der Delft believed that Wriothesley was the "head" of the council, but he was beginning to find it a little difficult to understand why more was not being done to restore "true religion". In fact Goodrich's appointment checked the growth of conservative power, and Wriothesley's illness in the latter part of November contributed to an uneasy truce.

By the end of the month it had become apparent to the conservative leaders that whatever understanding they thought they had with the earl of Warwick was not working, and if they were going to secure effective control, he would have to be removed. The prime mover of this plot seems to have been the earl of Arundel, and the imprisoned duke of Somerset became the means to achieve their end. It was later claimed that Arundel had intended to use the interrogation of Somerset, which he was then conducting, to implicate Warwick in the former protector's misdeeds, and thus to be rid of them both at a stroke[3]. However, if this was his intention, it was based on a wild miscalculation of the political realities. More soberly he may well have discovered the nature of the understanding between Cranmer and Warwick, and believed that by forcing Somerset's execution he could have driven a wedge between them which would have destroyed Warwick's ascendancy in the council. Whatever the truth, the plot was betrayed to Warwick by Lord St. John, in whom Arundel had rashly confided, early in December. The exact sequence of events is hard to reconstruct, but it seems that Warwick took advantage of Wriothesley's continuing incapacity to secure the appointment of his friend and ally Henry Grey, marquis of Dorset, to the council on 29th November. This forced the conservatives on to the defensive, and may well have convinced St. John, who was a pragmatist with an eye to the main chance, that Arundel's plot was doomed to fail anyway. He therefore seized the opportunity to ingratiate himself with the likely winner, and put the outcome beyond doubt. For a few weeks there was an atmosphere of febrile intensity as Warwick feared, or pretended to fear, a conservative *coup*. The council met at his bedside as he in turn endured a bout of illness, Arundel conspicuously absenting himself. On the 5th December Richard Scudamore, writing to Sir Philip Hoby from the court reported that Sir William Paget had recently been ennobled, and that Sir Anthony Wingfield had taken his place as controller. There were strong rumours that the duke of Norfolk would soon be released, through the intercession of his daughter the dowager duchess of Richmond, and possibly young Edward Courtney as well. The earl of Warwick was to be marquis of Pembroke and lord treasurer, the Earl of Arundel was to be lord great chamberlain, and Lord Paget, chamberlain[4].

If Scudamore's intelligence was correct, and he was usually well informed, St. John had not at that time alerted Warwick, and there was no open rift between the two parties. Indeed there seems to have been an intention to continue working together, at least on Warwick's part, from whose friends this probably came. On the other hand one well informed protestant divine who had left the country before the middle of November, claimed to have seen an official letter or proclamation promising further religious reform, and Richard Hilles, writing on the 17th declared "..we are hoping that Christ may yet remain with us"[5]. Whether Warwick was playing a double game during these weeks, or whether he was hoping to carry his council colleagues with him against their natural judgment, is not clear. Whatever his intention, St. John's revelations altered the situation, and brought the apparent consensus which had prevailed since early October to an end. For the time being Warwick kept his knowledge to himself, and arranged a showdown. On the 13th December Somerset signed thirty one articles of submission, and six days later Arundel, and Wriothesley, who was also in the plot, came to the council strongly urging the duke's execution. At that point Warwick suddenly declared that whosoever sought the blood of Somerset sought his own as well. The violence of his reaction produced a stunned silence, but there could be no doubt that it was a declaration of political war. The fate of the former protector thus became the occasion of a power struggle which had been inherent in the composition of the alliance which had overthrown him. The issue was decided in council by 2nd January 1550 when a bill for Somerset's fine and ransom was presented to parliament. On the 14th January Arundel and Wriothesley were placed under house arrest, and parliament ratified the ex-protector's submission.

Over the next month Warwick progressively consolidated his victory, reshaping the council to his own liking, and distributing rewards and punishments which had been earned in the last six weeks or so of 1549. On the 16th January Walter Devereux, viscount Hereford and Sir Thomas Darcy were admitted to the council, the former being a strong protestant and the latter a political ally. On the 19th Lord St. John became the earl of Wiltshire, and his colleague John, Lord Russell, who had joined Warwick's party at the same point, was created earl of Bedford. Richard Rich, the lord chancellor, not a natural friend to religious radicals, nevertheless accommodated himself to the new order and kept his office, for the time being. Darcy became vice-chamberlain and captain of the guard in succession to Wingfield, and Paget was left out in the cold. Exactly why the intention to make Paget lord chamberlain was abandoned is not clear. His peerage was presumably a reward for his part in negotiating Somerset's surrender, so his involvement with Arundel and Wriothesley must have been suspected. He remained on the council for the time being, and was soon endeavouring to make himself useful, but Warwick never trusted him[6]. Wriothesley and Arundel were formally expelled from the council on 2nd February, the same day upon which Warwick assumed the title of president. Arundel forfeited the office of chamberlain at the same time, and was replaced by Lord Wentworth. Sir Edward Peckam's career as a privy counsellor was short indeed. Introduced at the beginning of October, his attendance was last recorded on the 30th of that month. It is possible that he was the personal friend and nominee of Wriothesley, and that as soon as illness prevented the latter from attending meetings he was quietly dropped, not having the confidence of the other conservative councillors,

among whom he naturally belonged. There is no indication that
Warwick could have secured his dismissal at such an early date. On
the other hand Richard Southwell, whom appeared at the same time as
Peckam, was clearly a victim of Warwick's victory. He was dismissed
on the 29th December, and arrested shortly afterwards on a charge of
having written "certain bills of sedition". He was eventually pardoned
after paying a fine of £500, but played no further part in the politics of
the reign.

Somerset finally confirmed the terms of his submission on 27th
January. A few days later he was released upon a recognizance of
£10,000 to reside within four miles of his house at Syon, and barred
from access to the king. On the 18th February he received a free
pardon and the bulk of his estates were restored. The duke's rehabilitation is something of a mystery. It has been suggested that he was too
powerful to be permanently rusticated, and that Warwick feared him.
This cannot be disproved, but he had no friends of importance in
October 1549, and his popularity with the commons turned out to be
more of a liability than an asset. On the other hand he was a man of
considerable ability who, if he could be persuaded to work as a
member of the team instead of its master, might still have a great deal
to offer. It is hard to believe that he was more powerful, or a greater
potential danger than the heads of the old entrenched peerage families,
like the earl of Shrewsbury or the earl of Derby, neither of whom was
particularly sympathetic to the earl of Warwick. On the 18th April
1550 the duke was again received at court, and two days later he was
restored to the council. It is very unlikely that this was a negative
move, or that it was the result of intercession made by his wife. Given
her longstanding unpopularity, the duchess's advocacy would hardly
have helped her husband's cause[7]. The earl of Warwick, being
committed to a forward policy in religion, expected his erstwhile
friend and former opponent to accept the new situation, and to work
with the reconstituted council towards the aims which they were
supposed to share. The defeated conservatives, such as the earl of
Arundel who was about to compound for a heavy fine, were their
common enemies, and it was not unreasonable to expect Somerset to
appreciate the advantages of working with the new lord president
rather than against him.

The council to which Somerset returned was nevertheless different
in many respects from that which had rejected his leadership seven
months earlier. Changes in composition had made it more obviously
protestant, but more important, it was a real governing body. Warwick

had already made it clear that he intended to restore real conciliar rule. The protectorship had been abolished, not merely transferred from one incumbent to another. At some point late in 1549, almost certainly after the confrontation of December, a new commission had been drafted in the king's name, rehearsing the events of the previous three years, and confirming the need for a body to govern in the king's name during the balance of his minority[8]. The powers which had at first been vested in the executors, and subsequently in the lord protector, were then conferred on the council as a whole. This commission does not seem to have been formally issued, but it certainly reflected the thinking of Warwick and his supporters. It may well have been withheld, not because of any doubts about the ideas which it embodied, but simply because it was deemed to be unnecessary. If, as Gardiner had admitted, the king's authority was sufficient to govern his realm "though he were in his cradle", then it was sufficient to confer authority upon his council without special commission . This also had the great advantage, from Warwick's point of view, that it left the theoretical responsibility in the hands of Edward himself, and the practical responsibility with the council as a whole. From that position it would be increasingly possible to advance by exercising a personal ascendancy over the young sovereign, unimpeded by legal obstacles, and progressively convincing the young king that he was making all the important decisions himself. In skillful hands such influence could be extended well beyond the end of the minority. It remained to be seen whether Somerset could really be persuaded to work as a member of a team in such circumstances, or whether the temptation to recover his former ascendancy would prove irresistible. In April 1550 Warwick considered the gamble to be well worth taking.

The council had unequivocally reaffirmed its protestant commitment on the 25th December 1549, denouncing those who "...have bruited abroad that they should have again their old Latin services, their conjured bread and water, with such like vain and superstitious ceremonies"[9]. At the same time other aspects of the former protector's policies were abandoned, or sharply reversed. A new statute declared it to be treason for twelve or more people to assemble for the purpose of killing or capturing a member of the privy council, and felony for any similar group to break an enclosure, or to refuse to disperse when ordered to do so[10]. This was clearly provoked by the troubles of the summer, and what were seen as the fatal consequences of hesitation and delay. Somerset's sheep tax, which had been the statutory embodiment of the social programme of the "commonwealth" group, by endeavouring to reduce the profitability of sheep ranching, was repealed after representations from the clothiers' lobby, and the lost revenue replaced with an orthodox subsidy. Even more fundamental was an act for the improvement of commons and waste ground, which repealed most of the anti-enclosure legislation of the previous half century, and revived the statutes of Merton (20 Henry III c.4) and Westminster(13 Edward I, c.46)[11]. A lord might now enclose common and waste ground at his discretion, provided that enough remained for the lawful requirements of his tenants. Since it was very difficult to say in most cases what constituted a lawful requirement, and manorial courts were themselves the arbiter of custom, this gave the lords a clear advantage in what had been a contentious marginal area. It did not, of course, affect the protection that tenants enjoyed in respect of their tenements proper, and certainly did not lead to an orgy of depopulating enclosure. At the same time several sensible acts were passed by the parliament which accepted Somerset's submission, for improving the quality of cloth and for containing the problem of vagabondage. The protector's savage act against vagabonds was repealed, having accomplished nothing. All this had happened before the duke's return, and was undoubtedly more in line with current aristocratic thinking than anything which he had endeavoured to do. For the time being he had no leverage to work against such consensus, but there could be no certainty that he had abandoned his former, and strongly held convictions, or that another turn of the political wheel would not restore the influence and credibility of "commonwealth" thinking. There were many imponderables in the balance which had been achieved by May 1550.

12

Religious opposition; the Princess Mary

Mary had been eleven when her parents marriage began to break up. By the time her father remarried in 1533 she was seventeen, and fiercely loyal to her mother. Her refusal to accept Anne Boleyn as queen, or Elizabeth as heir led to the dismissal of her household in November 1533, and her own house arrest. This situation Mary decided to blame entirely upon Anne, and she regarded the latter's fall and execution in 1536 as the signal for her own rehabilitation. Catherine had died in January of the same year, but even before that Mary had surpassed her mother in political importance, and had become the symbol and figurehead of conservative opposition to Henry's policies. For this reason her reinstatement was no simple and automatic matter. Whatever reason may have prompted the establishment of the royal supremacy, by 1536 Henry was convinced that it truly represented the will of God in respect of England. Anne's disgrace consequently made no difference whatsoever, and Mary found, to her horror and astonishment that she could not recover her father's favour without submitting to the regiment which she had so long resisted. After a crisis of conscience which had been reflected in the court and council, in July 1536 she had submitted[1]. This cut the ground from under the feet of those who were anxious to use her against her father. The rebels of the Pilgrimage of Grace used her name in their demands, but she gave them no countenance or encouragement, and her relations with her cousin the Emperor Charles V, who had been her great supporter in adversity, gradually became more distant. During the last ten years of her father's life, Mary's relationship with him had varied from the dutiful to the enthusiastic, and she had become very friendly with his last queen, Catherine Parr, in whose household she was living, by choice rather then necessity, when he died in January 1547.

That a royal princess in full possession of her faculties should remain unmarried at the age of thirty one was an anomaly, and one which Mary herself felt keenly. The reason was mainly her ambiguous status. Bastardised by statute in 1533, and never restored, she had nevertheless been included in the succession after her half brother Edward, both in the succession act of 1543 and in her father's will. This was a situation which no one outside England could understand at all, and Henry had made matters worse by discouraging suitors. By the terms of his will she was only permitted to marry with the consent of her brother's council - an inevitable precaution - and she was allotted a marriage portion of £10,000. The difficulty was, of course that those to whom she would be most attractive were catholics who regarded her as legitimate; the least likely to win the consent of a protestant council. In another sense, however, Mary's status had been clarified by her father's death. Until that time, whether in favour or not, she had had no land or income of her own, but Henry's will settled on her a landed estate of about £3,000 a year. This was the income of a major peer, and appropriate to her rank. It also meant that for the first time she would be an independent figure, with her own affinity and the possibility of autonomous political action. Somerset honoured his obligation promptly, although it seems that he never showed Mary the will itself. At some point between April and July she was put in possession of an extensive patrimony, valued in the following year at £3819 18s 6d[2]. It may well have been that this process was speeded up by the fact that Mary's continued residence in Catherine's household became increasingly embarrassing as Lord Thomas Seymour's approaches became more ardent. Mary had almost certainly moved out by the end of April, when her own officers began to account, but she continued to receive payments out of the royal coffers for another three months. The estate of which she then became seized consisted of thirty three manors and lordships. With a few outlying exceptions, such as Shotwick in Cheshire, they were mainly concentrated in two areas; ten lay north and north east of London, in Essex and Hertfordshire, and another thirteen in Norfolk[3]. Most had belonged to the duke of Norfolk, and had come to the crown on his attainder, less than six months before Mary acquired them.

It soon became apparent that a significant part of the former Howard affinity had also transferred to the princess. Her officers, men such as Robert Rochester, Edward Waldegrave and Henry Jerningham, belonged to families with strong Howard connections. By the autumn of 1547 Mary was the strongest peer in East Anglia, so it was natural for established power seekers to gravitate towards her, but she also had another strong link to the Howards in her religious conservatism. Contrary to what is often supposed, Mary was not a lifelong reactionary. She had lived amicably with Catherine, who was a humanist reformer of fairly advanced views, and had taken part in her project for translating the scriptures. She was, however, a staunch defender of the mass, and of many popular and traditional pieties. In 1547 this aligned her with Stephen Gardiner and the other ecclesiastical conservatives, and made a confrontation with Somerset and Cranmer extremely likely. In June Van der Delft reported that she was hearing four masses a day, and if that was the case then she was literally making an exhibition of herself in order to encourage resistance to those protestant views which were beginning to attract official support. Somerset was proceeding cautiously, and his personal relations with Mary were good, so there was no immediate confrontation, but in December 1548 Van der Delft's secretary, Jehan Dubois reported that Mary had recently returned to London out of Norfolk, and "...wherever she had power, she caused the mass to be celebrated and the services of the church performed in the ancient manner." It was probably not accidental that the bill of uniformity was going through parliament at that point, and the council's intentions were an open secret. A council delegation waited upon Mary at about that time, but if their intention was to dissuade her from such gestures, then they were wasting their time. By then the princess had made her position clear to Somerset in a letter which no longer survives. From his response it is clear that she was expressing her defence of her father's religious settlement, and telling him that nothing could be changed until the king came of age. This was so similar to the views which had already been communicated by Bishop Gardiner that the protector understandably suspected collusion.

This may have been the case, but his two opponents differed in one very important respect. Mary placed no stress on the Act of Six Articles, or the *King's Book*, and was therefore quite unmoved by their repeal. As far as she was concerned the mass and the traditional rites of the church simply represented true religion, which her father had recognised in enforcing them. How she would have reacted if Edward had attained his majority and issued the same orders, we do not know, and the circumstance did not arise, but it looks as though the argument about minority was a mere smokescreen. On Whitsunday 1549, the day upon which the Prayer Book came into use, the parishioners of Sampford Courtney rioted, and Mary ordered mass to be celebrated with especial pomp in the chapel of her house at Kenninghall. At the time it must have been difficult to know which act of defiance was the more dangerous. On the 16th June the council wrote, remonstrating with her for her undutiful conduct and "evil ensample", and on the 22nd she replied, informing them blandly that she had broken no law "...unless it be a late law of your own making for the altering of matters in religion, which in my conscience is not worthy to have the name of law"[5]. In other words she was claiming the right to decide which laws she would obey, exactly as she had done in defying her father sixteen years earlier. Fortunately for her, Somerset did not have Henry's imperious temper, nor his weight of authority, and he was enmeshed in other problems. He was forced to temporise, not least because he could not afford a confrontation with the Emperor. As early as January Charles had warned the English council that he would expect his kinswoman and protege to be exempt from any heretical laws which they might be thinking of making. At that time the protector had replied that Mary was the king's subject, and must obey his laws like anyone else. In May Van der Delft was instructed to demand specific guarantees in writing that Mary's religious freedom would be respected. No government could yield to such blatant interference and retain its authority, so in spite of his mounting difficulties, particularly the French pressure on Boulogne, Somerset refused to issue any such guarantee. Instead Paget on his behalf gave a verbal undertaking that Mary's right to a private mass would be respected.

This was a sensible compromise, but it foundered on the definition of "private". Whatever Paget had meant at the time, the council subsequently glossed this to mean "in her own chamber and attended only by her personal servants", while Mary claimed indulgence for open celebrations in her household chapel for the benefit of anyone who wished to come . Skirmishing continued inconclusively throughout the summer. The council harried Mary's servants, particularly her chaplains, and she complained vigorously to Van der Delft, who in turn did his best to harry the council. Neither side wanted a breakdown of relations, but in October it seemed to the ambassador that his pressure had paid handsome dividends. Although Mary refused to become involved, the fall of the protector had at first every appearance of a conservative *coup*. The princess was sceptical, and told Van der Delft early in November that she did not believe that "religion" would be restored because the people were so infected with heresy. She was right, albeit for the wrong reason, and when the council showed its hand clearly in December, she likened it to the hardening of pharaoh's heart. A terrible judgment was about to descend on England, and Mary began to talk of fleeing the country, as she had talked in similar circumstances fifteen years before. Van der Delft became convinced that she was in serious danger, but the Emperor was not persuaded. To him she was a point of entry into English politics, a pressure point which he was perfectly willing to exploit. As a fugitive in Flanders she would be no use to him at all, and might even sacrifice her chance of the succession if Edward should unexpectedly die. One alternative to flight in the ordinary sense was marriage, and in the spring of 1550 two possibilities were under consideration. One was Dom Luis of Portugal, the younger brother of the king, who was a kinsman of the Emperor's and a good catholic, the other was the Lutheran marquis of Brandenberg. The second would have been acceptable to the council, but not to Mary or Charles. The first should have been acceptable to all parties. England would have been rid of a serious nuisance and the Emperor would have acquired a family claim to the English throne. However the reverse also applied. Charles would have lost his "pressure point" and England would be threatened with a Portuguese king. The negotiations consequently dragged on inconclusively. In April the council was considering further action to curb the luxuriance of Mary's "private" masses, and by early May she was working herself up into a state of hysteria.

Perhaps Charles became concerned for her mental stability, or perhaps he merely remitted the whole matter to the capable hands of his half sister, Mary of Hungary. For whatever reason, by the beginning of June an escape plan had been agreed. Van der Delft's health was failing and he was recalled. His successor, Jehan Scheyfve, was carefully told nothing of what was intended, so he could not be held responsible if the plot was discovered. The idea was that an Imperial warship should be sent to lie off the Essex coast on the pretext of chasing Scottish pirates, and that Van der Delft's secretary, Jehan Dubois should be sent ashore in a small boat in the guise of a corn merchant. Mary meanwhile would visit a small house that she had near Maldon, at Woodham Walter, and when Dubois signalled his approach would join him at Maldon, either in disguise or under cover of night. On 30th June Dubois duly arrived, spread his corn samples around Maldon, and sent word to Woodham Walter. Then things started to go wrong. Mary would not come, but asked Dubois instead to come to her. This he did at considerable risk, to find her in a desperate state of indecision, while her servants packed huge quantities of luggage. When Dubois demurred at the latter, and urged speed and secrecy, she began to draw back, while her controller, Robert Rochester, heightened her fears by lamenting the number and alertness of the "watches" which the council had ordered along the coast. Eventually, threatened with discovery, Dubois withdrew empty handed[6], leaving the situation as it had been before, except that the council soon discovered what had been intended, and set spies in the princess's household to prevent any repetition . At the end of July another of her chaplains was arrested, and Mary was interviewed by the council for some undisclosed purpose which was almost certainly another attempt to curb her mass. Soon after Scheyfve began the ritual of representation and protest where Van der Delft had left off. Thereafter an uneasy truce prevailed until the beginning of December.

At that point Edward himself, then aged thirteen and a half, began to take a personal interest in his sister's recalcitrance. Early in the month two of Mary's chaplains were arrested for saying mass in one of her houses for the benefit of her servants and during her absence. She, as usual, protested that this was covered by her immunity, which in turn provoked a lengthy epistle from the council, more than half protestant sermon and making patronising observations about the weakness of her theological understanding. This was followed on the 24th January by a personal letter from the king, about half in his own hand and reprimanding her in no uncertain terms;

> "...in our state it shall miscontent us to permit you, so great a subject, not to keep our laws. Your nearness to us in blood, your greatness in estate (and) the condition of this time maketh your fault the greater."[7]

This placed the princess in a very difficult dilemma, as it was no doubt intended to do, because a central pillar of her argument had always been that the king was too young to understand such matters, and that no one else could claim the right to constrain her conscience. Genuinely distressed, she became ill, and once again appealed to Scheyfve for the Emperor's protection. She was, she professed, willing to obey the king in all things "saving her conscience". Neither at this or any other time did she attempt to appeal beyond her father's settlement to the faith of the church universal, and the pope was never mentioned by either side. Presumably she believed the royal supremacy to be personal to her father, and acceptable because he had defended the mass - precisely the kind of conditional allegiance which the council could not afford to tolerate. Edward offered to instruct his sister, and the ambassador threatened the Emperor's displeasure, but the stalemate continued, and eventually the realistic Charles declared "If they may be brought to consent that she may hear mass privately in her own house without admitting any strangers, let her be satisfied with that...". Chastened by this evidence of disengagement on the part of her champion, the princess retreated slightly. Without making any ostensible concession, she confined her celebrations to her own household, and the council refrained from further pressure for several months.

In August 1551, however, the issue surfaced again. This was not on account of any provocation offered by Mary, but because deteriorating Franco-Imperial relations had given the council more room to manoeuvre, and they decided that the challenge that she represented could be ended without international repercussions. It was also convenient to make another demonstration of the king's personal indignation. Mary's "mass licence" was withdrawn altogether, and her household officers were summoned before the council and ordered to insist that the edict was obeyed. They refused and were imprisoned. The inevitable protests were flying thick and fast when, on 29th August a council delegation went down to Copthall to confront the Princess in person[8]. They were treated to a full range of histrionics, from exaggerated respect for the king's order to withering contempt for his representatives. Her father, she declared had "made the more part of you almost as nothing", and she had no more intention of obeying than she had had before. Mary kept her mass - just - but it was several months before her officers were released and her household restored to normal. Having at last successfully insisted that Mary's indulgence was confined to herself and her personal servants, the posturing on both sides subsided and there were no serious incidents during the last eighteen months of the reign. Mary had demonstrated her tenacity and her devotion to traditional religion beyond all doubt. She had also demonstrated her dependence upon her Habsburg cousin. What she had not done was to show the slightest interest in the pope or his jurisdiction.

13

Education, charity and the dissolution

of the chantries.

A chantry was an endowment to provide intercessory prayer. It was largely, but not entirely, dependent upon the customary belief in purgatory, that indeterminate place between heaven and hell where the souls of sinners were cleansed in preparation for their eventual acceptance into the kingdom of God. The prayers of the living could assist the passage of the departed through this experience, and many people left behind instructions that such prayers should be offered, and money to pay the priests who should say them. The wealthiest might endow a perpetual foundation, even a college of many priests who's main function was to offer prayers and masses for the souls of their benefactor and his or her kindred. Many chantries, however, were small, and the majority were of limited duration. At the lowest level a few pence might be left for a commemorative mass at the "months mind" or the anniversary. Henry had moved against purgatory almost as soon as he had moved against the pope. In 1535 the great pilgrimage shrines began to be destroyed. Their property was appropriated and the practice was forbidden. It has often been claimed that this had more to do with the king's greed for the jewels of Glastonbury and Walsingham than with any aversion to intercessory prayer, but such a claim is not entirely justified. In 1543 the *King's Book*, which was in many ways a very conservative manifesto, allowed intercessory prayer, but declared that purgatory was "not to be spoken of". Two years later all chantry foundations were dissolved by statute on the grounds that the king had need of "a mass of money", which certainly does not sound like a religious motive, but the fact remains that the king's enthusiasm for the mass did not extend to the protection of other peoples endowments[1]. Nine years earlier Hugh

Latimer had declared that the dissolution of the monasteries "argueth purgatory not to be", which did not show a very clear understanding of the *opus dei*, but was an accurate reflection of the attitude of the Henrician church[2].

For a number of reasons, including the king's death, the dissolution act of 1545 was never implemented. However the financial situation did not improve, and the attitude of the council towards intercessory prayer became markedly more hostile under the new regime. A new bill for the dissolution of the chantries was introduced into parliament in November 1547, this time coupling the king's financial needs with the elimination of superstitious practices. It was fiercely resisted, both in the lords and in the commons. The conservative bishops disapproved both of its purpose and its didactic preamble, but Cranmer also disapproved, probably because he did not trust the avowed intention to devote the newly acquired resources to charity and education. He had previously taken issue with Henry VIII over the secularisation of the monastic lands, and his view of the rapacity of the laity had not changed. In the commons the resistance came partly from those who feared for the survival of the craft guilds and academic colleges, and partly from the burgesses of specific towns, such as Coventry and King's Lynn, which had already diverted much of the endowment to civic purposes. Most of this opposition was bought off with concessions which were embodied in appendices to the act, and the bill became law on the 15th December[3]. It may be that the archbishop's scruples had been heeded, or perhaps the protector always intended to be conscientious, but commissions were immediately established under the great seal to survey the affected property, and to make suitable provision for those other functions that the intercessory foundations often performed. Where chantry chapels had served as "chapels of ease" in very large parishes, or where cantarists had also performed necessary parochial functions, these were to continue. Similarly endowed grammar schools were to be refounded, and where such secular purposes as the repair of highways or sea defences had been part of the founder's intention, then those functions were to continue also. Although the promoters of the act were protestants, not all conservatives were outraged by the disappearances of these foundations. They had, after all, appeared to load the salvation stakes very heavily in favour of the rich, and there was, at this stage, no attempt to outlaw intercessory prayer itself.

Although a sizable proportion of former chantry property was eventually sold or granted to laymen, much was absorbed by continuations or pensions, and much remained in the hands of the crown[4]. This was not necessarily intentional, and often resulted from the fact that the properties involved were very small and scattered, but it blunted the edge of later criticism. It would probably be an exaggeration to say that parishes which had lost large chantry foundations were better off without them, but a large church like that of Chester-le-Street in County Durham lost little if anything in terms of its spiritual functions. There a dean and eight prebendaries, most of whom were non-resident pluralists, were replaced with a vicar and two curates, who were required to devote their full energies to the service of the parish. Hardship and loss were incurred, however, when non-endowed functions disappeared. It was, for example, quite common for an underemployed cantarist to keep a school, which served the community and supplemented his stipend. Sometimes the removal of his main employment would force him to leave, and his school would close. But it would be a mistake to see the Chantries Act as having a devastating effect on English education. What it did do, to some extent, was to restructure the parochial clergy in a manner more appropriate for a protestant church. That would have been more effectively accomplished if the council had been willing to allow the continuation commissioners to be more generous in allocating stipends to the new vicars and curates. Too often the new payments were adequate by the old standards, but insufficient to attract the educated preaching ministers which the new church so desperately needed.

Because protestantism was predominantly a faith for the literate, it might be supposed that the reign of Edward VI would have seen a dramatic surge in new school foundations. This, however, did not happen. Education had been a favourite destination for charitable donations and bequests for many years. It was humanists like John Colet rather than protestants that created the fashion for a learned laity, a fashion which became firmly established at the court of Henry VIII with momentous consequences for the English aristocracy. By the end of his reign the grammar school, which had originally been intended to give potential priests a grounding in Latin, which would be their professional language, were increasingly filled by the sons of well to do merchants, officials and minor gentry, who had no intention of seeking a career in the church. So far had the pendulum swung that archbishop Cranmer, when he was drawing up regulations for a new school in Canterbury, had to fight off a demand that its intake should be exclusively confined to the sons of gentlemen. Education remained a gateway to the priesthood, but it had also become the essential preliminary to a wide range of secular careers, before it also began to be perceived as a pathway to salvation. Given the range of vested interests which were engaged, it is perhaps the paucity of school provision rather than its generosity which should surprise us. Most towns of any substance could boast a school, and London had several, but the attendance at each was counted in scores rather than hundreds and it is doubtful whether more than 5% of the population ever benefited from such provision[5]. Basic literacy extended well beyond this elite group, and may have reached as much as 15% of the population, but it is notoriously tricky to assess, because many who could read could not write, and many who could write their names could extend their skill no further. Broadly speaking the gentry, both male and female,were literate, and most urban householders, but in rural communities which made up over 80% of the population, literacy was patchy and unpredictable, often depending upon the skill and willingness of the local incumbent.

Unendowed and random village schools provided all the education most people were ever likely to get, but unlike the grammar schools, they catered for both boys and girls, and sometimes enjoyed surprising influence, especially after the English bible came along to reinforce the motivation of their pupils. The grammar schools could expect their intake, at the age of about eight or nine, to be literate in the vernacular, and they concentrated, as before, upon Latin, although by 1550 it was the Latin of the renaissance and classical antiquity rather than that of the church. Classical literature and the Christian faith were the staple items of the school curriculum, whether the regime was catholic or protestant, and both sides in the reformation controversy were equally concerned to control the schools. Consequently in Edward's reign new foundations tended to flaunt their evangelical credentials, but to remain firmly under lay control. Bodies of governors and trustees were looked to maintain the integrity of the founder's intentions. Most of these foundations were the work of private individuals, but the crown was by far the largest single benefactor, distributing a capital sum of about £21,000 in this way. To keep this generosity in proportion, it represented no more than $3^1/_2$% of the capital value of the chantry property confiscated under the act of 1547, which has been calculated at a little over £610,000[6].

In spite of the switchback effects of the reformation changes, English schools were expanding and flourishing in the mid-sixteenth century, but the same was not true of the universities. A growing gentry involvement had taken the young Thomas Wyatt to St. John's college Cambridge in the early days of its foundation, and by the early seventeenth century was to turn both universities into aristocratic preserves. But in 1550 the original purpose of ordination training was still predominant, and they were consequently in the front line of ideological conflict. Two blows both delivered in the 1530s, had been particularly severe. In 1535 a royal edict, engineered by Thomas Cromwell, had prohibited the study of canon law and discontinued the award of degrees in the subject. This destroyed at a stroke the largest faculty in each university, and the whole profession which had depended upon its graduates. The halls which had catered for the canon lawyers disappeared, taking with them about 40% of the students and teaching staff. When the monasteries were dissolved, between 1536 and 1540, the monks and friars also vanished from the university scene, and most of the remaining halls, which were the cells of religious houses, or friaries in their own right, were closed down and disposed of. This left the colleges, which had previously been only one element in the structure of the universities, in not-so-splendid isolation. Matriculation figures slumped as ecclesiastical careers seemed increasingly unattractive and uncertain. Neither Henry nor Cromwell had any intention of damaging the country's two centres of higher education. In 1540 Regius professorships on the French model were established in Greek, Hebrew and Divinity, and by 1546 new colleges on the grand scale had been founded in both Oxford and Cambridge. Christ Church was a re-foundation of Wolsey's Cardinal college, but Trinity was an entirely new initiative, and did something to restore the student numbers which earlier royal policy had so drastically reduced.

In educational terms the dominance of the colleges was not altogether a good thing. Apart from the religious foundations, which had their own discipline, the halls were little more than hostels. The colleges, on the other hand, were very carefully structured. Moral tutors not only provided academic guidance but strict personal control. A tutor would be responsible for about twenty young men - or more accurately boys - aged between thirteen and eighteen. They lived under his personal supervision; their behaviour, their movements and their reading, were all subject to careful scrutiny. This was not a regiment designed to produce independent minds, and the turbulent intellects of the mediaeval universities largely disappeared. Doctrinal orthodoxy became an obsession. During the theological disputes of the fourteenth century university men had been allowed to say more or less what they liked, so long as they said it in Latin, but between 1549 and 1552 visitations were conducted which resulted in numerous expulsions. Prayer Book services were imposed upon college chapels, and new statutes drawn up which removed the traditional rites of intercession. Nor did the rise of humanism lead to any liberalisation of the curriculum. The study of classical texts, and of the scriptures, was as strictly regimented as ever that of the commentators and glossators had been. From the 1530s onwards university intellectuals had an important role to play in the affairs of state, but it was to defend the orthodoxies of obedience, not to undermine them with criticism or dissent. Sir John Cheke's *Hurt of Sedition* was the kind of utterance which was expected of a Regius professor. Civil law survived the departure of the canonists, but students were few, and there were no concessions to more modern preoccupations. Both music and medicine remained strictly traditional higher studies, and there were no faculties for modern languages, or anything which we would recognise as science[7]. At the same time the colleges developed a powerful sense of corporate identity, and defended their privileges and immunities tenaciously against both patrons and intrusive vice-chancellors. As a result the balance of power in both Oxford and Cambridge began to shift away from the universities and towards these constituent institutions, with important consequences for the future. No new colleges were founded in Edward's reign, but foundations recommenced under Mary in Oxford and under Elizabeth in Cambridge. Strict religious and moral discipline was characteristic of the charters of these new colleges, and both Sir Thomas White (Trinity Oxford, 1555) and Sir Walter Mildmay (Emmanuel Cambridge, 1584) saw themselves as planting seminaries of true religion.

Cambridge had a protestant tradition going back to the 1520s, when the so-called "White Horse group" had gathered to discuss the writings of Luther and the other new ideas which were convulsing Germany. It was allegedly scholars imported from Cambridge to staff Wolsey's new foundation in Oxford who first contaminated the older university with heresy. By 1550 there was a significant, but still minority, protestant presence in Cambridge, particularly in colleges like St. Johns which had a strong humanist tradition[8]. Martin Bucer was welcomed as Regius professor of Divinity, and although he only survived the fenland climate for a little over two years, enjoyed an immense influence which was remembered by his students many years later. Peter Martyr Vermigli, who held a similar position in

Oxford, had a much more difficult task. There were protestant cells in colleges such as Brasenose, but Martyr was harried and obstructed by conservative opponents far more than his colleague. At the same time, because his brand of theology was more acceptable to the Swiss than that of Bucer, it was to Oxford that young friends and followers of Heinrich Bullinger migrated when the pressures of study nearer home became too great. So we find John Stumphius and John and Conrad ab Ulmis writing from Oxford to complain what a lame and uncertain process the advance of godliness was in England, and praising Martyr's efforts under great difficulties[9]. Both universities were undergoing a very painful of adjustment between 1540 and 1560. Each successive government professed the desire to promote good learning, but none had any concept of the kind of intellectual freedom which was to prevail, for instance, at Leyden after 1580. Each wished to see the universities as training schools for loyal and orthodox clergy of its own persuasion. Meanwhile, in courtly humanism and in the increasing aristocratic interest in education as a means of secular advancement, the seeds had already been sown for that process which was to turn the colleges into tightly controlled finishing schools for the sons of gentlemen, and even noblemen. For some time after 1560 these two ideals were to live side by side. By 1600 the universities were producing as many graduate clergy as the church could absorb, while at the same time the aristocratic practice of spending a year or two in residence as a means of acquiring a fashionable veneer of learning, before proceeding to an inn of court or the grand tour, was already well established. There never was any intention under Edward of dissolving the university colleges, and the campaign which was once supposed to have earned their reprieve was largely a myth, but it would be hard to point to any action , either by Somerset or Northumberland, which actually strengthened or promoted them. The number of students was probably halved between 1530 and 1550. It would be twenty years before Cambridge recovered its former size, and over thirty before Oxford did the same . The revolution in higher education owed a lot to Henry VIII, and a lot to Elizabeth, but not very much to Edward VI.

14

The foreign policy of the Earl of

Warwick

In spite of the advantageous timing of their move against Boulogne, in October 1549 the French were making little headway. Their galleys had been heavily defeated off Jersey in August, leaving the English navy in complete command of the channel, and the Emperor had issued a solemn warning that any attempt to extend hostilities to Calais would force him to honour his treaty obligations. Chatillon had managed to sever communications between Calais and Boulogne, but since the latter was supplied almost entirely by sea, that made little difference . Moreover, it remained to be seen whether Warwick could succeed where Somerset had failed, in establishing a more positive relationship with Charles V. The fall of the protector appeared to reopen the whole question of Anglo-Imperial relations. Charles, however, was not to be drawn. Even while it still seemed likely that Somerset's religious policy would be reversed, he was refusing to alter his position over Boulogne, and extremely reluctant to allow even a modest recruitment of mercenary soldiers. Nevertheless as England's domestic crisis eased it became possible to reinforce both Calais and Boulogne, while plague and financial difficulties were handicapping the French assault. Neither side wanted a protracted stalemate. By December it had become clear that Chatillon could not take the town by assault as long as it could be supplied and reinforced by the sea, but the English could not raise the siege without Imperial support. Both sides were ready for negotiations, but neither was willing to take an open initiative. Consequently a Florentine named Anthony Guidotti, long resident in London, was sent across to Paris to put out secret feelers[1]. The response was positive, and after Christmas Guidotti made a second trip, this time with some tangible proposals, which were alleged to include a marriage between Edward and Henry's daughter, Elizabeth. Eventually at the end of January, both sides were sufficiently convinced to appoint commissioners for a formal negotiation.

Lord Paget headed the English delegation, accompanied by Russell, Petre and Mason, and in spite of recent problems it is clear that he had the full confidence of the council. Shorn of their rhetoric, his instructions were to surrender Boulogne for the best terms that he could get; to haggle, but not to risk coming away without an agreement. The demand was the full ransom agreed at Cercamp, plus the rasing of the fortifications. Warwick was even prepared to make another attempt to persuade Henry to accept the Anglo-Scottish marriage, offering in return to give up the remaining English strongholds in Scotland. The French, who held the stronger hand, refused to discuss Scotland at all, except on the basis of an unconditional English withdrawal. Paget's assessment of his negotiating position is usually described as "realistic", but he may have underestimated the French anxiety for an end to hostilities[2]. In the event all he was able to get was a ransom for 400,000 crowns (about £100,000), to be paid in two instalments. Agreement along these lines was reached on the 24th March, and proclaimed in England on the 28th. The formalities of ratification took some time . Hostages were exchanged; Lord Clinton handed the town over to Chatillon on 25th April, and the first instalment of the ransom was paid in Calais on the same day. Given that it cost about £30,000 to pay off the garrison and the civilian work force, Warwick did not gain much disposable cash from the first stage of this transaction, and the treaty was generally regarded as a surrender resulting from political weakness. It was called "dishonourable" both at the time and since, but in truth Boulogne was a liability, which had cost a fortune to acquire and maintain. The only valid criticism which could be made was that it did not contain any provision for a dignified end to the protector's unfinished Scottish business, which remained on the agenda for another occasion.

In one sense the loss of Boulogne left Calais more exposed, but there were two ways to protect the "old conquest". One was to continue to rely on the Imperial guarantee of 1543, which had recently been renewed. The other was to cultivate the friendship of France, thus hopefully removing the threat. The latter policy was contrary to Tudor custom, although Henry had tried it briefly, both in 1514-18 and 1527-9. At neither time had it paid significant dividends, but it did

have the immense advantage of reducing England's vulnerability to
Imperial pressure. At a time when relations with the Emperor were
strained by religious differences , and when Mary of Hungary, at
least,was casting predatory eyes upon a kingdom which she thought
"would not be impossible to conquer, especially now that it is prey to
discord and poverty"[3], friendship with France was not such a bad idea.
Once the issue of Boulogne was out of the way, it became at least a
realistic option, and as early as May 1550 a certain warmth was
injected into the exchange of honorific missions which completed the
process of ratification. Warwick did not, however show any
inclination to rush to premature conclusions. Henry II had not
suddenly become anglophile, and there was no reason to suppose as
yet that his designs on Calais had been abandoned. A joint boundary
commission was established in July to forestall any sudden pretext for
a confrontation, but the council continued to feed money, armaments
and reinforcements into the pale in small quantities throughout the
remainder of the year. Whatever hopes may have been entertained of
improving relations with France the Calais guard had not been
lowered. Tension arising from border infringement occurred at regular
intervals, and at the end of October 1550 1000 fresh troops were sent
across to strengthen the garrison. However, neither side wished to
escalate these irritations, and at the end of November the border
commission was reactivated to continue with its work of defusing
potential trouble. At the same time an attempt was made to tackle the
endless complaints of piracy which constantly soured relations
between the mercantile and maritime communities on both sides.
Part of the problem was caused by tension and disagreements within
France. The powerful Guise faction was implacably hostile to
England. Ostensibly this was for religious reasons, but probably had
more to do with the position of Mary of Guise in Scotland, and the
fact that her daughter was betrothed to the dauphin. The constable,
Anne de Montmorency, on the other hand, was a pragmatist whose
eyes were mainly on the next round of hostilities with the Emperor.
To him England, heretical or not, was a potential ally. English
diplomats also tended to be divided. In February 1551 Sir John Mason
reported on a long conversation with the king and the constable, which
had convinced him of their genuine desire for amity, and perhaps an
explicit alliance. But at about the same time Nicholas Wotton, who
was very experienced in continental affairs, warned that Henry had no
intention of giving up his claim to Calais , and would be at best an
unreliable and short term ally[4].   He strongly urged friendship

with the Emperor. As a religious conservative he had little sympathy with Warwick's domestic policies, and would not have regretted renewed attempts to modify them. By April 1551it seemed that Montmorency's influence was in the ascendant in the French court. A French mediator the Seigneur de Lansac, had finally negotiated a more or less graceful English withdrawal from Scotland, and good progress was being made with the long standing commercial disagreement. In April also Henry II was elected, and accepted election, to the Order of the Garter. The Emperor's agents watched this rapprochement with a scepticism not untinged by alarm. England was not a military power to be feared, but her navy was powerful and her strategic position guaranteed that it could be used to good effect. Simon Renard, Charles' ambassador in Paris believed that a marriage between Edward and Elizabeth was in an advanced state of negotiation.

He was almost right. In May a large and honorific mission, headed by the marquis of Northampton, was instructed to proceed to France to confer the Garter upon the king. Northampton, who was accompanied by a stiffening of seasoned diplomats, was also to treat for the marriage, asking for the enormous dowry of 800,000 crowns and a *dot* of 12,000 marks a year[5]. At the same time it was indicated that a similar mission, headed by the Marshal de St. Andre, would visit London to confer the Order of St. Michael upon the king of England. These very positive developments did not please everyone at Edward's court, and the pro-Imperial party in the council found a powerful advocate in the person of the newly rehabilitated duke of Somerset. As protector he had had little option but to seek what Habsburg protection he could get, but, like many other Englishmen, he was temperamentally averse to any closer relations with France, and in a strong position to undermine Warwick's policy if he chose to do so. Northampton's mission, however, succeeded reasonably well. He had no chance of extracting a dowry of 800,000 crowns, but haggled for nearly two months before accepting 200,000, which was the most that Montmorency was prepared to concede. The treaty was signed on the 20th July, and the marquis and his retinue then immediately returned home to something approaching a hero's welcome. Meanwhile St. Andre's much simpler mission had been even more successful. He was an affable and good natured man, and a magnificent showman. Little more was required, because Edward was as delighted with his new decoration as any normal child would be with a new toy[6]. The marshal arrived in London on 11th July, and the order was conferred at Hampton Court on the 16th. The king's *Journal* testifies to his enthusiasm and to the good impression that St. Andre made. Lavish entertainment followed and a series of private audiences in which the professions of good will and mutual admiration flew thick and fast. It was all very well for Wotton to write from Frankfurt that the French were never to be trusted, and their diplomats least of all. The king was completely captivated by his new friend, and that suited the purposes of the earl of Warwick very well.

Any improvement in Anglo-French relations produced a suspicious reflex in Brussels, but in the summer of 1550 Charles had no particular need for English friendship, and had so low an opinion of English power that he could regard the possibility of hostility with equanimity. His own health was not particularly good, and beyond condoning the abortive plot to whisk Mary away from Woodham Walter, he took no action at all. The replacement of Van der Delft by Scheyfvre as ambassador did nothing to strengthen the Imperial influence on London, and apart from continuous commercial disputes, there was little diplomatic exchange between the courts for several months. If Scheyfve was a poor substitute for Van der Delft, Richard Morrison was an even worse replacement for Sir Philip Hoby. Hoby was tactful and experienced, and his dispatches showed a sound grasp of political reality. Morrison was conceited and opinionated, flaunting his protestantism in a manner that the Emperor found particularly irritating. He had no feeling for the environment in which he was operating, and no means of obtaining reliable information. If Warwick was deliberately trying to run down his relations with the Emperor, then he chose the right man to do it. In so far as there was any thrust or direction to Imperial policy during the early part of 1551, it came from the regent, and was distinctly hostile to England. In January the commercial disputes sharpened as Mary threatened reprisals against English merchants in Antwerp for the alleged depredations of English pirates. In fact the new lord admiral, Lord Clinton, seems to have been taking effective action to police the narrow seas, and unsupported accusations that he was himself implicated in piratical activity did nothing to sweeten relations[7]. However the regent soon discovered that any action which she might take against English merchants would severely damage the commercial prosperity of her own subjects, and by June the pressure had eased in spite of the continued and ritualistic posturing about princess Mary and her mass.

In September 1551 when the threatened hostility between France and the Empire eventually broke out, Mary of Hungary was not quite so blase about the English attitude. Charles sought, and received, assurances that Edward would abide by his treaty obligations, and would not provide shelter for French privateers, but Mary was more aggressive. This was the time, she felt, to capitalise upon the weakness of England and the friendship of her namesake. The control of at least one English port was necessary to secure the safety of Imperial shipping, and if it could not be secured by friendship, then it must be seized by force. No such attack came, and indeed it was the regent rather than the Emperor who tried to stem the exodus of English merchants from Antwerp following a harsh new series of "placards" or edicts against heresy. Religion continually threatened to undermine Anglo-Imperial relations, quite independently of England's growing amity with France. Charles's ambassador in London enjoyed complete immunity to practice his catholic faith within the privacy of his own residence, but when Warwick demanded a reciprocal arrangement for the English ambassador in the Low Countries, it was angrily and indeed contemptuously refused. Morison had partly brought about this rebuff by preaching at the Emperor, but even when he was recalled and replaced by the diplomatic Wotton, there was no change. Warwick threatened to withdraw Scheyfve's privilege if his own demand was not met, but his bluff was met by Charles's continued intransigence and his own reluctance to force a complete breakdown in diplomatic relations. There was every reason in October 1551 for the regent to fear that her strenuous efforts to maintain the prosperity of Antwerp would founder as England entered the war on the French side.

The duke of Northumberland (as Warwick became in November 1551) had every reason to avoid becoming embroiled. Some of Henry's allies the German protestant princes, appealed directly for English aid, and a force of 400 English volunteers served as mercenaries under the duke of Aumale, but that was the full extent of English participation. The marriage treaty between Edward and Elizabeth was confirmed at the end of December, and an exchange of rich gifts followed in January 1552, but there was no military alliance. In March England reaffirmed her neutrality and since this position was more beneficial to France than to the Empire, both sides were reasonably content. The second fall of Somerset at the end of 1551, and the exclusion of Paget from the council had led the Emperor to fear the worst of Northumberland's intentions, and he was therefore relieved to have no worse an outcome. By the summer the duke was clearly attempting to pursue an isolationist policy, and some of

England's ambassadors felt that he was doing so by the simple expedient of ignoring them[8]. However it was a difficult stance to maintain, especially since England had a mutual aid treaty with the Emperor, which the latter had been willing to honour as late as 1550. It was the regent who first invoked this treaty, pointing out in a letter of the 5th July that the borders of her state had been violated, and calling upon the English council to provide immediately the 5000 foot to which they were committed. This embarrassing request was evaded for as long as possible, using the excuse of a royal progress, but eventually, on the 31st of the month it was met with a flat refusal. Edward neither could nor would honour his father's treaty, although he professed a willingness to negotiate one of his own. At the same time, in spite of the continued professions of goodwill, it seems that the council did not entirely trust its friendship with France. Large troop movements in Picardy produced the reflex action of sending reinforcements to Calais, even though it was quite clear that the mobilisation was against the Low Countries. In the autumn of 1552 English policy was in a state of flux. Whether this was the result of increasing participation by the young king himself, or of fundamental disagreements within the council is not clear[9]. There had always been a party that disliked the French connection, and wished to return to the old alliance with the Emperor. This party was given a strong boost in November when the letters passing between French officers in Scotland and members of the council in Paris revealed that whatever Henry II might profess, or intend, the Guise party was determined to press its advantage in Scotland, and seize any opportunity to act against English interests. This further undermined English confidence in French integrity, which was already fragile, and caused new signals to be sent to the Emperor. Charles was by this time heavily embroiled in the siege of Metz, but he gave a cautious welcome to this change of direction. The only tangible sign of improved relations was an easing of commercial restrictions, but by the end of 1552 England was certainly not looking to France for protection against the Habsburgs. Having disposed of the duke of Somerset, Northumberland found himself at this point almost back to the protector's policy of 1548. If his intention was to preserve a convincing air of neutrality, then he was succeeding, and in consequence was fully trusted by neither side.

15

The court and the council, 1550-1553

It has often and correctly, been observed that the earl of Warwick restored concilar government after the virtual autocracy of the protectorate. There were a number of reasons for this, but constitutional propriety was not one of them. By February 1550 he had established a firm ascendancy over the council. The dismissal of Arundel and Wriothesley, and the appointment of Hereford and Darcy gave him sufficient control to enable him to alter the membership at will thereafter. This meant that he could enjoy the security of collective responsibility without sacrificing his freedom of action. By confining himself to the title of lord president, he signalled that he was merely *primus inter pares*, while ensuring that his will would prevail when it mattered. At the same time he was aware, as Somerset had not been, that executive authority could only be effective when it was exercised with the co-operation of the majority of the ruling class. To maintain that co-operation imposed certain restraints on his policies, but these could be lessened if members of the council were willing to carry the message into their countries, mobilising the support of the gentry for the regime, and maintaining the kind of disciplinary vigilance which had been neglected with such disastrous consequences in 1548-9[1]. In other words, the privy council became his team - a necessary agency and support - but there could be only one leader, and dissent which amounted to a challenge could not be tolerated, as both Paget and Somerset discovered to their cost in the autumn of 1551. There was also another dimension to Warwick's method. Soon after the king had achieved his fourteenth birthday in October 1551 he began to appear at council meetings, and to be exposed to public business. It even began to be hinted that he was old enough to make important decisions himself. This was almost certainly part of a long term strategy on Warwick's part to convert himself from a regent into a trusted chief minister. Personal influence over Edward was the key to his method , and another means of avoiding the exposure which Somerset had deliberately created, but which in the end proved fatal to him.

The former protector was restored to the council on 10th April 1550, and it is very unlikely that this was either a sentimental gesture or a sign of weakness. There must have been some understanding that the two men would work together in the new situation, and Warwick was sure enough of his position to be willing to take the political risks involved. On the 19th April Sir John Mason was also added; formerly a protege of Paget, but by this time already linked to Warwick, a man of sound bureaucratic experience and diplomatic expertise. The next recruit was Edward Fiennes, Lord Clinton, who had just succeeded Warwick as lord admiral, an old companion in arms of the earl, and one of his most trusted associates. He was sworn on 4th May. George Brooke, Lord Cobham, who joined on the 23rd May was a somewhat less obvious recruit. An experienced soldier, and presently lord deputy of Calais, he had no particular connections with Warwick, and may have been advanced as a means of persuading him to re-align his loyalties[2]. If that was the case, the manoeuvre seems to have succeeded. Francis Hastings, earl of Huntingdon, who was sworn on 4th September 1550, represented Warwick's determined attempt to expand his power base within the established nobility. He had a modest record as a soldier, but was a powerful man in Leicestershire and there were not too many major peers who were willing to stand beside Warwick in public. Similar considerations probably explain the elevation of the earl of Westmorland on 26th February 1551. Henry Neville was a member of the "old" (pre-Tudor) nobility, and a great man in the sensitive border regions against Scotland. He had a record of eccentric behaviour suggestive of mental instability, and had been in the Fleet at the time of Henry VIII's death on suspicion of plotting to murder his father[3]. But he had served successfully against the Scots in 1548, and Warwick was in urgent need of a powerful local man in the far north to replace Cuthbert Tunstall, the aging bishop of Durham. Tunstall had opposed very step of the Edwardian reformation, discreetly but with determination, and was arrested in August 1550, ostensibly for concealing a treasonable plot, but in reality for being too recalcitrant to act as an agent for Warwick's policy in the north[4]. Westmorland was sent north immediately after his appointment with instructions to monitor the conservative rumblings of discontent in that region.

Warwick's other council appointments were of a different nature.

Sir William Cecil became a privy councillor on the 5th September 1550, when he was appointed as one of the two principal secretaries. Cecil had been briefly imprisoned after the fall of the protector, but had successfully ingratiated himself with the new regime. He was a man of great ability, which had already been recognised, and an honest supporter of the reformed religion. Sir John Gates was similarly an *ex officio* appointment, when he became vice-chamberlain on 8th April 1551. Gates was Sir Anthony Denny's brother in law, and had been a gentleman of the privy chamber since before Henry's death. He had been sufficiently trusted by the reforming party to be named as one of those authorised to use the old king's dry stamp in the last months of his life, and had been given actual custody of the stamp itself. Consequently it is not surprising to find Warwick promoting him to such a sensitive and important court office. Sir Philip Hoby, who was sworn at some point between May and August 1551, was a professional diplomat, and his appointment probably had more to do with enhancing his status abroad than with any service he was expected to perform at home. He may also have been recruited to strengthen Warwick's party against the duke of Somerset, with whom a showdown was looming by August 1551. He had deserted the protector at the time of his fall, and relations between the two men were notoriously bad. Sir Robert Bowes was a soldier and administrator with great experience of the north, and a considerable following in Yorkshire. Like Westmorland, he was recruited to strengthen the council's hand in dealing with the marches, where there was little sympathy with Warwick or his policies. He was sworn on the 25th September 1551. Sir Richard Cotton, who became a counsellor in May 1552 was a financial expert, who shortly after became cofferer of the household, and the last appointment was that of Sir John Cheke on 2nd June 1553 when he was briefly named to a third secretaryship. Warwick thus added eleven permanent members to the council after securing his ascendancy in January 1550, and dismissed five, not counting the duke of Somerset under either of these headings. The council thus numbered thirty two or thirty three in the summer of 1553, half as big again as that which had dismissed the protector; but it was, or appeared to be, an effective working team which kept domestic unrest under firm control, and even began to tackle the crown's serious financial problems with some evidence of success[5].

Some appointments were made, however, which do not fit in to this pattern. The rehabilitation and eventual destruction of Somerset is an issue in itself, but there was also the curious temporary co-option of the earls of Arundel and Derby on the 9th August 1551. Arundel had been an important councillor before his fall early in 1550, but Derby had never been a member, and had to take a special temporary oath. It may be that their brief appearance was part of Warwick's strategy against Mary, which was going through a fresh convolution at this point; or it may have been the formal culmination of discussions which had been going on for some months about preserving security in some of the more remote parts of the realm. If there was one issue upon which Warwick was likely to see eye to eye with the staunch and powerful conservatives, it was surely the need to prevent any recurrence of the upheavals of 1549. When faced with an unruly commons the nobility must stand shoulder to shoulder, no matter what their differences. The final and cardinal sin that the protector had committed was to call upon the commons to defend him. Whether he was aware of the strength of feeling which his proclamation had generated is unknown, although it featured in the charges against him. Somerset was neither particularly alert nor particularly sensitive to his own errors. In April 1550 Warwick was looking to him as a chastened ally, who would support a regime which was committed to further the religious reform programme which had meant so much to him. In return he would have to accept the fact that it was not committed either to his social programme or his foreign policy. Within a few weeks, before the end of June, Warwick was beginning to drop hints that he found the duke's demeanour in council unsatisfactory. He was pressing for the release of Gardiner, and boasting of the king's affection for him, of which "...he is by some fondly persuaded". These hints were conveyed to Cecil, with the clear intention that they should be passed on[6]. If Somerset wished to be a full participant in the process of government, then he would have to accommodate himself to working with the council. If he chose to "take private ways by himself", then he would again find himself exposed to the danger from which he had so recently and narrowly escaped. The message seems to have been received and understood, but it did not resolve the growing problem. Somerset, had, and knew he had, a valid point of view on a number of issues which was different from that of Warwick. When others agreed with him , it inevitably looked as though he was trying to form a party.

The duke had never been noted for his tact or discretion, and when he tried to insist upon the recall of parliament, which Warwick was anxious to avoid, it looked as though he was seeking to use that body to recover his ascendancy. In the autumn of 1550 both the French and Imperial ambassadors reported that Somerset was seeking to gain friends within the council, and was accusing Warwick of a harsh and repressive social policy. Over the next few months rumours of hostility persisted, but there was no open rupture. In March 1551 Sir Ralph Vane, who was a close friend of Somerset's, picked a rather gratuitous quarrel with Warwick and was briefly imprisoned. Scheyfve believed at one point that the duke was about to retreat to the north and make common cause with the conservatives, but there is no hard evidence of any such intention, which is intrinsically improbable. Both were heavily involved in the court ceremonies attendant upon the reception of the order of St. Michael, which effectively stifled any signs of discord for several weeks. If Somerset had been intent on mounting a challenge to Warwick for the control of the council, then by September it must have been clear to him that he had failed. No significant group was supporting him, and men who had recently been trying to keep a foot in both camps, like Sir William Cecil, had cautiously backed off. By early October the rumour mongers in London had picked up a new theme. Instead of Somerset conspiring to overthrow Warwick, it was now the earl and his supporters who were plotting the downfall of the duke. This time the reports had more substance, although the timing of Warwick's blow remains something of a mystery. Perhaps he had waited for Somerset's rather ham-fisted attempts at regaining power to run into the sand, or perhaps he had simply lost patience with a rival who was clearly a nuisance, if not a serious threat. For whatever reason, Somerset was arrested on the 16th October, and charged with treasonable conspiracy.

A dozen or more of the duke's supporters were also rounded up at the same time, in a series of concerted moves resembling a modern police operation. At the same time the council released to the ambassadors in London a prepared statement explaining that Somerset had plotted to seize the Tower, raise the commons and launch a team of hired assassins against his colleagues. When Scheyfve expressed astonishment, he was blandly informed that no one else could understand the motivation behind so dastardly a plot either[7]. But the council had had their eye on the conspirators for some time, and had made no mistake. The timing of the strike, which seems to have taken Somerset completely by surprise, seems to have been contrived to coincide with Warwick's elevation to the dukedom of Northumberland, which had taken place on the 11th October which the former protector had attended. The two events were linked by something more substantial than symbolism, because on the day of the ceremony Northumberland was already in possession of the testimony by Sir Thomas Palmer upon which the charges were based. It is hard to avoid the conclusion that Somerset was framed, especially as Northumberland himself was to confess *in extremis* that the charges had been fabricated, but it may not have been simply the latter's ambition which led him to so drastic a step. To judge from the tone of one of the entries in his journal, Edward was convinced that his uncle intended to harm him, a suspicion which may well have been lurking in his mind since his dramatic removal from Hampton Court to Windsor two years before[8]. The one thing that the council could not afford in the face of so many difficulties and pressures, both at home and abroad, was a split in its own ranks. If forced to choose between Somerset and Northumberland the young king would not have hesitated. Somerset's challenge had failed, but nobody could be sure that he would not try again. In words later used of the earl of Stafford "stone dead hath no fellow". If the choice lay between judicial murder and continued political instability, the Northumberland was not the man to be squeamish.

Palmer turned out to be an unreliable witness, and began to change his story, but it was not long before fear, and possibly cupidity among those who had been arrested began to produce corroboration of a sort. William Crane, a servant of Somerset's, produced all kinds of circumstantial detail about the intended assassinations , which had been intended for August, but he did not explain why they had not, in the event, been attempted. Accusations and recriminations flew thick and fast. Paget was implicated, and the earl of Arundel, and Lord Strange, the earl of Derby's son. However hysterical accusations were not quite the same thing as evidence, and it was hard to avoid the fact that neither Somerset nor his alleged accomplices had actually done anything at all. The nearest thing to sober testimony which survives comes from the earl of Arundel, who confessed that he had discussed with Somerset the possibility of arresting Warwick and charging him with misgovernment - a reversal of the *coup* of 1549. It seems that several such conversations took place, and that others may have been involved. That was probably the core of Somerset's plot. The assassinations and popular uprisings were so much garish embellishment to a very optimistic intention of displacing Warwick as the head of the council. He had at some point, probably in April 1551, entertained a hope of putting his counter *coup* into effect, but he had abandoned the whole idea of his own volition when some of his agents began to talk indiscreetly. Warwick probably knew of these intentions soon after they were expressed, but bided his time, and possibly worked on the king, in order to give his riposte the maximum impact. No one outside England found the charges at all plausible, although Henry II expressed polite concern in a message to Edward when informed of the latter's narrow escape. Northumberland's international credit benefited not at all, and the Emperor feared that his actions might be part of a deep laid plot to justify further action against Mary.

On the 23rd November the marquis of Winchester was appointed high steward for Somerset's trial. The indictments had been handed down on the 16th, alleging conspiracy to deprive the king of his royal dignity, to seize his person, and to exercise the government in his place. This was to be accomplished by imprisoning the duke of Northumberland and other members of the council and by arousing the citizens of London to rebellion[9]. No mention was made of intended assassinations. The trial took place at Westminster on the 1st December, and there was an embarrassing disarray among the peers who acted as judges. Somerset denied all the charges, and impugned Sir Thomas Palmer's character, which was an obvious line of defence . Conspiring to imprison Northumberland was the only charge for which any substantial corroboration could be produced, and that did not amount to treason, as Northumberland himself was the first to admit. The peers refused to be convinced that the intention behind the plot was treasonable, and Somerset was acquitted on the main charge. However conspiring to imprison councillors was a statutory felony, and of that he was convicted. When news of the first verdict leaked out, there was rejoicing in the city, but the true state of affairs soon became apparent. Felony also carried the death penalty. Northumberland's main purpose was achieved, and his rival went to the block on 22nd January, the day before parliament reconvened after many prorogations. In spite of the character assassination which had accompanied and followed his death, it is generally acknowledged that Somerset was unjustly executed. However, his destruction must be seen as a political act, not a judicial one. Whether the two dukes could have continued to serve in the same council without splitting it down the middle and dragging it into civil war must remain an open question. Northumberland thought not, and chose what appeared to be the lesser evil. The king supported him, and if Edward had lived this *coup* might have been seen as the one which established the Dudley ascendancy at his court. His death left Northumberland exposed to charges of judicial murder, but eighteen months without serious challenge gave him time to establish his credentials as a ruler, ambition or no ambition.

16

The Second Book of Common Prayer.

The Prayer Book of 1549 had satisfied nobody, not even its principal author. In spite of the elegance of Cranmer's liturgical language, it
showed every sign of having been designed by a committee. So
imprecise was its wording on a number of key issues that Stephen
Gardiner pronounced it to be capable of a fully catholic interpretation.
Those who had rioted against the replacement of the mass with a
communion service did not see it in that light, but their objections had
been to the changes of usage and language, rather than to the underly-
ing teaching. On the other hand John Hooper and those who thought
like him, regarded it as "very absurd" and "full of popish errors and
superstition". By the time the book came into use at Whitsun 1549,
Cranmer already knew it would have to be revised, and indeed his
own thinking on the eucharist had moved appreciably in the direction
of Zurich since he had first drafted the prayer of consecration in 1548.
Both Martin Bucer and Peter Martyr were invited to comment on the
first book, which they presumably read in Latin, since neither of them
had much English, in spite of their protestant principles about vernacular liturgy. Bucer produced a lengthy *Censura*, to which Martyr
seems to have contributed, making a few comments of his own only
when he disagreed with his colleague[1]. On the whole he found the
work "very agreeable both with God's word and the observance of the
ancient churches", but he wished to see all the services simplified ,
and every gesture which could be misconstrued specifically prohibited. Bucer was particularly concerned about the clandestine continu-
ance of private masses, thinly disguised as Prayer Book eucharists and
celebrated in non-parochial chapels. He believed that the communion
should be celebrated frequently, but only in parish churches and other
places of public resort. He also deplored the weakness of the parochial
ministry, while understanding the reasons for it. An old priest could
not be turned into a new preacher overnight. There was a desperate

need for more preachers, but until they could be trained, more emphasis should be placed on the use of the *Homilies* which Cranmer had written in 1547, and more should be prepared. The plunder of the church would have to stop, so that when resources were taken from bishops and rich cathedrals, they must be channelled into the universities, or into an equalisation scheme for poor livings, a point which Cranmer had been making since the 1530s. The English church also needed a clear and unequivocal statement of its doctrinal position, not in liturgical form, but set out as a formal confession, like that of Augsburg.

After the earl of Warwick had secured control of the council in January 1550, Cranmer progressively withdrew from secular affairs. By 1552 he was clearly at odds with the council on a number of issues, but there is no reason to suppose that his retreat was initiated by any aversion to Warwick or his policies. Bucer had convinced him, if he needed any convincing, that his priority must be the reform and rehabilitation of the church. In November 1550 he launched a vigorous campaign for the removal of stone altars from all churches and their replacement with wooden communion tables[2]. At the same time, with the close co-operation of his friend Nicholas Ridley, the bishop of London, he was struggling to maintain discipline within the episcopate. The cause of this problem was the earl of Warwick's protege, John Hooper, who had been nominated for the see of Gloucester. Hooper strongly objected to the reformed ordinal which had been issued earlier in the year, on the predictable grounds that it was insufficiently protestant. He particularly objected to the vestments he was required to wear for his consecration, and the council was prepared to put pressure on the archbishop to dispense him from the requirement. Cranmer was saved from this humiliation partly by the powerful advocacy of Ridley, who pointed out that the church's credibility and authority could not be subject to such erosion, and partly by the unreasonable intransigence of Hooper himself, who eventually exasperated even his warmest supporters. In January 1551 he was committed to prison, and submitted after a few weeks. This victory, and the strong support which he received from the council over the removal of altars gave an appearence of harmony which was not altogether justified. When Stephen Gardiner was eventually deprived of the see of Winchester, and the preferment was given to John Ponet the latter was required to surrender the entire endowment of the bishopric, worth some £3,000 a year in return for a stipend of 2000 marks (£1333 6s 8d). This was precisely the kind of transaction which Cranmer found most unacceptable, but he was not consulted and it was clear that he had failed to protect the church from further plunder. In this context it is not surprising that the archbishop found the reshaping of the liturgy a positive and attractive task. Unlike the first Book, the revision seemed to be almost entirely his own work. Apart from Bucer and Martyr, he certainly consulted John Cheke, Richard Cox and Nicholas Ridley[3]. Others may have advised on specific points, but the text was principally his own composition. Peter Martyr reported that he had seen the new text early in February 1551, and understood that it contained many amendments, although not all the suggestions in the *Censura* had been adopted. He was unable to comment specifically, because of his ignorance of English. Cranmer passed it around amongst his episcopal colleagues for comment, and was once againd criticised from both sides. The draft also seems to have been considered by the commission which had been recently re-established to formulate the revision of the canon law, although no substantial amendments seem to have been proposed. Whether this was because of consensus or because the commission had no status in this context is not clear.

The revised Prayer Book was not submitted to convocation, or formally approved by the church in any way. Like the first book, it was introduced as an appendix to an Act of Uniformity in religion. This act was passed, not without a certain amount of opposition and redrafting, between the 6th and 14th April 1552. It did not repeal its predecessor, and was careful not to impugn it. Instead it was declared that "diverse doubts" had arisen about the interpretation of the earlier liturgy, and that there was therefore need for amendment and clarification. Apart from introducing the new Prayer Book, the new act differed principally in imposing penalties on the laity for non-attendance at their parish churches. This statute was not due to come into force until November, partly because it was hoped that seven months would give Cranmer time to complete the articles of religion upon which he was engaged, and partly in the hope that a conference of leading protestant divines could be convened in England during the summer. The archbishop had been intending to summon such a "council" for some time, intending both to raise the profile of the English reformation, and to attract recognition and support. Both Bullinger and Melanchthon were invited, but both eventually declined feeling that they could not be spared from their own missions. As Bucer died in February 1551, Peter Martyr was the only foreign reformer of standing in England in 1552 and the idea was abandoned. The articles were completed, but they were not promulgated until June 1553. This was not because Cranmer had been remiss, but because of disagreements and other preoccupations within the council. Eventually the delay in issuing the Prayer Book must have seemed rather pointless, but it did give the people a little more time to get used to a liturgy which was far more radical in form and feeling than its predecessor. The eucharist was now renamed the lord's supper, the chrisom was banished from the rite of baptism, and the sign of the cross from confirmation. All prayers for the dead were forbidden, and the service of burial was simplified. The whole liturgy was unequivocally protestant, and the artifices which had been used to disguise the previous book in a catholic mask became impossible.

Cranmer's approach, as always, was moderate and persuasive. An introduction explained that many familiar ceremonies had now been abolished because they had grown up spontaneously, without sufficient thought for their true meaning, and had overlaid the word of God with superstitious distractions. The new order was based exclusively on scripture and would, it was hoped, set an example which the other churches might follow. However the order was for England only

> "...we condem no other nation, nor proscribe anything but to our own people only. For we think it convenient that every country should use such ceremonies as they think best to the setting forth of God's honour..."[4]

This was hardly a sentiment to which Hooper or Knox would have subscribed, and their influence was steadily increasing as the summer of 1552 advanced. The printing and the distribution of the new book, which was a very large task by the standards of contemporary publishing practice, was entrusted to Richard Grafton. By October the work had also been translated into French for use in the Channel Islands and, hopefully, the foreign congregations in London. There was then a significant hitch. Several radicals, including Hooper, had made representations against the rubric which required the sacrament to be recieved in the kneeling position. John Knox then preached a series of sermons on the same theme in Newcastle-upon-Tyne, and won the support of the duke of Northumberland, then in the north discharging his duties as warden general of the marches. As a result the council wrote to Cranmer and Ridley, asking them to reconsider the matter, despite the fact that the book had been approved by parliament and was in an advanced state of preparation. The archbishop refused, and with unwonted anger denounced the "unquiet spirits" who had pressed for this change, accusing them of anabaptist leanings[5]. Knox immediately responded that kneeling was fit only for slaves and not for the communion of the free sons of God. The council ordered Grafton to suspend printing and issued an explanatory proclamation declaring that the gesture of kneeling was only for the sake of seemly order, and did not imply and superstitious reverence for the elements. This explanation was then included in the Prayer Book as the so-called "black rubric". A compromise of a sort had been reached, but Cranmer never forgave Northumberland for this public affront to his authority and his relations with the council became increasingly cold and distant. This was bad news for a regime whose religious policy could only command minority support at the best of times, and not particularly good for the duke because the archbishop was the only man who could challenge him for the trust and affection of the young king. It did not, however, impede the introduction of the new Prayer Book, black rubric and all, which took place as scheduled on the 1st November. All over the country churches were stripped of their last remaining ornaments, and the bleak cerebral rites if the reformers replaced the last traces of the colourful rituals familiar to generations of worshippers. There was remarkably little reaction, except that attendances at services declined dramatically in spite of all coercive efforts, and outside London ordinations virtually ceased.

Meanwhile the articles of faith provided another bone of contention. Unlike the liturgy, Cranmer had approached this task of doctrinal definition with reluctance, partly because it was bound to be contentious and partly because his own cast of mind did not run to that sort of clarity. He became convinced of its necessity when Hooper started issuing his own set of articles and he was confronted by the spectre of a different doctrine in every diocese. At some time towards the end of 1551 he circulated the draft of forty two such articles to some at least of the bishops, but it was not until May 1552 when the council ordered him to submit them for examination that they entered the public domain. They were then sent to the royal chaplains - a notoriously radical group - for comment, and return to the archbishop for revision . In exactly what way they were revised we do not know, but they grew in the process from forty two to forty five, and were then resubmitted in September. Further revision followed, which brought the number down to forty two again, and on the 24th November Cranmer sent his final version, with a pointed request that the articles now be given royal authority to set "...a concord and quietness in religion", which was much needed[6]. Nothing happened. Having badgered and fidgeted for over a year, the council simply sat on Cranmer's document. Perhaps it was intended to submit the articles to the parliament which met in March 1553, or to the convocation which accompanied it, but no such action was taken. The agenda may have been too crowded, but that seems unlikely. Probably the radicals were again unsatisfied and obstructed promulgation, just as they had obstructed the issuing of the Prayer Book, but if so we do not know what the particular points of contention were. Eventually they were issued in June 1553, just a few weeks before Edward's death, pretending the collective authority of the bishops, to which they were not entitled[7]. Cranmer protested against the misrepresentation, but in the circumstances the point was academic. It was not until they were reissued in the reign of Elizabeth that the articles of religion became an important part of the anglican tradition.

If Cranmer was frustrated over the articles, he was even more distressed by the fate of his cherished scheme for the revision of canon law. The establishment of the royal supremacy had made nonsense of much of the traditional law of the church, and the law which was being administered by the ecclesiastical courts at the end of Henry's reign was a thing of shreds and patches. The king had been well aware of this, and had issued a commission to devise a new law for the English church. By 1545 a new code, which was largely Cranmer's work was in existence, but it was never submitted either to parliament or to convocation. Given the religious division in Henry's court and council at the time, that was not surprising, but the new regime of 1547 did not pick up the project with the enthusiasm which might have been expected . Protestants tended to argue that the bible was sufficient law for the Godly, and the politically powerful common lawyers had no desire to witness the recovery of a rival code from whose debility they were deriving considerable benefit. Significantly, a proposal by the bishops to reactivate Henry's commission was defeated in parliament in November 1549. They persisted, however, arguing the deplorable state of ecclesiastical discipline, a sentiment with which the radicals could hardly disagree, and in February 1550 passed an act for the establishment of a new commission[8]. Cranmer was bitterly opposed to this, partly because it meant discarding the code upon which he had spent so much labour, and starting again, and partly because he feared that the new commission would be dominated by laymen. In the event he need not have worried. The commission consisted of thirty two members, divided equally between laity and clergy, but it accepted his leadership, and largely accepted his earlier work. On the other hand, the whole business proceeded with infuriating slowness. It took the council over six months to name the commission, and two years for it to authorise it to start work. Since the commission was due to expire in 1553, this looked supiciously like sabotage. Nevertheless, in spite of all obstacles Cranmer had his proposed code ready to submit to parliament in March 1553, only to be met with a blank refusal by the duke of Northumberland to let it on the agenda. The reason for this was that the common lawyers , and probably Northumberland himself, saw the canon law as a means of restoring a degree of jurisdictional autonomy to a church which was presently subject completely to lay control. The code was shelved and the commission expired with nothing accomplished. It is not surprising that relations between the archbishop and the lord president of the council were glacial by the summer of 1553.

By then even advanced reformers were beginning to feel that the church was under seige , and Hooper and Knox had abandoned praise of Northumberland for denunciation of "carnal gospellers". Paradoxically one of the reasons for this was a policy to which they ought to have had no objection - the confiscation of superfluous church plate and ornament. Such an appropriation had been on the cards since 1549, when inventories of such church goods were first ordered. At that time nothing had been done, but in March 1551 it was declared that the king needed "a mass of money" and commissions were established to recieve all plate and other goods not needed for the Prayer Book services. Feet were obviously dragged heavily in all quarters , because in January 1552 the instructions were reissued , and followed up a year later with a peremptory order to complete the process. The reformers had no affection for "massing gear", but what they were witnessing was the removal of valuables which should have been sold for the benefit of the poor or the payment of preachers, and the principal recipient was not even the king's exchequer - it was the private pockets of the commissioners and their agents. In other words the secular control of the church, which they had established to humble the pride of priests and prelates, was being used to reduce the priority accorded to spiritual matters, and to withdraw the material support without which the process of evangelical conversion would wither and the protestant ideal itself would die.

17

Religious radicalism

By the time that he came to draw up the Forty Two Articles
Cranmer was almost as worried about anabaptist subversion as he was
about catholic opposition. Strictly speaking, anabaptists were those
who rejected the practice of infant baptism, and thus became, in the
eyes of the orthodox, "re-baptisers". This was an ancient heresy, for
which the death penalty had been decreed by the Emperor Theodosius.
The implication of such a belief, and the reason why it had always
been so fiercely persecuted, was that there could be no such thing as a
church which was co-extensive with a civic society. Membership of a
"baptist" church could only follow a voluntary confession of faith
made after achieving the age of discretion. It was essentially a
sectarian or gathered view of the church, which had no place for the
Christian Empire, or even a Christian city. Not all those who were
called anabaptists in the sixteenth century actually held that view.
Some rejected baptism altogether as a meaningless ceremony; others
rejected all sacraments. Some were scriptural fundamentalists, who
believed every word of the bible to be inspired and literal truth; others
rejected the scriptures altogether, as having been superseded by the
direct intervention of the holy spirit. What they all had in common,
however, was a complete disconnection between the life of the spirit
and the everyday life of the secular community. The true believer,
while continuing to live in the world, ceased to be a part of it. No
believer would hold office, or swear an oath, or play any part in public
life. Sometimes this extended to withholding taxes, both clerical and
lay, and refusing to acknowledge any allegiance to a superior
authority. Many such sectaries also rejected formal education as being
both unnecessary and misleading. At the same time very few were
anarchists in the modern sense, and the moral discipline within their
own congregations was often extremely rigorous.

These radicals were a rogue element within Christendom which had surfaced from time to time throughout its history. They were particularly numerous in the early sixteenth century because the authority of the traditional church had been weakened by the challenges of Luther, Zwingli and other reformers. Luther was as hostile to the radicals as any catholic, and published in 1525 a vehement tract *Against the Heavenly Prophets,* but there is no doubt that his actions had stirred them up, and some of the most notorious "anabaptist" leaders of the 1520s, such as Andreas Carlstadt and Thomas Muntzer, began their careers as his followers. There is no doubt that their convictions were subversive of established order, but their enemies consistently overestimated the danger which they represented. The very nature of the radical groups made them incapable of large scale organisation or institutional architecture. They nearly always appeared in response to the charismatic preaching of an individual , and changed their size and location with bewildering rapidity. Muntzer called himself "the sword of the Lord and of Gideon", and was a violent social revolutionary, but the vast majority of "anabaptists" were quietists who remained true to their unworldly convictions, even under the most extreme persecution[1]. In the unsettled religious climate of the 1530s and 1540s groups of these radicals can be found all over western Europe, and their real numerical strength is impossible to assess, but it is unlikely that they formed more than 10% of the population, even in the worst affected areas. Unfortunately they received vast notoriety for their role in two very disturbing events. The first if these was the great German peasant uprising of 1525, which was largely social and economic in its genesis, but in which the preaching of Muntzer and his followers played a conspicuous part. The second was the "kingdom" of Munster. In 1533 the quarrels between the bishop of Munster in Westphalia and the Lutheran townsmen enabled a group of radicals to seize control of the town. They were then swiftly overtaken by charismatic leaders from the Netherlands, who established a bizarre regime of polygamy and community of goods, in the midst of which the ultimate leader, Jan of Leyden, kept an old testament court. Besieged by both Lutheran and Catholic authorities, they held out with fanatical heroism for several months. In their willingness to take political action, these Munster revolutionaries were quite untypical of the radicals as a whole, but their actions sent shockwaves across the whole continent, and led to the creation of myths like the "great anabaptist conspiracy". This joined a febrile gallery of other horrors, involving Jews, witches, the Turks and (in catholic countries) heretics; all prepared to do the devil's work in the world for the overthrow of Godly order.

England never suffered from more than a pale reflection of this paranoia. The indigenous English radicals were called Lollards, and were the followers of the fourteenth century Oxford divine, John Wycliffe. Wycliffe's original ideas had been expressed in tortuous and obscure Latin, but they had been swiftly translated into English, and much simplified in the process[2]. He had condemned the wealth of the church, and its claims to temporal authority, including those of the papacy. He had also rejected transubstantiation, and with it the sacramental power which the clergy were believed to exercise *ex officio*. The implications of these ideas were extremely radical, but they had never been systematically thought out. For about thirty years, from 1380 to 1410, Lollardy had enjoyed considerable social and intellectual strength, but the hostility of the Lancastrian monarchy and the Oldcastle rebellion of 1414 had driven it under ground. By the early sixteenth century it was a grassroots movement, with numerous scattered groups of adherents, but no coherent theology and no leadership. It has been correctly described as more a state of mind than a creed[3]. Nevertheless the existence of Lollardy, particularly in London and the home counties, provided patches of fertile ground in which the seeds of the protestant reformation took root. It also provided a climate which was receptive to some of the more radical ideas which were being preached by the anabaptists of the Low Countries. By continental standards English persecution was never particularly severe, so even when Thomas More as chancellor was mounting a special campaign against dissent, between 1530 and 1532, the south east of England was still safer than Flanders or Picardy, and once More was gone it was a veritable haven. Hundreds, perhaps thousands, of these relatively harmless folk lived in London, Norwich and many other towns between the Wash and the Solent. A few, like Jan Mattijs, were arrested tried and burned; and some who had lived temporarily in England, like Anneke Jens, were caught and executed when they returned home[4]. But considering their numbers and the extreme nature of some of their views, they made remarkably little impact upon the English ecclesiastical records. Occasionally meetings of "anabaptists" were detected and broken up, like that at Bergholt in 1536, but Lollardy had to some extent inoculated the English against such extremism, and the execution of native radicals was rare, because Lollards were seldom made of the stuff of martyrs.

One of the problems with anabaptism is that we have so few inside accounts. The alleged beliefs of such radicals nearly always have to be reconstructed from the charges brought against them, or from hostile polemic. A statute against heresy listed eight points, which also occur in many individual denunciations. These included the community of goods among Christian men, adult baptism, the rejection of office by Christians, and a denial of the human nature of Christ[5]. Ten years later John Hooper was writing that certain London anabaptists were arguing that God had a secret agenda, beyond that which he had revealed in the scriptures. Hooper found these people a particular embarrassment, not because he agreed with them but because of the way in which catholic polemicists insisted in calling them protestants, and then using them as a means of exaggerating the genuine difference which existed among the reformers. As Miles Huggarde was to write during the Marian reaction,

> "But if these good felowes wyll nedes be of Christes churche
> as arrogantly as they presume by their own confession;
> they must have one unitie of doctrine as ye churche hathe,
> whiche surely they have not...The punishments are not
> so divers in hell (as Vergill described) as are the sundry
> opinions of these Protestants..."[6]

The English reformers certainly did not encourage anabaptism, or at least they did not intend to, but because some Lollard ideas were so similar to their own, they may not have been sufficiently alert to its unacceptable face. It may have been this which Cranmer had in mind when he prayed after Mary's accession "O good Lord be merciful unto us, for we have been too remiss in punishing offenders, and many things we have winked at..." Only two anabaptists were burned in England during Edward's reign. One was a Dutch fugitive named George van Paris and the other was Joan Bocher, who was executed in April 1550 for denying the incarnation. The main reason for this was not a lack of orthodox zeal, but the relatively low priority accorded to such a vague and disorganised movement. Joan Bocher is alleged to have claimed that a thousand in London were "of her sect", but if she used any such words, they seem to have meant no more than that there were a lot of eccentric ideas around in the capital. The Edwardian authorities detected many individuals and small groups of radical dissenters, but nothing which could be dignified as a sect. There was Thomas Cole and his friends, who admitted to the privy council in 1551 that they had not attended communion for over two years. The reason for their dissent was not made clear , but they were not catholics[7]. There were groups in Bocking and Faversham which were described as "anabaptist", but which seem to have consisted of followers of Henry Hart. Hart held none of the classic "anabaptist" views, but refused to accept the orthodox protestant teaching on predestination. For that reason he was known as a "freewiller", and was fiercely disliked, particularly by those who followed the Swiss teaching , but he could not fairly be described as a radical[8]

The freewillers practised a form of seperatism, calling each other "brother" and "sister" after the manner of the later sects, but they had no ministry of their own , and if they ever drew up a confession of faith it has not survived. In this they were the authentic heirs of the Lollards, most of whom can be described as "occasional conformists", who for all their variety of radical ideas, never withdrew from the church or attempted to set up an alternative. In spite of the anxiety expressed by both Hooper and Cranmer, and the intermittent energy deployed by the council, there is no evidence that "gathered" or covenanted radical churches existed in England before the reign of Elizabeth. It was therefore the power of heretical ideas rather than the power of the heretics themselves which the archbishop was endeavouring to counter in the Articles of religion. This he did principally in article 28 "Of Baptism"; article 36 "Of the Civil Magistrates"; article 37 "That the goods of Christians are not common"; article 38 "It is lawful for a Christian to take an oath"; and article 27 "The wickedness of the ministers takes not away the efficacy of Divine Institutions." Infant baptism was specifically advocated, and the civil magistrate was declared to be "...ordained and approved by God, and is therefore to be obeyed not only for fear of wrath, but also for Conscience sake..." In declaring a Christian's right to individual property the false opinions of the anabaptists were specifically denounced, but in defence of oaths it was merely said that "a man may swear when the magistrate requireth"[9]. Article 27 was directed not so much against the anabaptists as against the Lollards, because it had long been one of their favourite propositions that the efficacy of a priest's ministry depended not upon his orders but upon his state of grace. This of course removed an objective criterion and replaced it with a subjective one . No one could properly determine another's state of grace, but in practice it was assumed that the decision would be made by those to whom he was ministering. In another context Cranmer had been willing to admit that ordination was not strictly necessary to ministry, but in this article he was just as insistent as the catholics upon the *ex officio* authority of the minister.

Perhaps it is significant that, in article 24, he was so careful to insist that it was the "public authority" which had the right and authority to call men to the ministry, not the congregation which they were to serve.

Northumberland's use of the royal supremacy during the latter part of his tenure of office made the archbishop particularly sensitive to issues of authority, and therefore keenly aware of the radical challenge. Like Luther he feared the solvent affect of any direct appeal to the holy spirit, and like him realised that the best way to counter the logic of such a challenge was to test the spirit by the letter, and to refuse to countenance any authority which ran counter to the scripture. However he had an additional problem in that he was also bound to recognise the voice of the king as the authentic instrument of God. That the king's authority might be subject to the test of scripture and found wanting was something which he was not prepared to contemplate. To him it was axiomatic that God spoke through the king, but it was also axiomatic, as it was to all protestants that the scripture needed no "lively expositor", being sufficient in itself. As long as Edward lived he could console himself with the thought that so Godly a prince would never deviate from the path of truth, and that Northumberland's anti-ecclesiastical animus was merely a temporary aberration. When Edward died, he found himself face to face with an ungodly prince, committed to the restoration of superstition and idolatry and the crisis of his conscience had arrived. Because of the nature of their beliefs, the radicals had no significant secular backing. Indeed, almost without exception they were humble and uneducated men, but their German cousins had provided a warning of what could happen when a group of ordinary men and women believed that they had found their own way to God. If no principle of obedience to authority was built into a structure of faith, then there was no guarantee how that group would behave. They would become literally "masterless men", which was synonymous with outlaw. It was not their eccentric Christology, nor even their contempt for sacraments which most worried the Edwardian church about the anabaptists. It was their rejection of the king's authority. There was scarcely such a thing as a true catholic in England after 1547; reformers and conservatives alike accepted the royal supremacy, but an example of principled defiance even from so insignificant a group, could prove infectious. There was no chance that the anabaptists could have overthrown the church, but every chance that an alternative form of authority to the king would prove appealing.

Cranmer's failure to suppress radical dissent created in time a serious historical ambiguity. Under Mary all protestantt and anabaptist groups were dissenters. The church did not recognise any distinction, and later protestant historians such as John Foxe were prepared to describe all dissenters as protestant in order to lengthen the martyrology and boost the roll-call of the Godly who were prepared to stand up and be counted. With the accession of Elizabeth radical nonconformity reappeared wearing its true colours, but radical seperatism was slow to develop. Even Richard Fritz's congregation which was denounced in 1571 for " establishing a private religion..." appealed to the queen to "bryng home the people of God to the purity and truth of the Apostolyke church"[10], and it may be questioned whether they should not simply be classed as puritans. It was not until the appearance of the Brownists and the Barrowists in the last fifteen years of the reign that sectarianism finally emerged, and not until the following century that it became briefly important. During the reign of Edward anabaptism was principally a bogey to discredit unwelcome challenges to a precarious ecclesiastical ascendancy.

18

Financial reforms and retrenchment.

Henry's wars in the last five years of his reign cost in the region of £2,100,000. This massive expenditure he had endeavoured to cover in a variety of ways. £656,000 came from unusually generous parliamentary subsidies, £270,000 from forced loans, which were always unpopular, and about £700,000 from the sale of monastic property. Each of these sources of revenue carried a political price tag. Subsidies mortgaged the king's freedom of action by increasing the indispensability of parliament. Forced loans bred resentment, and the sale of monastic land deprived the exchequer of an income which could have amounted to £75,000 a year. Moreover they left him almost half a million pounds short of his expenditure level, and the gap had to be bridged by still more damaging expedients. Some £363,000 had been raised by debasing the currency, a proceeding which helped to create inflation and massive commercial disruption, and well over £100,000 had been borrowed on the Antwerp exchange at between 10% and 12% interest[1]. When Henry died, he had owed about £100,000 in Antwerp, and probably half as much at home, mostly in London. The protector paid no heed to these warning signs, and continued with the same policies. Between 1547 and 1549 military expenditure ran at over £580,000, in addition to the heavy cost of defending Boulogne and maintaining the navy. Consequently the revenue expedients continued also, although at a somewhat lower level, enforced by the government's shortage of political and financial credit. The debasement of the coinage continued undiminished, and by 1550 the pound sterling had declined from twenty six shillings Flemish on the exchanges to thirteen - which would be rather like the contemporary pound suddenly going down to eighty cents against the dollar. When the earl of Warwick took over the reins of government at the beginning of 1550 the accumulated debt probably stood at nearly £300,000, and the ordinary revenue of the crown at around

£150,000 per annum.

These figures alone suggest a compelling reason why the new lord president should have been looking for ways of cutting his losses in foreign policy. The surrender of Boulogne not only saved some £30,000 a year in defence costs, it also brought a one-off bonus of £133,000. Nevertheless in a dangerous world there were limits to the retrenchment which could be undertaken in this area, and for the remainder of the reign military expenditure continued to run at some £200,000 a year, which was very high for peace time. At the same time revenue became more difficult to find. Crisis in the cloth trade, and the serious outbreaks of sweating sickness in 1551 and 1552 made subsidies difficult and forced loans impossible. Parliament granted only some £300,000 in the entire reign, and a proportion of that was never collected. Sales of crown lands continued, to a capital value of over £400,000, but Warwick made his own position worse by granting away almost as much land to purchase the political support of his fellow peers[2].Given his situation, it is not easy to see how that could have been avoided, but there is no doubt that it hampered his efforts to put the king's finances on a sound footing. For all these reasons Warwick was forced to continue Somerset's practice of debasing the coin, although he knew perfectly well what a deleterious effect such action was having. By the time that he eventually desisted in 1551 he had milked the mint for a further £250,000, bringing the total since 1547 to some £530,000. A stock taking at the end of that year disclosed an accumulated debt of just over £240,000, of which £132,000 was owed in Antwerp on a short term obligation of a few months, and the balance in London on a variety of obligations[3]. Debt at this level cost about £26,000 a year to service and it is not surprising that the council addressed itself earnestly to the task of getting it down.

In June 1551 Warwick declared a financial policy. Regular income must cover regular expenditure, and the king's debts must be liquidated. He may have heeded the advice of his city experts such as Thomas Gresham, or he may have been told bluntly that without a radical policy of retrenchment he could expect no more support or co-operation from that quarter. There are certainly signs of understanding. Instead of futile and counter productive attempts to "cry down" the debased currency, the council began to issue sound coin of full weight. This did not solve the problem, because it was judged that a full re-coinage could not be afforded, and the bad money drove out the good, but it was a step in the direction of restoring confidence, and enabled Gresham to claw back some credibility for sterling in Antwerp, which he then claimed was worth tens of thousands of pounds to the exchequer. In 1552 the council also withdrew the long established privileges of the Hanseatic League, against which the merchant adventurers had been campaigning for many years. In return the city continued to underwrite the royal debts in Antwerp, and also provided short term commercial loans of their own. The survey already referred to at the end of 1551 declared the crown's net ordinary revenue to have been £168,000, and ordinary expenditure £131,000, but such figures, even if accurate, give no sensible picture of the real situation. Extraordinary income was running at £130,000 a year, and extraordinary expenditure at over £200,000, leaving a deficit in the region of £40,000. On 23rd March 1552 a more ambitious enquiry was initiated "for the survey an examination of the state of all his majesty's Courts of Revenue". The commissioners of this enquiry produced startlingly different figures for what purported to be the same ordinary balance; income £272,000, expenditure £235,000[4]. Clearly "ordinary" and "extraordinary" did not mean the same thing to the two sets of commissioners. However the real purpose of the second survey was to put pressure on the king's creditors rather than to present an accurate balance, so it does not follow that the higher figures are more trustworthy.

The commissioners, who reported eventually towards the end of 1552, made a number of draconian recommendations for economies particularly in the household and military budgets, which do not appear even to have reached the council, let alone been implemented[5]. The duke of Northumberland paid off his very expensive German and Italian mercenaries, a step which may well have cost him dear in the summer of 1553, but close investigation does not reveal much sign of the severe reductions in expenditure which used to be postulated. Instead of being slashed to the bone and largely neglected - "left to rot at its moorings" as one scholar put it - we now know that the navy was maintained to a high standard for peace time at a cost of over £20,000 a year[6]. In the summer of 1552 it looks as though the council was scrabbling around trying to find a few hundred pounds for immediate expenses, but the appearance may be deceptive, and in any case a cash flow problem is not the same thing as a financial crisis. By comparison with Charles V or Henry II of France, the financial problems of Edward VI were insignificant. The overall debt was brought down to about £180,000 by the end of the reign, and thanks to skillful management the English council was always able to borrow money in Flanders at the standard rates of interest. By the end of the decade both Henry and Philip II were bankrupt - the latter thanks to his father's debts which he had just inherited - but neither Edward nor Mary defaulted upon their obligations. If the 1552 commission was really designed to convince the propertied classes of the need for them to rally round a beleaguered government, then it very largely failed. When parliament was asked for a subsidy in March 1553, a move for which there was every justification, there was considerable grumbling and resistance. A single subsidy was eventually voted, but collection was spread over two years. So strong was the general conviction that this taxation was unnecessary that Mary remitted the second instalment, a quixotic gesture which her ministers were soon to regret.

Parliament in fact did very little to dig Northumberland out of the hole in which Somerset had left the treasury. The two most important elements in the rehabilitation which began in 1551 were the absence of war and the continued sale of crown lands. About £145,000 was gained by this means in the last six months of the reign, which at the standard rate of twenty years purchase meant sacrificing a revenue income of some £8,000 a year. Northumberland was also fortunate in having, in Thomas Gresham a financial agent of genius, who had the confidence of bankers in both London an Antwerp, and whose skillful manipulations were largely responsible for the healthy state of English credit. Gresham's technique was based on borrowing a considerable number of relatively modest sums, and staggering the repayments as widely as possible. He had very little ready money at his disposal, and funded the majority of his repayments with fresh borrowing, but he did have two big assets. The first was the support of the city of London, which underwrote the debts that he incurred on the king's behalf, and the second was the merchant adventures annual cloth shipment, which in a good year was worth £300,000. 1552 was not a good year, in fact it was a very bad year following the slump of 1550-51, but the cloth fleet was still a major factor in the Antwerp economy. These securities enabled Gresham to get through a very tight bottleneck between March and July 1552, when £106,000 fell due, and the government could provide virtually no cash. He reborrowed over £90,000 and found the balance out of the accumulated credits[7]. After that it could only get easier. In August 1552 Edward's total indebtedness in Antwerp stood at £108,000, and Gresham decided to spread the load by developing a new strategy.

The idea was that the council would advance him £1,200 weekly, which he would discreetly feed into the market at a rate of about

£200-£300 a day, accumulating Flemish pounds, and creating a shortage of bills on London in the Antwerp market. This money was supplied out of the sale of crown lands, and was sufficient to sustain a healthy exchange rate, and enable Gresham to make a modest profit on his transactions . By 1552 he had managed to squeeze the exchange up from 13 shillings, where it had stood in 1550, to 19 shillings. By April 1553 it had reached 23 shillings and 4 pence, and was steady. By that time Edward could borrow at 12%, while the Emperor whose resources were infinitely greater, was forced to pay 16%. In the autumn of 1552 Gresham had almost complete control of the credits arising from the cloth shipment, which amounted to some £60,000, and he was able to pay off over £36,000 in crown debts on the due rates without re-borrowing[8]. By the summer of 1553 the total royal debt in Antwerp had been substantially reduced, and bullion was actually flowing into England, in spite of the fact that no complete re-coinage had taken place and there was still a considerable amount of base metal in circulation. The price for this success was paid by the merchant community, whose profits were delayed by the need to provide Gresham with credits. On the other hand they were able to charge a political price for their financial services. Shutting out the Hanseatic League was a part of that payoff; another was the abandonment of any plan to make custom revenues more realistic by increasing the dues on cloth. The customs continued to run at £23-25,000 throughout Edward's reign. When Mary's council grasped this nettle in 1557 the revenue shot up to over £80,00 a year on a very similar volume of trade,   so the services which the Merchant Adventurers in particular rendered to the minority governments were by no means unrewarded. The council also supported the city authorities over the sensitive issue of policing the city, where unemployment and religious division created constant tension.

In addition to accumulating war debts, the protectorate had also failed to maintain a tight control on financial administration. The most notorious example was the peculation of Sir William Sharrington at the Bristol mint, but he was by no means the only culprit. In January 1551 Sir Martin Bowes, the sub-treasurer of the London mint, was found to be no less than £10,000 in arrears with his account, while John Beaumont had milked the court of wards and liveries of a similar sum during a five year tenure of office from 1545 to 1550. The earl of Warwick brought in a new team to remedy this situation. William Paulet, marquis of Winchester, may well have become lord treasurer in February 1550 for political rather than administrative reasons, but his brief was a reforming one. How effective he would have been on his own may well be doubted, but he was ably supported by Sir William Cecil, who seemed to have been responsible for the detection of most of the malfeasance, and Sir Walter Mildmay. In addition to proceeding against a number of individual defaulters, this team was also responsible for the commission of 1552. Although ineffective in many ways, this investigation did put its finger on one very important source of the weakness which was evident in the running if the king's financial affairs, and that was the multiplicity of revenue courts[9]. These courts had been created by Thomas Cromwell, partly to divert money away from the treasury of the household, and partly to divide control in a manner more amenable to his own management. The existence of five separate and independent accounting bodies had been recognised as clumsy and inefficient for some time, but the officers of each court constituted a substantial vested interest which could not easily be removed. Augmentations and general surveyors had been merged in 1547 into a new court of augmentation, but the main problem remained.

The commission recommended merging the five remaining institutions - exchequer, augmentations, first fruits and tenths, wards and liveries and the duchy of Lancaster, into one. This, it was estimated, would save over £18,000 a year in fees and salaries as well as improving the administration of the revenue. Winchester, or possibly Northumberland, was convinced by these arguments and the last parliament of Edward's reign tackled the issue. First, it was enacted that all revenue officers should be placed under sufficient bonds for the proper discharge of there duties. Secondly prompter and more reliable audits were ordered, and thirdly the king was authorised by his letters patent to merge and dissolve the existing revenue courts as he thought fit[10]. The king's illness and early death prevented this statute from taking effect, but it was re-enacted by the first parliament of Mary's reign. In 1554 by the queen's letters patent augmentations and first fruits and tenths were merged into the exchequer, the other two remaining independent. Winchester had retained his office as lord treasurer, and this pattern almost certainly reflected his priorities. Whether the exchequer would have been given similar prominence if Edward had lived to carry out the reforms himself may be doubted. The last years of Edward's reign saw a general tightening of procedures. A systematic docquet book was kept, and memoranda of business to be transacted by the council became more numerous. This energy did not only affect financial matters, but it was particularly noticeable there. The reason for this is debatable. Professor Jordan argued it was the result of the young king's personal involvement, and he pointed to a number of examples of transactions in which Edward was alleged to have made the critical decision himself. He also pointed out that memoranda became less numerous after the end of November 1552, at which point Edward also abandoned his journal, probably on account of his deteriorating health[11]. On the other hand neither the direction nor the drive of the council's reform programme changed after this date. It seems very likely that the king, who at this time was fifteen, was displaying an increased interest in affairs of state during 1552, and that he was encouraged to do so by Northumberland. His involvement in decision making, however, was probably more apparent than real. Given the duke's influence over his young master, and the fact that it was in his interest to exaggerate Edward's energy and capacity, it seems likely that the king's somewhat improbable urge for financial reform was to cover for Northumberland's own programme. He had learned from Somerset's mistakes that the English would accept decisions from an anointed king that they would not accept from a subect, no matter how powerful, especially if he was building up a private power base at the same time.

19

Overseas Trade and Exploration

It was axiomatic to any sixteenth century commentator that a healthy economy was a closely regulated one. This was a social theory rather than an economic one because it was based on the perception of the craft workers and merchants as socially cohesive groups, with their own discipline and sense of responsibility. From this it followed that a well ordered and prosperous town depended upon strong guilds, and the vested interests of established companies and corporations were consistently supported . Competition was strictly discouraged, whether from "merchant strangers" or from individual craftsmen who sought to escape from the suffocating security of the guilds by abandoning the corporate town for the countryside. Quality control was the standard excuse for this restrictive attitude. Guild inspection was supposed to be the guarantee of quality, and any possible desire on the part of the consumer to purchase an inferior item at a vastly lower price was regarded as a manifestation of original sin. The author of the *Discourse on the Commonweal of England*, written in 1549, expressed the orthodox view succinctly

> "...another thing I reckon would much help to relieve our towns decayed, if they could take order that all wares made there should have a special mark, and the mark to be set to none but to such as be truly wrought"[1]

It would be an exaggeration to say that either of Edward's minority governments had economic policy, or was pro-active in this matter of control, but the council, and parliament, were amenable to lobbying by the interested parties. Every session saw the emergence of statutes providing regulation, sometimes in minute detail, for the manufacture of hats, caps, gloves, shoes or woollen cloth. If a rival lobby proved successful in the next session, the statute might be repealed;

but that seldom, if ever, reflected a change of mind on the part of the government.

The crown could, and did, create new chartered boroughs with a view to extending this process of control[2], but prosperity could be created neither by statute nor by letters patent. Prosperity depended upon trade, and trade upon the vagaries of supply and demand. Politics could have a disruptive effect on trade, but very seldom promoted it. Henry VII had used what little muscle he had to promote the interests of his merchants in Spain and the Low Countries, but his sons priorities were elsewhere. English trade with Spain had suffered severely from the king's Great Matter, and so angry had some Southampton merchants become with the attitude of the Spanish authorities that in 1545 one of them, Robert Reneger, had taken the law into his own hands, and seized a richly freighted Spanish ship inward bound from America. For this act of piracy he was mildly rebuked by the English council, and the life of the English community in San Lucar became even more impossible. War with France repeatedly disrupted the wine trade between Bristol and Gascony, and the occasional quarrels with the authorities in the Low Countries resulted in embargoes on the cloth trade. These could be damaging but were seldom long sustained because the English could, with difficulty, sell their cloth elsewhere, while the finishing industry in the Netherlands was absolutely dependent on supplies from across the Narrow Seas. War could create its own pattern of demand. Henry VIII's agents had bought saltpetre, sailcloth and rope in Danzig and Hamburg. Thomas Gresham mixed his skilful interventions in the Antwerp exchange with substantial purchases of almain rivets and pikes. Those who had contracts to feed or clothe armies did well out of war, then as now, but the merchant community as a whole was consistently opposed to war, whether it was Somerset's adventures in Scotland, or the risks which Northumberland took with the Emperor. Northumberland's good relations with the city of London were not only the result of his success against the Hanseatic League, but also of his success in avoiding armed conflict on any front.

In 1549 England exported some 150,000 broadclothes, of which about 80% passed through Blackwell Hall on their way to Antwerp. A hundred years before the total had been 57,000, and less than half had gone out from London[3]. These changes had brought prosperity to Suffolk and the Cotswolds, as well as to the capital, but some outports, such as King's Lynn, had languished. The big money was in cloth, but concentration in London was not the result of government policy. Wherever possible the council endeavoured to protect the outport merchants against the bullying tactics of the merchant adventurers. Both Newcastle and Bristol adventurers retained their independence, and in 1552 the latter were granted their own charter. Nor was cloth the only export. Tin, hides, fish and some manufactured goods also feature in the port books, and not all the coal going out of the Tyne was destined for London. In spite of a lack of official encouragement, the merchants of Bristol had maintained in a small way that interest in the Atlantic that had caused the Cabots to base their voyages there in 1497 and 1498. There was a regular trade with the Azores and with Madeira, and Bristol also sent out a significant part of the fishing fleet which annually made its way to the Newfoundland banks. Despite all urging, Henry VIII had shown no interest in supporting exploration, or risky ventures in long distance trade, but soon after his death the signals became more encouraging. In 1547 Sebastian Cabot returned to England. He was an old man and had not worked in England for almost fifty years, but the initiative for the move seems to have come from him[4]. For many years he had been Charles V's pilot major, and he had been in charge of the navigational school at Seville. He was immensely knowledgeable about all maritime matters, and Charles was understandably chagrined at his departure. At first he refused to believe that the old man had gone of his own free will, but so it undoubtedly was.

In spite of his advanced years, Cabot was full of energy and ideas, and had already set about the task of persuading the conservative merchant oligarchy of London to broaden their horizons before the Antwerp crisis of 1550-51 gave them an additional and compelling reason to do so. His natural allies were the privateers, or more accurately pirates because there was no state of war, who were already operating in the Atlantic as far south as the coast of Guinea. These captains needed no urging to go further afield in search of rich pickings, and since they nearly always doubled as respectable merchants, their attitude began to affect the merchant community at large. The first English trading voyage to Morocco was probably made in 1551, and the following year three ships traded along the Barbary coast, using the services of Jewish middlemen. In 1553, in defiance of Spanish protests, several more ships, accompanied this time by two royal warships, attempted to trade as far south as El Mina[5]. To what extent, if at all, Cabot was behind these ventures is not known, but he possessed an unrivalled knowledge of the Atlantic, and of Spanish maritime activity. If this sudden access of adventurousness was a coincidence, it was a remarkable one. Cabot was not, however, the only man in London eager to promote maritime enterprise. Shortly after his appearance the enigmatic John Dee returned from a tour abroad. Dee, a mathematician and cosmographer who was later accused of necromancy was a remarkable and visionary intellectual, who already enjoyed the respect and friendship of the influential William Cecil. Cecil introduced Dee to Northumberland, who employed him as a tutor and listened to his advice. Both Dee and Cabot advocated the establishment of a new route to the Indies. China particularly was a vast untapped market, but a route needed to be discovered which was not already claimed by other and more powerful seafaring nations.

Spain had already made clear its displeasure at any intrusion into the waters which it claimed as its own. Small scale defiance was a realistic and attractive option, but no major trade could be established without risking a war which England was in no position to fight. Portuguese power in the far east was in full decline by 1550, but this was not known or understood, and in any case the English had no equivalent to the vast Portuguese carracks, whose seaworthiness and capacity made the long voyage around the Cape of Good Hope a realistic proposition. So although protestant England ostentatiously refused to recognise Pope Alexander VI's division of the world into Spanish and Portuguese spheres of influence, there seemed to be no way in which the existing Imperial powers could be challenged. The alternative, advocated by both Dee and Cabot, was a route around the North Cape and along the northern shore of Asia. It was known that the north cape was ice free, and this prompted optimistic speculation that, in summer at least, an open channel could be found for the whole distance. With two such renowned cosmographers backing the scheme, and Northumberland leading a group of councillors and courtiers in support, a company was formed and the merchant community could hardly refuse to participate. A capital of about £6,000 was subscribed[6], and a small fleet was commissioned, with instructions to explore the coastline "towards Cathay", and to establish friendly commercial relations with any "civil" people they might find along the way. Sir Hugh Willoughby, a soldier with virtually no maritime experience, was licensed by the lord admiral to command this fleet. His job was partly to ensure discipline, and partly to make a respectable diplomatic presence, should the expedition encounter persons of consequence. It must be remembered that they were hoping to appear before the Emperor of China. The practical leadership of the expedition was placed in the hands of the pilot major, Richard Chancellor, a man whose skill and experience were fully equal to the responsibility.

It is said that Cabot himself wished to serve, but was persuaded that he was too old for the rigours of such a voyage. Instead he contented himself with drawing up the ordinances. A council was prescribed, to be presided over by Willoughby, and the behaviour of all the members of the expedition was to be that expected by men who were ambassadors of their country. The services of the *Book of Common Prayer* were to be strictly followed, but all manner of religious controversy, either within the expedition or between its members and those whom they might encounter, was strictly forbidden[7]. Formal letters missive were drawn up in a variety of languages, including Latin and Greek authorising Willoughby to discover and claim lands in the name of the king of England, and a letter commendatory hopefully addressed "towards the mighty Emperor of Cathay". The company, of which Cabot was the titular head, then equipped and fitted out three small ships - the *Bona Esperanza* of 120 tons, commanded by Willoughby himself, the *Edward Bonaventure* of 160 tons commanded by Chancellor, and the *Bona Confidentia*, commanded by Cornelius Danforth. The whole complement of the fleet was no more than 110 men, of whom 18 were merchants. Although guns were carried, it is clear that no serious fighting was anticipated, as fighting ships were manned at twice that level, and the careful conservation of supplies was more important than defence. Presumably it was hoped that pirates did not operate so far north. In spite of his deteriorating health, Edward showed a keen personal interest in the preparations for this voyage, and when at last it was ready to set off, on the 11th of May 1553 he was propped up at an open window of Greenwich palace to see the ships drop down the river, their departure heralded by salvos of gunfire.

The history of this voyage scarcely belongs to the reign of Edward VI, because before the ships had even cleared the coast of Norfolk on their outward voyage, the king was dead. However, as an enterprise launched with his encouragement, and the full support of his council, its achievements should be credited to his servants. Willoughby's log records that they reached the Lofoten Islands in the middle of July, and were already running dangerously late to accomplish their mission before the onset of winter. Early in August the three ships were separated by a violent storm somewhere to the north of North Cape, and Willoughby never saw the *Edward Bonaventure* again. In company with the *Confidentia* he sailed blindly west and south in search of land, on several occasions sighting coasts that were too forbidding to make a landfall. Eventually, on the 14th September they were able to land, probably at a place later called Arzina in Lapland. Because the *Confidentia* was leaking badly, and because the first snows of winter had already set in, Willoughby decided to remain in what was, apparently, a secure haven[8]. The ships were victualled for eighteen months, and there was abundant fish and game, so starvation did not seem to be a danger. He had, however, reckoned without the fierce cold of winter at such a high latitude. The seamen failed to find any sign of habitation, and were thus left to their own resources. Whether because of disease, or because they simply did not know how to survive in spite of abundant food and fuel, both crews died to a man, and their bodies (including Willoughby's log) were found by Russian fishermen in the spring of 1554. By the time that this had happened, the Russians already knew about the English expedition, because Chancellor, more fortunate, or possibly more skilful, had made his landfall at Archangel[9], on the southern shore of the White Sea. There he and his men were hospitably received, and when improving weather made travel possible, despatched south to Moscow in the care of local guides.

Fortunately for him, Tsar Ivan IV was always on the look out for openings to the west, for both commercial and political reasons, and therefore welcomed a mission which must have been unsure of its reception. He was even prepared to receive with equanimity an letter of commendation addressed to the Emperor of China! Chancellor was consequently cordially received, and presented with a letter for Edward VI, inviting him to establish commerce between their two countries. The Tsar was even prepared to offer "...free mart with all free liberties through my whole dominions". Since the expanding empire of Russia by this time stretched from the Urals to Dneiper, the opportunities which this offered seemed almost limitless. Chancellor returned to his ship at Archangel and sailed home, to find that Edward VI was dead, and several of the councillors who backed the voyage were either dead also, like the duke of Northumberland, or in disgrace like William Cecil. It soon transpired however, that support for this enterprise had not been specific to the regime. Cabot and his London colleagues quickly persuaded Mary's council to take up the offer, and in February 1555 the Muscovy company was chartered, with Cabot as its governor. By the summer the *Edward Bonaventure* was returning to Russia with Chancellor in command, and a number of merchants on board to act as the new company's permanent factors. In October 1555 Ivan granted the English merchants their promised charter of privileges, and when Chancellor returned to England in the summer of 1556 he was accompanied by an ambassador from Ivan to the court of Philip and Mary. On the voyage the entire fleet was lost, and Chancellor was drowned, but the ambassador survived to take up his post, and the Muscovy company duly commenced trading. It never became a great company in terms of its financial turnover, but it was a critically important pioneering venture which helped to initiate a steady diversification of English trade in the second half of the sixteenth century.

Richard Chancellor was not the only Englishman who was endeavouring to expand his country's commerce at the time. Before Edward ascended to the throne, in 1546, Anthony Jenkinson had set out from London with the intention of re-opening the trade of the eastern Mediterranean, which had long since succumbed to the discouragements of piracy and competition. After extensive, and apparently fruitless, travels in 1553 he secured an audience in Aleppo with the Sultan Suleiman the Magnificent, who was prepared to grant concessions similar to those which Chancellor was securing in Russia. In this case, however, it was to be twenty five years before the Levant Company was formed to follow up this initiative , partly because the Muscovy Company had stolen a march, and partly because Jenkinson himself took over Chancellor's role, finding Moscow a more promising route to the East than Istanbul. Although the climate was changing, the merchant adventurers of London were not yet prepared to support several such exotic ventures at the same time.

20

Northumberland and the succession crisis of 1553

Nobody knew that Edward VI was going to die until about a month before it happened. Rumours that the king's sickness was mortal began in January, but were not based upon any knowledge of the real state of his health. Edward's death had been reported several times during the previous five years, not because his health was particularly fragile, but because he represented England's tenuous hold on political stability. The king's death was feared, like the sweating sickness, as a manifestation of divine judgment. In January and February 1553 the rumour was that the duke of Northumberland was poisoning him, a tale which brought several men and women to the pillory, and some before the council[1]. Northumberland was unpopular for a variety of reasons. He was blamed, with some justice for the death of the "Good Duke" of Somerset, and for what many saw as the harsh and repressive policies with which he had succcessfully maintained domestic order since the end of 1549. Folk memories of Richard of Gloucester and the former earl of Warwick, Richard Neville, conspired with a more rational dislike to turn him into a sinister and conspiratorial figure with designs upon the crown. In fact Northumberland's whole position depended upon the king's life, and his plots were directed, not to seizing the crown but to establishing himself as the guide and mentor of a new and formidable Tudor king. Far from plotting Edward's death, all the evidence suggests that he was refusing to countenance such an appalling prospect, even when it had become a real possibility. It was the king himself, not Northumberland, who played around with the possibilities for the succession, in drawing up his notorious Device, probably in January 1553.

The surviving text is a strange palimpsest of a document, drawn up with no thought of early implementations, and probably as an exploration of the possibilities. The main problem was the same as that which confronted Henry VIII. Beyond the present incumbent there was no sign of a male heir. Edward had two half sisters, Mary and Elizabeth, both illegitimate by statute, but included in their father's succession act of 1543. He also had a legitimate cousin, Mary, the grandaughter of his father's sister, Margaret, and presently the queen of Scotland in her own right. Mary had been excluded from Henry's act on the grounds of her foreign birth, and a prolonged attempt to secure her as a bride for Edward had ended in frustration in 1548. In 1553 she was living at the French court , and betrothed to the Dauphin Francis. The king also had two other female cousins, the daughters of his father's younger sister, Mary, through her second marriage to Charles Brandon, duke of Suffolk. The elder of these, Frances, was married to Henry Grey, presently the duke of Suffolk and was the mother of three daughters, Jane, Catherine and Mary. The younger, Eleanor, was married to Henry Clifford, earl of Cumberland, and the mother of one daughter Margaret. The nearest male heir was Henry Stewart, Lord Darnley, the grandson of Margaret Tudor's second marriage, to Archibald, earl of Angus. The "Suffolk line", the descendants of Henry's younger sister, had been included in the 1543 act, but not Margaret's descendants by either marriage. Confronted by this unpromising array of females, Edward resorted to solutions which owed more to fantasy than political fact. If he were to die without heirs of his own , the crown was to pass to any son who might subsequently be born to the Lady Frances, and failing that to any son who might be born to one of her daughters[2]. Failing that to any son of the Lady Eleanor, or to any son of any daughter of the Lady Eleanor. The exclusion of the Scots in favour of this rather far fetched projection had a certain political sense. Not only had Henry excluded them, but the prospects of being ruled by a young lady who would one day become the queen-consort of France , and might very well seek to hand over her inheritance to her husband, was not to be endured. However the exclusion of Mary and Elizaeth made much less sense. The reason subsequently given was that, as both were unmarried they might take foreign husbands and bring the realm into subjection; but the real reason seems to have been that Edward was not willing to contemplate any woman as heir. Should there be no male available at the time of his death, then the Lady Frances was to hold a regency until such time as one of her daughters managed to perform the magic feat.

　　Such a bizarre proposal creates a doubt as to whether the device in its original form was ever anything more than idle jotting. It is hard to imagine so practical a statesmen as the duke of Northumberland contemplating a plan which would, in effect, have placed the monarchy in abeyance . When Edward's last parliament convened in March 1553, the Device was not mentioned. The king was unwell but there was no reason to suppose that his illness was particularly serious, and although a succession act might have been a sensible precaution, no serious plan existed which could have been submitted for ratification. During the spring of 1553 Northumberland himself was frequently ill, and far from plotting assiduously with his allies to assume absolute power, was talking despondently of retiring into private life[3]. These bouts of depression need not be taken too seriously, because the Duke had been something of a hypochondriac for several years, but between January and April it is likely that Winchester and Cecil were taking most of the decisions . Cranmer had long since retreated from the council, and the king, even if he had had the will and capacity to direct the affairs of state himself , can seldom have had the physical energy to be effective. By April, however, the duke was sufficiently recovered to complete the arrangements for the marriage of his only unmarried son, Guilford, to Lady Jane Grey on the 21st May, He had been pressing for this match for sometime, and it has often been supposed that he had done so in order to ensure that the much needed male heir would also be his grandson. However, that is to be wise after the event. Northumberland must have known of Edward's Device, but we do not know if he took it seriously. The fact that nothing had been said to parliament suggests not, and the marriage was not made with the succession in mind. Rather, it was part of a general strengthening of domestic ties among several noble families, because Jane's sister, Catherine was married to Lord Herbert and Guildford's sister (also Catherine) to Lord Hastings on the same day. Contrary to growing custom, the young people themselves do not seem to have been consulted, and Jane heartily disliked the man into whose bed she was forced by her unsympathetic parents. If anyone was calculating that Jane could bear a son in time to rescue the Tudor succession, then he did not know Jane, who was every bit as determined and obstinate as the king.

He did not know much about Edward's health either, because within a fortnight the king had taken a turn for the worse, and by the 7th June his doctors were saying gloomily that he could not live more than three months[4]. Untreated pulmonary tuberculosis is a cruel disease in that it progresses in spasms, with many remissions, and periods of apparent recovery. Had contemporary diagnosis been more effective, the council might have been told by January or February that they should prepare for the worst. As it was they were pitched into a sudden crisis early in June, and it soon became clear that even three months was an extremely optimistic prediction. Edward's resolute faith seems to have protected him from an ordinary mortal's fear of death, but he became desperately concerned about the succession, and his speculative ideas quickly became a serious political agenda. By the 12th June he had accepted that there was not going to be a male heir born in his lifetime. Nor was there going to be time to convene a parliament and legislate a new settlement. The king summoned the chief justices and other law officers to his sick bed, and ordered them to draw up a will on the basis of the Device, which he had recently altered to suit the new circumstances[5]. Frances Grey was now dismissed from consideration, along with Mary, Elizabeth, and the young queen of Scots. Instead the crown was to pass to "the Lady Jane and her heirs male". It is not surprising that the law officers, and many councillors looked askance at this quixotic decision. It had neither law nor logic to support it. A normal minor could not make a valid will, and no precedent existed to exempt a king from that limitation. Nor could any adult king demise the crown by his own unsupported authority. When Henry VI had agreed to bequeath the crown to the duke of York instead of to his son, the decision had been unacceptable to a large section of the nobility, and the result had been civil war. When Henry VIII reserved the right to alter the succession by his last will and testament, he had the authority of parliament to do so. If the crown had to pass to a female the obvious choice was Mary, who was already the lawful heir. If, as seems to have been the case, Mary was unacceptable to Edward because of her religious position, and a pretext had to be found to set her aside, then the next in line was Elizabeth against whom no such objection could be raised. Even if Elizabeth were set aside, and Mary of Scotland unacceptable, then the next heir was not Jane but her mother. There seem to be only two possible explanations for the king's action. One is that his hand was guided by the unscrupulous and ambitious duke of Northumberland, who could not resist the temptation of a crown matrimonial for his son. The other is that Edward was still obsessed by the idea of finding the quickest possible route to a male heir. Mary, in addition to all other considerations was already thirty seven and unmarried. Elizabeth was a suitable age, but showed no inclination to marriage, and in any case there was no suitable partner in sight. Frances, long married, was probably past the child bearing age, or at least it was reasonable to suppose that she might be so. Jane was young, healthy, and suitably married within the realm. Moreover, of all the women in question, she was the one who possessed the strongest and most articulate protestant zeal[6]. Edward knew her better, and probably liked her better than any of the others.

If the Device in its final form was really a political plot laid by the duke of Northumberland, then it was an extraordinarily scrambled and botched affair. On the other hand we know that the duke's influence over the young king remained extremely strong almost to the end. Perhaps the eventual settlement was a compromise. At least it avoided the absurdity of a regency for a hypothetical king who had not been born. It also avoided having the duke and duchess of Suffolk as king and queen, without any guarantee of a male succession. The real problem is the exclusion of Elizabeth. Was it because Northumberland felt he could not dominate her, as he could his daughter-in-law? Or was it because Edward himself believed that no statutory settlement could overcome the taint of illegitimacy? If that was the case, why did neither he, nor anyone else say so? Whatever the true explanation, during June 1553 the king bent all his failing energies to the task of forcing or persuading his council to accept the Device, and in that he was fully supported by Northumberland. On the 15th the law officers were again summoned to the royal bedchamber, and commanded upon their allegiance to draw up a will in due form. Their reluctance was not a convenient trick of later memory. Both Sir Edward Montague and John Gosnold, the attorney general, in yielding to the king's "sharp words and angry countenance" warned the council that, no matter how correctly the will was drawn up, it could not abrogate the Henrician succession act. On the other hand, it was clearly treason to refuse the king's express command. Six days later, on the 21st June, Edward played his last card. Summoning all his councillors and officers of state, including Archbishop Cranmer, twenty two other peers, the judges, his household officers, the lord mayor and aldermen of London and the sheriffs of the neighbouring counties, he commanded them all to "observe, fully perform and keep" the order of succession which he had laid down. Meanwhile news of the Device had leaked out. Antoine de Noailles, the French ambassador, probably knew because Northumberland had told him, soliciting his master's assistance to keep out Mary, who could plausibly be represented as an Imperial puppet[8]. But Scheyfve also knew, and so did Mary, who was not deceived by the friendly and informative messages which she was receiving from Northumberland. Before the end of June her friends and affinity were preparing to challenge the king's will.

When Edward at length died on the 6th July, everyone had hard decisions to make. The dukes of Suffolk and Northumberland, who had the most to gain, immediately made it clear that they would stand by the Device. Their resolution ostensibly carried the remainder of the council with them and on the 8th July Jane was duly proclaimed queen. The following day Mary, who had retreated to Norfolk as the king's death became imminent, proclaimed herself queen and wrote to the council in London commanding their allegiance. As the crisis approached she had done what she always did in such circumstances, and sought the advice of the Imperial ambassador; but Scheyfve did not know what to say, and in the event she acted on her own determination. A few days before Edward died a special Imperial embassy had arrived, ostensibly to commiserate upon his illness, but really to watch events after his death[9]. Charles's instruction were typically cautious. If the country seemed disposed to accept Jane, then they were not to jeopardise future relations by insisting upon Mary's superior claim. If, on the other hand, Mary appeared to have a real chance of success, then they were to support her as discreetly as possible. The ambassadors' first appraisal, written on 12th July, was that the council was solidly for Jane, and commanded all the available resources. Mary had no chance. The real situation, however, was very different. Strongly on Jane's side was the habit of obedience, and the fact that everyone of importance seemed to be supporting her. Less strong, but still of considerable importance, was the seriousness with which the oath had been taken. Cranmer, deeply unhappy about the legality of the settlement, supported it because he had sworn an oath to do so. Also on her side, but much less strong than had been expected, was the protestant suspicion of Mary's conservative religious convictions. On Mary's side, first and foremost, was the undoubted fact that she was the heir by law, and that Edward's Device had no legal or constitutional validity. Almost equally important was the unpopularity of Northumberland and his friends, who were widely and ridiculously blamed for the king's death. Finally her religious conservatism, much as it may have alienated her brother, was widely popular and generated much support. The first few days were critical. Mary's carefully prepared defiance was unexpected. Her normal reaction to crisis was to run away, collapse, or appeal tearfully for Imperial support. But Northumberland should have remembered how tough she had been in resisting her father twenty years earlier. When her conscience was fully engaged she could be extremely resolute, and that was the situation now. Swiftly her supporters began to muster at Kenninghall and Framlingham. East Anglian gentry at first, but soon peers such as the earl of Bath, and contingents from all over the country. According to her sympathetic chronicler, Robert Wingfield, nobles were forced to declare for her by their recalcitrant servants, and captains by the men under their command[10]. In fact the core of her support seems to have come from the gentry, and as it became apparent that a military campaign was going to be necessary to defeat her, the cracks in Jane's support became increasingly clear to see. Northumberland was the best soldier in England, but he could not be in two places at once. He needed to be in London to overawe those councillors who were disposed, once Edward was dead, to remember that they were no longer protected by the necessity to obey him[11], but he also needed to be in Norfolk to defeat the rebels. The latter task was probably the easier, but Jane forced it upon him by refusing to allow her father to go. In the short time at her disposal, Jane demonstrated some of her potential toughness as queen, because she also categorically refused to concede to her husband the crown matrimonial. In the latter case she may have been justified, but in the former her judgment was at fault. No sooner was Northumberland out of London than the earls of Arundel and Pembroke led a defection from the council. Between the 16th and the 18th of July they gathered and assessed their strength, and on the latter day proclaimed Mary in London amid general rejoicings. The following day, trapped at Cambridge and with his army deserting, Northumberland surrendered.

The foreign observers in London watched this debacle with incredulity. They were used to peasant revolts, and to magnate faction, but this was neither. It was a "gentleman's rebellion" in defence of established legal and constitutional procedures against the pretensions of an extremely exalted prerogative. It is unlikely that the duke of Northumberland ever set out with the deliberate intention of overthrowing the supremacy of statute. He set out to obey his king, and was then trapped by a mixture of loyalty and self interest into maintaining a position which was legally untenable. However, it is easy to be wise after the event. The *coup* represented by Edward's Device could easily have succeeded, and the whole subsequent history of England might then have been different. Edward VI could well have gone down in history as the king who established royal absolutism in England without ever exercising it himself.

NOTES

CHAPTER 1

1. Document no. 1

2. Glyn Redworth, *In Defence of the Church Catholic; the life of Stephen Gardiner*, pp. 239-40.

3. Henry's surviving will is dated 30th December, and there is no conclusive evidence that it was altered after that date, so it may have been presented merely for confirmation. Having examined the original, W.K. Jordan believed that it had been signed, not stamped (*Edward VI: the young king*, p.55), so it is possible that there may have been two versions. On the other hand the use of a stamp on 30th December is intrinsically probable, as well as being supported by other evidence. See also Document no. 2.

4. The sixteen were: Thomas Cranmer, archbishop of Canterbury, Thomas, Lord Wriothesley, lord chancellor, William, Lord St. John, lord great master, John, Lord Russell, keeper of the privy seal, Edward Seymour, earl of Hertford, great chamberlain, John, viscount Lisle, lord admiral, Cuthbert Tunstall, bishop of Durham, Sir Anthony Browne, master of the horse, Sir William Paget, principal secretary, Sir Edward North, Sir Edward Montague, Sir Thomas Bromley, Sir Anthony Denny, Sir William Herbert, Sir Edward Wotton and Dr. Nicholas Wotton.

5. The other peers created were: Sir Thomas Seymour (the Protector's brother) as Lord Seymour of Sudeley; Sir Richard Rich as Lord Rich of Leighs; Sir William Willoughby as Lord Willoughby of Parham; and Sir Edmund Sheffield as Lord Sheffield,

6. When this council settled down, it included thirteen former executors (Wriothesley, Bromley and Nicholas Wotton having been dropped) and eight former assistants. D.E. Hoak, *The King's Council*

under Edward VI, pp. 36 42, 47.

CHAPTER 2

1. S.T.C. 4827

2. Document no. 6.

3. Gardiner to Cranmer, 12th June 1547; J.A. Muller, *The Letters of Stephen Gardiner*, p.299.

4. Document no. 7.

5. P.L. Hughes and J.F. Larkin, *Tudor Royal Proclamations*, I, pp.413-15.

6. For a full discussion of the impact of these changes upon the spirituality of traditional communities, see E. Duffy, *The Stripping of the Altars*, pp. 478-503.

CHAPTER 3

1. One of the few identifiable causes of this recovery was a drop in the average age of marriage, leading to improved fertility and a marginal decline in infant mortality. J. Hatcher, *Plague, Population and the English Economy, 1348-1530*.

2. For a good discussion of this, and other legal issues, see Eric Kerridge, *The Agrarian Problem in the sixteenth century and after*, passim.

3. Voices were occasionally raised in defence of enclosure even in the sixteenth century, but always in the context of improved arable yields. For example:
    Example by Leicestershire take
    What soil can be better than that
    For anything heart can desire?
    And yet it doth want ye see what:

Mast, covert, close pasture and wood
And other things needful as good.
All these do enclosure bring,
Experience teaches no less....
R.H. Tawney and Eileen Power, *Tudor Economic Documents*, III, p.63.

4. A "demesne copyholder" also held a copy of court roll, but it conveyed no security because all demesne land was legally in the lord's hand, and anyone else occupying it could only be a tenant at will. This was not always understood by those who were in that situation.

5. Robert Crowley on the causes of Kett's rebellion, *Tudor Economic Documents*, III, pp.57-60.

6. For presentments before these commissioners, see Document no. 9.

7. *A Discourse on the Commonweal of this Realm of England*, ed. E. Lamond, p.130.

CHAPTER 4

1. One of the reasons for Henry's insistence on this meeting was that James had failed to appear at York during the summer progress of 1541, when he had been expected. Henry had felt rather childishly humiliated by this fiasco.

2. See Grafton's account in Document no. 8.

3. The full list of garrisons actually established runs:
Broughty Crag
Dundee
Inchcolm
Inchkeith
Haddington
Yester castle
Dunglass castle
Fast castle   East coast and East March
Eye mouth
Billie Tower

Ayton castle
Lauder
Hume castle
Kelso
Roxburgh
Jedburgh
Hermitage castle   Middlemarch
Moffat
Langolm
Castlemilk   West March
Lochwood castle
Dumfries
Cockpool

Garrisons were also intended, but never established, at: Montrose, Arbroath, Perth, Burntisland, Edinburgh, Leith, Inveresk, Musleburgh, Aberlady, Whitekirk, Dunbar, Lochmaben castle and Kirkcudbright. M.L. Bush, *The Government Policy of Protector Somerset*, pp. 13-17.

4. Lord Wharton was particularly cantankerous, and was eventually replaced by his bitter enemy, Lord Dacre. Jordan, *The Young King*, p.296.

5. Also French titles. The earls of Huntly and Argyle became members of the Order of St. Michael, and the earl of Arran became duke of Chatelherault.; Jordan, *The Young King*, p.272.

6. Bush, *Government Policy*, pp.17-18.

CHAPTER 5

1. *Acts of the Privy Council*, III pp.4-5

2. It was standard practice after 1540 for the clerk, who took the minutes to be excluded from all discussions of a sensitive nature. The record therefore only contains notes of administrative business and never of political advice, even if that was proffered from a regular meeting.

3. Northamptonshire Record Office, Fitzwilliam MS C.21, cited by

D.E. Hoak, *The King's Council under Edward VI*, p.103. Paget went on to urge, significantly "youe must often altre your determinacions" as a result of such consultations, which was precisely what the Protector was unwilling to do.

4. See Document no. 4.

5. W.K. Jordan, *The Young King*, pp. 368-381.

6. D.E. Hoak, *The King's Council*, from which much of the information in this lecture is taken.

CHAPTER 6

1. BL. Cotton MS Titus B ii, 47, ff.79-81; cited Jordan, *The Young King*, pp.230-31.

2. See Document no. 10.

3. For a fuller discussion of this point, see chapter 12.

4. *Calender of State Papers, Foreign, Edward VI*, 51; cited Jordan, *The Young King*, p.236.

5. This point and its consequences, is fully discussed in M.J. Rodriguez Salgado, *The Changing Face of Empire*, passim.

6. Northampton Record Office, Fitzwilliam MSS, Paget Letter Book, 5,7 ; B.L. Beer and S.I. Jack, "The Letters of William, Lord Paget of Beaudesert", *Camden Miscellany*, 25, 1974, pp.

CHAPTER 7

1. D.M. Loades, *Politics, Censorship and the English Reformation*, p.134.

2. Hughes and Larkin, *Tudor Royal Proclamations*, I, pp.181-6.

3. The stationers' company was not actually chartered until 1557,

but it was in existence for nearly a century before that. It had originally consisted of paper sellers, but it was prepared to receive the new printers when the scriveners refused, and was eventually taken over by them. Cyprian Blagden, *The Stationers Company, a History, 1403-1959.*

4. P. Took, "Government and the Printing Trade, 1450-1560." (Unpublished London Ph.D,1978) p.331 and Appendix II.

5. *A Short Title Catalogue of Books Printed in England, Scotland and Ireland...and of English Books Printed Abroad,1475-1640*, ed. A.W. Pollard and G.R. Redgrave, and revised by W.A. Jackson, F.S. Ferguson and K.F. Pantzer, no. 1462.3, sig. C6v.

6. D.M. Loades, *The Reign of Mary Tudor*, pp. 262-303.

7. See particularly E.C. Whitaker, *Martin Bucer and the Book of Common Prayer*, passim.

8. For a full discussion of these churches, see Andrew Pettegree, *Foreign Protestant Communities in Sixteenth Century London*, pp.77-112.

9. Hughes and Larkin, *Tudor Royal Proclamation*, I, p.515.

CHAPTER 8

1. Sixteen out of twenty seven vacancies which occurred in the diocese of Bangor in 1554 and 1555 were deprivations for marriage, but since bishop Skevington had also had problems with illicit clerical marriage before 1533, this does not necessarily represent the spread of protestant ideas. In the further corners of Wales the Hildebrandine reforms had never taken effect. A.I. Pryce,*The Diocese of Bangor in the sixteenth century*, pp.12-14.

2. Jordan, *The Young King*, pp.312-13

3. For a distinctly pessimistic view of the reception of the Edwardian changes, see E. Duffy, *The Stripping of the Altars*, pp. 478-503.

4. Gilbert Burnet, *A History of the Reformation*, II,ii, pp.133-149.

5. Even the moderate Dryander wrote to Bullinger "You will also find something to blame in the matter of the Lord's Supper; for the book speaks very obscurely, and however you might try to explain it with candour, you cannot avoid great absurdity". *Original Letters relative to the English Reformation*, ed. H. Robinson, I, pp.350-51.

6. *Original Letters*, I, pp.72-3

CHAPTER 9

1. His enlargement of Savernake Park was particularly controversial, although compensation was offered. M.L. Bush, *The Government Policy of Protector Somerset*, p.63 n.124.

2. Jordan, *The Chronicle of Edward VI*, p.12

3. Jordan, *The Young King*, p. 448.

4. Richard Polwhele, *The History of Devonshire*, I, p.254; Jordan, *The Young King*, p. 456.

5. This council had been set up in 1538, on the lines of the council in the marches of Wales, apparently on the grounds that the south west formed a "march" area which needed special control. There was probably never any real need for it, and it was quietly abandoned after a few years. Joyce Youings, "The Council in the West", *Transactions of the Royal Historical Society*, 5th series, 10, pp. 41-60.

6. Cranmer, *Works*, ii, pp. 163-87.

7. Diarmaid MacCulloch, *Suffolk and the Tudors*, pp. 300-304.

CHAPTER 10

1. *Calendar of State Papers, Spanish*, IX, p. 448. Van der Delft also reported that Warwick had been speaking warmly about the need for the Emperors friendship - as well he might since the French had just

declared war!

2. Jordan, *The Young King*, pp.500-503. Jordan believed that the earl of Warwick was the chief conspirator, but the evidence which he adduces does not make that clear,

3. College of Arms, Petyt MS, xlvi, f.466

4. Somerset sent Petre with a message for the Lords on 6th. October and he did not return, thus escaping any further involvement. Smith stayed at his post, and was eventually imprisoned and deprived of his office.

5. Grafton, *Chronicle*, p. 523.

6. Two days later the common council did make 500 men available to the lords, but support for Somerset was strong in the city, and the men never seem to have been raised. The speed of events in any case made further action unnecessary.

7. Grafton, *Chronicle*, p. 523.

8. British Library, Harleian MS 353, 23, f.77; Jordan, *The Young King*, p. 519.

9. *Acts of the Privy Council*, III, p. 343.

CHAPTER 11

1. *The Chronicle of Edward VI*, p. 18.

2. Van der Delft's reports; *Calendar of State Papers, Spanish*, IX, pp. 469-70; X, p. 7.

3. Henry James, "The aftermath of the 1549 coup, and the Earl of Warwick's intentions", *Historical Research*, 62, 1989.

4. Richard Scudamore to Sir Philip Hoby, 15th December 1549; Advocates Library of the National Library of Scotland, MS Adv. 34.2.14, f.31; edited by Susan Brigden in *Camden Miscellany*,

Vol.XXX (1990), pp. 99-102. See Document 13.

5. *Original Letters*, I, pp. 267-68.

6. He was sent off to France early in February, as one of the commissioners to negotiate the treaty of Boulogne.

7. Van der Delft believed that the duchess had made a successful approach via the countess of Warwick; *Cal. Span.*, X, p.14.

8. British Library, Cotton MS Titus B ii, 49, ff. 91-94.

9. Jordan, *The Threshold of Power*, pp.29-30.

10. 3 & 4 Edward VI, c. 5.

11. 3 & 4 Edward VI, c. 3.

CHAPTER 12

1. BL Cotton MS Otho C x, f.289; *Letters and Papers of the reign of Henry VIII*, Vol. X, 1136

2. *Calendar of the Patent Rolls, Edward VI*, Vol. II, p. 20.

3. D.M. Loades, *Mary Tudor; a life*, p. xi.

4. D.M. Loades, *Mary Tudor*, p. 143.

5. Mary's letter to the council is printed in J. Foxe, *Acts and Monuments of the English Martyrs*, Vol. VI, p. 7.

6. Dubois subsequently sent a full report of his misadventure to Mary of Hungary, no doubt to excuse himself for having failed in his mission. *Calendar of State Papers, Spanish*, Vol. X, p.127.

7. Foxe, *Acts and Monuments*, Vol. VI, pp.11-12. See Document 16.

CHAPTER 13

1. Statute 37 Henry VIII c.4.

2. The *opus dei* was the whole work of prayer to which the religious life was supposed to be dedicated. It might include intercession, particularly for benefactors, but that was not its sole or even its main, purpose.

3. Statute 1 Edward VI c.14; G.R. Elton, *The Tudor Constitution*, pp. 391-94.

4. If the pensions bill alone had been met, it would have absorbed over £200,000, or about one third of the total capital value of the acquisitions. Perhaps as much as a half of the income of former chantry properties was absorbed by pensions and continuations together.

5. W.K. Jordan has calculated that there were 272 endowed schools functioning in 1553, of which 154 were of chantry origin by one route or another. The population of England and Wales at this time was around three million. Jordan, *The Threshold of Power*, pp. 229-34. See also David Cressy, *Literacy and the Social order*.

6. According to Jordan, private almsgiving during the reign amounted to some £105,000, of which education absorbed about £19,000. The accuracy of these figures may be questioned, but their approximate scale is probably correct. Jordan, *The Threshold of Power*, p.206.

7. It was not until the foundation of Gresham college in the reign of Elizabeth that an institution of higher education in England offered technical or scientific instruction. The universities did not follow suit until the nineteenth century.

8. H.C. Porter, *Reformation and Reaction in Tudor Cambridge*.

9. *Original Letters*, Vol. II, pp.377-427.

CHAPTER 14

1. *Calendar of State Papers, Spanish*, Vol. IX, p. 469; Edward VI, *Journal*, p. 20.

2. BL Landsdowne MS 2, f.33; Jordan, *Threshold of Power*, p.121.

3. See Document 18.

4. Mason to the council, 7th February 1551; *Calendar of State Papers, Foreign, Edward VI*, no. 289. Wotton to the council, 23rd. February 1551; ibid, no. 295.

5. *Calendar of State Papers, Foreign, Edward VI*, nos. 349, 351.

6. Edward VI, *Journal*, pp. 72-73.

7. Jordan, *Threshold of Power*, p. 140.

8. See, for example, Sir William Pickering's letter to the council of 12th. October 1552; *Calendar of State Papers, Foreign, Edward VI*, no. 570.

9. There is ample evidence that the young king was becoming more actively involved in affairs towards the end of 1552, but it is debatable how much independent influence he exercised. On this point compare Jordan, *Threshold of Power*, p.166, and B.L. Beer, *Northumberland*, pp. 124-25.

CHAPTER 15

1. The extraordinary guard which Edward reviewed on 7th December 1551 consisted of bands of horsemen raised by the councillors and other leading courtiers. This was intended both for the security of the king and as a mobile police force. Edward VI, *Journal*, p.100. Sir Thomas Wyatt had also proposed a "select militia" of a similar nature to preserve order in the countryside. *The Papers of George Wyatt*, ed. D.M. Loades (Camden Society, 4th series, vol.5), pp. 163-180.

2. Hoak, *King's Council*, p.62.

3. Neville's problem was debt, arising from his chronic addiction to gambling. He had resorted to alchemy and necromancy as well (allegedly) as conspiracy to murder. Ibid, p. 63.

4. On the removal of Tunstall, see D.M. Loades, "The Last Years of Cuthbert Tunstall, 1547-1559", *Durham University Journal*, 66, 1973, pp. 10-21.

5. See below, pp. 130-137.

6. Public Records Office, SP10/10 f. 9; Jordan, *Threshold of Power*, p. 75.

7. *Calendar of State Papers, Spanish*, X, pp. 384-86; 18th October 1551.

8. Edward VI, *Journal*, pp.88-89.

9. Ibid, p.89. The king recorded these charges without comment, and it is difficult to know whether he believed them or not.

CHAPTER 16

1. E.C. Whitaker, *The Censura of Martin Bucer*, passim.

2. As Hooper never tired of pointing out, the retention of altars also retained the notion of sacrifice in the mass, an extreme form of idolatry to protestants. Hooper to Bullinger, 27th March 1550; *Original Letters*, I, pp. 78-85.

3. J. Strype, *Cranmer*, II, pp. 898-901; Cambridge University MS, MM4, 14 no.6; cited Jordan, *Threshold of Power*, p.346.

4. *The Two Liturgies...of the reign of Edward VI*, ed. Joseph Ketley, p. 199.

5. P.R.O. SP10/15 f.15; 7th October 1552

6. Cranmer, Writings, II, p. 441.

7. They were entited *Articles agreed upon by the bishops, and other Godly and Learned men,* which clearly implied approval by convocation. When Cranmer protested, he was told that the Articles should have been issued "in the time of convocation", although no explanation was offered as to why that had not happened.

8. Statute 3 & 4 Edward VI, c. 11.

CHAPTER 17

1. The anabaptists proper seem to have originated in Zurich with teachers such as Conrad Grebel, and Zwingli, the Zurich reformer, persuaded the council to launch a fierce persecution against them. See G.R. Potter, *Zwingli*; M. Mullet, *Radical Religious Movements in Early Modern Europe.*

2. K.B. McFarlane, *John Wycliffe and the beginnings of English Nonconformity.* It is doubtful whether any of the English works ascribed to Wycliffe were actually written by him.

3. By J.A.F. Thomson in *The Later Lollards, 1414-1520.*

4. Cornelius Krahn, *Dutch Anabaptism,* p. 215.

5. *Statutes of the Ream,* III, p. 812.

6. Huggarde, *The Displaying of the Protestants* (1556) p. 14.

7. There seems to have been more than one man with this name active in radical circles in Kent and Essex. C. Burrage, *The Early English Dissenters,* II, pp.5-6. I. Horst, *Radical Brethren,* p. 123.

8. J.W. Martin, *Religious Radicals in Tudor England,* pp. 71-82.

9. G. Burnet, *The History Of the Reformation of the Church of England,* II, pp. 209-219.

10. Richard Cox to Rudolph Gualter, 12th February, 1572; *Zurich Letters,* ed. H. Robinson, II, p.221.

CHAPTER 18

1. C. E. Challis, *The Tudor Coinage*, pp. 81-111.

2. *Historical Manuscripts Commission, Salisbury MSS*, I, pp. 91-104; 29th September 1552.

3. British Library Lansdowne MS 2, no. 55, f. 122; cited by Jordan, *The Threshold of Power*, p. 457.

4. W.C. Richardson, ed. *The Report of the Royal Commission of 1552*, pp. 393 ff.

5. J.D. Alsop, "The Revenue Commission of 1552", *Historical Journal*, 22, 1979, pp. 511-33.

6. T. Glasgow. "The maturing of the Naval Administration, 1656-1564", *Mariners Mirror*, 56, 1970; D, Loades, *The Tudor Navy*, p.155.

7. *Acts of the Privy Council*, IV, p. 27.

8. Ibid, pp. 183, 199. *HMC, Salisbury MSS*, I, p. 117.

9. Jordan, *The Threshold of Power*, pp. 446-47.

10. 7 Edward VI cs, 1, 2.

CHAPTER 19

1. *A Discourse of the Common Weal of the Realm of England*, ed. E. Lamond, p. 130.

2. Robert Tittler, "The emergence of urban policy, 1536-1558" in J. Loach and R. Tittler, eds., *The Mid-Tudor Polity, c. 1540-1560*, pp. 74-93.

3. D.M. Loades, *The Mid- Tudor Crisis, 1545-1565*, p. 89.

4. Some mystery surrounds Cabot's decision. He was offered, and accepted an annuity of 200 marks from the English council but that

would hardly have been sufficient in itself to tempt him. Perhaps he was beginning to feel the officiousness of the Inquisition threatening, and it may be significant that he had no scruples about prescribing the use of the Prayer Book in his instructions for the Cathay voyage. *Acts of the Privy Council*, II, p. 137, October 9th 1547.

5. Jordan, *The Threshold of Power*, p. 489.

6. 240 shares at £5 each. Sir William Foster, *England's Quest for Eastern Trade*, pp.8-9.

7. Cabot's ordinances and instructions are printed in Richard Hakluyt, *Principle Voyages and Navigations* II, pp. 206, 212-214.

8. At the time this haven was known as the Bay of Nokujeff.

9. The port of that name did not exist in the sixteenth century. The village which received Chancellor was called Nenuska.

CHAPTER 20

1. *The Acts of the Privy Council*, IV, pp. 220, 232, 234, 257, 258-9, 266-7, 269.

2. Or to any son who might be born to one of her granddaughters; the time scale envisaged is highly flexible. The original text of the Device is overlaid with corrections and the order in which they were made requires ingenious reconstruction. The Inner Temple MS Petyt xlvii, f. 316, ed. J.G. Nichols in *The Literary Remains of King Edward VI*, II, pp. 571-72.

3. Jordan, *Threshold of Power*, pp. 497-98.

4. At exactly what point the royal physicians came to this frightning conclusion is not known, but Sir John Cheke, writing to Bullinger on 7th June clearly knew the truth. *Original Letters*, ed. H. Robinson, I, p. 141.

5. Jordan, *Threshold of Power*, p.516. The relevant alterations are not made in the king's own hand, but it is clear from contemporary

accounts that they represented his wishes.

6. See particularly her letters to Bullinger in 1551 and 1552. *Original Letters*, I, pp. 4-8.

7. According to Edward Montague it was during one of these sessions that the duke called him a traitor, and threatened "to fight in his shirt with any man living" who opposed the king's wishes. *Historical Manuscripts Commission, MSS of Lord Montague of Beaulieu*, p. 4.

8. *Ambassades des Messieurs de Noailles*, ed. R.A. de Vertot, II, pp. 47-49. When Northumberland talked to Noailles on 26th June he was vague about the king's health, but before Edward actually died he had decided to accept direct aid from France. His decision was far too late to make any difference.

9. These ambassadors, Thoulouse, Courrieres and Renard, were instructed on the 23rd June and arrived in London a few days later. Renard's subsequent despatches form one of the best sources for the history of subsequent events.

10. "The *Vita Mariae Reginae* of Robert Wingfield of Brantham", ed. D. MacCulloch, *Camden Miscellany*, XXVIII.

11. When the charges were brought against Northumberland and his supporters, no treason was alleged before 6th July 1553. Their treason lay, not in accepting the Device, but in maintaining it after Edward's death. P.R.O., KB8/23, Baga de Secretis.

Document 1

The immediate occasion for this third succession act was the king's determination to wage war in France in his own person, and the need to settle the succession in case the hazards of campaigning should prove too much for him. It is remarkable mainly for two things; firstly that both Mary and Elizabeth are included, although both had been declared illegitimate, and secondly that it totally ignores Margaret Tudor's descendants by both her marriages. The king is also authorised to make a final determination of the succession by his last will and testament.

Document 1: The third succession act of Henry VIII. 35 Henry VIII ca. l. *Statutes of the Realm*, III, pp. 955-58. *Extracts*.

An acte concerninge thestabilishment of the King('s) Majesties Succession in the Imperiall Crowne of the Realme.

Where in the Parliament holden at Westmynster the eight daye of June in the xxviij[th] yere of the raigne of our most dread Soveraigne Lorde Kinge Henrie theight an Acte was had and made for the establishment of the succession of the Imperiall Crowne of this Realme of Englande, by w[ch] Acte emong(s) divers other thing(s) it was enacted, that thimperiall Crowne of this Realme withe all dignities honors p'hemynenc(s) p'rogatives auctorities and jurisdiccons to the same annexed or belonginge shoulde be to the Kinges Majestie and his heires of his bodye laufullie begotten, that is to saye, to the firste sonne of his bodie betwene his Highnes and his then laufull Wyef Quene Jane nowe deceased begotten, and to the heires of the bodye of the same firste sonne laufullye begotten, and for defaulte of suche heires, then to the seconde sonne of his Highnes bodye and of the bodye of the saide Quene Jane begotten, and to the heires of the bodye of the same seconde sonne begotten, with div'se other lymitacons of thestat conveyaunce and remaynders of the saide Imperiall Crowne and other the p'misses; And it was also enacted further by the saide statute, that for lacke of issue of our said Soveraigne Lorde the King('s) bodye laufullye begotten, that then his Highnes sholde and myght give will lymytt assigne appoynte or dispose the saide Imperiall Crowne and other the p'misses to what p'son or p'sons, and give the same p'son or p'sons such estate in the same, as it shoulde please his Majestie by his gracious l'tres patent under the great Seale, or by his laste Will in writinge signed with his most gracious hand; as by the same Acte emong div'se other thing(s) therein conteyned more at large it doeth appeare: Sythen the makinge of w[ch] Acte, the Kyng(s) Majestie hathe [one] onlye yssue of his bodye laufullye begotten betwixte his Highnes and his saide late Wief Quene Jane, the noble and excellente Prince, Prince Edwarde whom Almyghtie God longe p'serve; and also his Majestie hath nowe of late sithen the death of the said Quene Jane, taken to his Wief the most vertuous and gracious Ladye Katherine nowe Quene of Englande, late Wyef of John Nevyle Knight Lorde Latymer deceased, by whom as yet his Majestie hath none yssue, but maye have full well when it shall please God; And forasmuche as our saide most dread Soveraigne Lorde the Kinge upon good & just ground(s) & causes, entendeth by Gods grace to make a voyage royall in his Majesties most royall Parsone into the Realme of France, againste his auncient Enemye the Frenche Kinge, his Highnes most prudentlye & wisely consideringe and callinge to his remembrance howe this Realme standeth at this p'sent tyme in the cace of succession, and paysinge and wayinge further with himselfe the great truste & confidence that his lovinge subject(s) have had and have in him, puttinge in his handes hollye thordre and declaracon of the Succession of this Realme, recognisinge and knowleginge also that it is the onlye pleasure and will of Almyghtie God howe longe his Highnes or his saide entierlye beloved sonne, Prince Edwarde shall lyve, and whether the saide Prince shall have heires of his bodie laufullye begotten or not, or whither his Highnes shall have heires begotten and p'created betwene his Majestie and his saide moste deare and entierlye beloved Wief Quene Katherine that nowe ys, or any laufull heires and yssues hereafter of his owne bodye begotten by any other his laufull Wief; And albeit that the King('s) most excellent Majestie, for defaulte of suche heires as be enheritable by the saide Acte, myght by thauctoritie of the saide Acte, give and dispose the saide Imperiall Crowne and other the p'misses by his l'tres patent under his great Seale, or by his last will in writinge signed with his most gracious hande to any p'son or p'sons of suche estate therein as shoulde please his Highnes to lymytt and appoynte, yet to thintent that his Majesties disposicon and mynde therein shoulde be openlye declared and manifestlie knowne and notyfied, aswell to the Lordes sp'uall and temporall as to all other his lovinge and obedient subject(s) of this his Realme, to thintent that their assent and consent myght appeare to concurre with thus farre as followeth of his Majesties declaracon in [his] behalfe; His Majestie therfor thincketh convenient afore his departure beyonde the Seas, that it be enacted by his Highnes withe thassent of the Lordes sp'uall and temporall and the Comons in this p'sent Parliament assembled and by auctoritie of the same, and therefore be it enacted by thauctoritie aforesaide, that in case it shall happen the Kinges Majestie and the saide excellent Prince his yet onlye sonne Prince Edwarde and heire apparaunte, to decease without heire of either of their bodies laufullye begotten (as God defende), so that there be no suche heire male or female of any of their two bodyes, to have and inherite the said Imperiall Crowne and other his D'nions, accordinge and in suche manner and forme as in the foresaide Acte and nowe in this is declared, That then the saide Imperiall Crowne and all other the p'misses shalbe to the Ladye Marie the Kinges Highnes Daughter and to the heires of the bodye of the same Ladye Marie laufullie begotten, withe suche condicons as by his Highnes shalbe lymitted by his l'tres patent under his greate Seale, or by his Majesties laste Will in writinge signed with his gracious hande; and for defaulte of suche issue the saide Imperiall Crowne and other the p'misses shalbe to the Ladye Elizabeth the King('s) seconde daughter and to the heires of the bodie of the saide Lady Elizabeth laufullye begotten, withe suche condicons as by his Highnes shalbe lymitted by his l'tres patent under his greate Seale, or by his Majesties laste Will in writinge signed with his gracious hande; any thinge in the saide Acte made in the saide xxviij[th] yere of our saide Soveraigne Lorde to the cont[a]rie of this Acte notwithstandinge.

....

And forasmuche as it standeth in thonlye pleasure and will of Almightie God, whither the Kinges Majestie shall have any heires begotten and p'created betwene his Highnes and his saide moste entierly beloved Wief Quene Katherine, or by anye other his laufull Wief, or whither the saide Prince Edwarde shall have yssue of his bodye laufully begotten, or whither the Ladye Marie and Ladye Elizabeth or any of them shall have any yssue of any of their sev'all bodyes laufulye begotten, and if suche heires shoulde fayle (whiche God defende) and noe p'vision made in the King('s) lief who shoulde rule and governe this Realme for lacke of suche heires as in this p'sent Acte is afore mencioned, that then this Realme after the King('s) t[a]nsitorie lief and for lacke of suche heires, shoulde be destitute of a laufull Governour to order rule and governe the same; Be it therfore enacted by thauctoritie of this p'sent parliament, that the King('s) Highnes shall have full power and auctoritie to give dispose appoynte assigne declare and lymitt, by his gracious l'tres patent under his great Seale, or els by his Highnes laste Will made in writinge and signed withe his most gracious hande, at his onely pleasure from tyme to tyme hereafter, the Imperiall Crowne of this Realme and all other the p'misses, to be remayne succede and come, after his deceasse & for lacke of laufull heires of either of the bodyes of the King('s) Highnes and Prince Edwarde begotten, and also for lacke of laufull heires of the bodyes of the saide Ladye Marie and Ladye Elizabeth to be p'created and begotten as is afore lymytted in this Acte, to suche p'son or p'sonnes in remaynder or rev'con as shall please his Highnes, and accordinge to suche estate and after suche manner and fourme fashion ordre or condicon as shalbe exp'ssed declared named and lymited in his Highnes l'tres patentes, or by his laste Will in writinge signed with his most gracious hande as is aforesaide; any thinge conteyned in this p'sent Acte or in the saide former Acte to the cont[a]rie thereof in anywise notwithstandinge.

....

Document 2

This letter was written in 1566, when the author was trying to persuade Cecil of the legitimacy of Mary Stewart's claim. Maitland's argument refers to the statute of 1543 only as authorising Henry VIII's will, which he then goes on to argue was invalid. He shows detailed knowledge of the circumstances of 1546/7, but ignores the succession act itself, which would undermine his case. As far as we know Cecil was not impressed or persuaded.

Document 2: Sir William Maitland of Lethington to Sir William Cecil, concerning the title of the Queen of Scots to the Crown of England. Gilbert Burnet, *The History of the Reformation of the Church of England*, I, ii, pp.267-270. Extracts.

I cannot be ignorant that fome do object as to her Majefties Forreign Birth, and hereby think to make her incapable of the Inheritance of *England*. To that you know for anfwer what may be faid by an *Englifh* Patron of my Miftrifs's Caufe, although I being a *Scot* will not affirm the fame, that there arifeth amongft you a Queftion; Whether the Realm of *Scotland* be forth of the Homage and Leageance of *England*: And therefore you have in fundry Proclamations preceding your Wars-making, and in fundry Books at fundry times, laboured much to prove the Homage and Fealty of *Scotland* to *England*. Your Stories alfo be not void of this intent. What the judgment of the Fathers of your Law is, and what commonly is thought in this Matter, you know better than I, and may have better intelligence than I, the Argument being fitter for your Affertion than mine.

 Another queftion there is alfo upon this Objection of Forreign Birth; that is to fay, Whether Princes inheritable to the Crown, be in cafe of the Crown exempted or concluded as private Perfons, being Strangers born forth of the Allegiance of *England*.

....

 The Contract of Marriage is extant betwixt the King, my Miftris's grandfather, and Queen *Margaret*, Daughter to King *Henry* the *7th*, by whofe Perfon the Title is devolved on my Sovereign; what her Fathers meaning was in beftowing of her, the World knoweth, by that which is contained in the Chronicles written by *Polidorus Virgilius*, before (as I think) either you or I was born; at leaft when it was little thought that this Matter fhould come in queftion. There is another Exception alfo laid againft my Soveraign, which feems at the firft to be of fome weight, grounded upon fome Statutes made in King *Hen.* 8. time, (*viz.*) of the *28th*, & *35th* of his Reign, whereby full power and authority was given him the faid King *Henry*, to give difpofe, appoint, affign, declare, and limit, by his Letters Patents under his Great Seal, or elfe by his laft Will made in writing, and figned with his hand at his pleafure, from time to time thereafter the Imperial Crown of that Realm, &c.

Which Imperial Crown is by fome alledged and conftantly affirmed to have
been limited and difpofed, by the laft Will and Teftament of the faid King
Hen. 8. figned with his hand before his death, unto the Children of the Lady
Francis; and *Elenor*, Daughter to *Mary* the French Queen, younger Daughter
of *Hen.* 7. and of *Charles Brandon* Duke of *Suffolk*; fo as it is thought the
Queen, my Soveraign, and all others, by courfe of Inheritance, be by thefe
Circumftances excluded and fore-clofed.
....
  Now let us examine the manner and circumftances how King *Hen.* 8.
was by Statute inabled to difpofe the Crown. There is a form in two forts
prefcribed him, which he may not tranfgrefs, that is to fay, either by his
Letters Patents, fealed with his Great Seal, or by his laft Will, figned with his
hand: for in this extraordinary cafe he was held to an ordinary and precife
form; which being not obferved, the Letters Patents, or Will, cannot work the
intent or effect fuppofed. And to difprove, that the Will was figned with his
own hand; You know, that long before his death he never ufed his own
figning with his own hand; and in the time of his Sicknefs, being divers times
preffed to put his hand to the Will written, he refufed to do it. And it feemed
God would not fuffer him to proceed in an Act fo injurious and prejudicial to
the right Heir of the Crown, being his Niece. Then his death approaching,
fome as well known to you as to me, caufed *William Clarke*, fometimes
Servant to *Thomas Henneage*, to fign the fuppofed Will with a ftamp, (for
otherwife figned it was never); and yet notwithftanding fome refpecting more
the fatisfaction of their ambition, and others their private commodity, than
juft and upright dealing, procured divers honeft Gentlemen, attending in
divers feveral Rooms about the King's Perfon, to teftifie with their hand-
writings the Contents of the faid pretended Will, furmifed to be figned with
the King's own hand. To prove this diffembled and forged figned Teftament,
I do refer you to fuch Trials as be yet left. Firft; The Atteftation of the late
Lord *Paget*, publifhed in the Parliament in Queen *Mary's* time, for the
reftitution of the Duke of *Norfolk*. Next, I pray you, on my Sovereigns behalf
that the Depofitions may be taken in this Matter of the Marquefs of
Winchefter, Lord Treafurer of *England*, the Marquefs of *Northampton*, the
Earl of *Pembroke*, Sir *William Petre*, then one of King *Henry's* Secretaries,
Sir *Henry Nevill*, Sir *Maurice Barkley*, Doctor *Buts*, *Edmond Harman Baker*,
John Osborn Groom of the Chamber, Sir *Anthony Dennis*, if he be living,
Terris the Chirurgion, and fuch as have heard *David Vincent* and others
fpeak in this cafe; and that their Atteftations may be enrolled in the
Chancery, and in the *Arches*, *In perpetuam rei memoriam*.
  Thirdly; I do refer you to the Original Will furmifed to be figned
with the King's own hand, that thereby it may moft clearly and evidently
appear by fome differences, how the fame was not figned with the King's
hand, but ftamped as aforefaid. And albeit it is ufed both as an Argument and
Calumniation againft my Sovereign to fome, that the faid Original hath been
embezelled in Queen *Mary's* time, I truft God will and hath referved the fame

to be an Inftrument to relieve the Truth, and to confound falfe Surmifes, that thereby the Right may take place, notwithftanding the many Exemplifications and Tranfcripts, which being fealed with the great Seal, do run abroad in *England*, and do carry away many Mens minds, as great prefumptions of great variety and validity. But, Sir, you know in cafes of lefs importance, that the whole Realm of *England*, Tranfcripts and Exemplifications be not of fo great force in Law to ferve for the recovery of anything, either real or perfonal: And in as much as my Soveraign's Title in this cafe shall be little advanced, by taking exceptions to others pretended and crafed Titles, confidering her precedency, I will leave it to fuch as are to claim after the iffue of *Hen*. the 7*th*, to lay in Bar the Poligamy of *Charles Brandon* the Duke of *Suffolk*; and alfo the vitiated and clandeftine Contract, (if it may be fo called) having no witnefs nor folemnization of Chriftian Matrimony, nor any lawful matching of the Earl of *Hertford* and the Lady *Katharine*. *Laftly*; The femblably compelling of Mr. *Key*, and the Lady *Mary* Sifter to the Lady *Katherine*.
....

For my particular, as I have always honoured you as my Father, fo do I ftill remain of the fame mind, as one, whom in all things not touching the State, you may direct, as your Son *Thomas Cecil*, and with my hearty commendations to you, and my Lady, both, I take my leave. From *Striveling*, the 14*th* of *January*, 1566.

Document 3

Ostensibly this act was designed to lighten the burden of Henry VIII's treason legislation, but its more practical effect was to repeal the Act of Six Articles and the other statutes against heresy, thus opening the way for the advancement of protestantism. The repeal of the statutes creating new felonies was more in the nature of a public relations exercise, and it is an illustration of Somerset's desire for greater popularity.

Document 3: An Act for the repeal of certain statutes concerning Treasons. 1 Edward VI, ca. 12. *Extracts*.

No thinge being more godlie more sure more to be wisshed and desired betwixte a Prynce the Supreame Hed and Ruler and the Subgect(s) whose Gouverno^r and Hed he is, then on the Prynces p'te great clemencye and indulgencye, and rather to muche forgivenes and remission of his royall power and just punishment, then exacte severitie and justice to be shewed, and on the Subject(s') behalfe that theye shoulde obeye rather for love and for the necessitie and love of a Kinge and Prynce, then for feare of his streight and severe Lawes; yet suche tymes at some tyme comethe in the comonwealthe that it is necessarie and expedient for the repressinge of the insolencye and unrulynes of Men, and for the foreseing and provyding of remedyes against rebellyon insurrection, or suche mischief(s) as God sometyme with us displeased for o^r punishment dothe inflicte and laye uppon us, or the Devill at Godds p'mssion to assaye the good and God('s) electe dothe sowe and sett among us the which Allmightie God wth his helpe and mans pollicye hath allwaies bene content and pleased to have stayed that sharper lawes as a harder brydle shoulde be made to staye those men and fact(s) that might ell(s) be occacon cause and aucthors of further inconvenyence; The which thing cawsed the Prynce of most famous memorie Kinge Henry theight father to o^r saide Soveraigne Lorde the King, and other his Highnes progenito^{rs}, with thassent of the Nobles and Comons at divers p'lement(s) in theire severall tymes [holden] to make and enacte certaine lawes and Statutes which might seme and appere to men of exterio^r Realmes and manny of the King('s) Ma^{tes} Subgect(s) verie streighte sore extreme and terrible, allthoughe theie were then when theye were made not wthowt great consideracon and pollicye moved and established and for the tyme to thadvoyd^{a}unce of further inconvenyence verie expedyent and necessarie, But as in tempest or winter one course and garment is convenyent, in cawlme or warme weather a more liberall rase or lighter garment bothe maye and ought to be followed and used, so we have seen divers streight and sore lawes, made in one p'lament the tyme so requiringe, in a more cawlme and quiet reigne of a nother Prynce by like aucthoritie and p'liament repealed and taken awaie; the which moste highe clemencye and Royall example of his Ma^{tes} moste noble progenito^{rs}, The King('s) Highnes, of his tender and godlie nature moste given to mercye and love of his Subgect(s) willing to followe, and p'ceiving the hartie and syncere love that his moste lovinge subject(s) bothe the Lordes and Comons dothe beare unto his Highnes now in this his Majesties tendre age, willing allso to gratefie the same therfore, and myndinge further to provoke his saide Subgect(s) with greate indulgencye and clemencye shewed on his Highnes bihalfe to more love and kyndnes towardes his Majestie (yf it maye be), and uppon trust that theie will not abuse the same, but rather be encouraged thereby more faithefullie and with more diligence (yf it maye be) and care for his Ma^{te} to serve his Highnes now in this his tender age, is contented and pleased that the severitie of certaine Lawes here followinge be mitigated and remitted. Be it therefore ordeigned and enacted by the King o^{r} Soveraigne Lorde with thassent of the Lordes sp'uall and temporall and of the Comons in this present p'lament assembled and by thauctoritie of the same, That from hensfurthe, none acte dede or offence, being by Acte of p'lament or Statute made Treasone or petit Treasone by wordes writing cipring dedes or otherwise what so ever, shalbe taken had demed or adjudged to be highe Treasone or petit Treasone, but onelie suche as be treasone or petit Treasone in or by the Acte of p'lament or Statute made in the xxv^{th} yere of the Reigne of the moste noble Kinge of famous memorie Kinge Edwarde the thirde touching or concerninge Tresone or the Declaracon of Treasones, And suche offences as hereafter shall by this present Acte be expressed and declared to be Treasone or petit Treasone, and none other; Nor that anny paynes of deathe penaltie or forfaiture in anny wise ensue or be to anny of the offendo^{rs} for the doing or comittinge anny Treasone or petit Treasone, other then suche as be in the saide Estatute made in the saide xxv^{th} yere of the reigne of the saide King Edward the thirde, or by this present Estatute, ordeyned or provyded; Anny Acte or Actes of p'liament Statute or Statut(s) had or made at anny tyme heretofore, or after the saide xxv^{th} yere of the Reigne of the saide late King Edwarde the thirde, or anny other declaration or matter to the contrarie in anny wise notwithstanding.

    And allso be it enacted by thauctoritie aforesaide, that all Actes of p'lament and Estatutes towchinge mencyoninge or in anny wise concernynge Religion or opinyons, That is to saie aswell the Statute made in the [first] yere of the Reigne of the King('s) noble progenito^{r} Kinge Richarde the Second, and the Statute made in the Seconde Yere of the Reigne of King Henry the fifthe, and the Statute allso made in the xxv^{th} Yere of the Reigne of Kinge Henry theight concerninge punishment and reformacon of Heretykes and Lolardes, and everie provision therein conteyned, and the Statute made for the abolishment of diversitie of opinions in certaine artycles concerninge Christian Religion comonlie called the Six Articles, made in the p'lament begonne at Westmestre the xxviijth daie of Apryll in the xxxjth yere of the Reigne of the moste noble and victorious Prynce of moste famous memorie Kinge Henry theight father to our saide moste drad Soveraigne Lorde the Kinge that now is, and allso the acte of p'lyament and Statute made at the p'lament begoonne at Westmestre the xvjth daye of Januarye in the xxxiiijth yere of the Reigne of the saide late King Henry theight and after that proroged unto the xxijth daye of Januarye in the xxxiiijth yere of the Reigne of the saide late King Henry theight, touchinge mentioninge or in anny wise concerninge bookes of the old and newe Testament in Englishe, and the pryntinge utteringe selling giving or delivering of bookes or writing(s) and reteyninge of Englishe bookes or writing(s), and reading preaching teaching or expownding of Scripture or in anny wise touching mentionynge or concerninge anny of the same matters, And allso one other Statute made in the p'lament holden at Westmestre in the xxxvth yere of the Reigne of the saide late King Henry theight, concerninge the qualificacon of the Statute of Sixe Articles, and all and everie other Acte or Act(s) of p'lament concerninge doctryne [and] matters of Religion, and all and everie br^aunche artycle sentence and matter paynes and forfaitures conteyned mentioned or in anny wise declared in anny of the same act of p'liament or Estatutes, shall fromhensfurthe be repealed and utterlie voyde and of none effecte.

And be it further ordeyned and enacted by thauctoritie aforesaide, that all Offences made felonye by anny Acte or Act(s) of p'lament Statute or Statut(s) made sithens the xxiijth daie of Apryll in the first yere of the Reigne of the saide late King Henry theight, not beinge felonye before, and allso all and everye the br^aunches and articles mentioned or in anny wise declared in anny of the same Statut(s) concerninge the making of anny Offence or Offences to be felonye not being felonye before, and all paynes and forfaitures concerninge the same or anny of them, shall from hensfurthe be repealed and utterlye voyde and of none effecte.

And be it allso ordeyned and enacted by thauctoritie aforesaide, that one Acte made in the p'lament holden at Westmestre in the xxxjth yere of the Reigne of the saide late King Henry theight, that p'clamacons made by the King('s) Highnes by thadvise of his honnorable Councell shoulde be obeyed and kepte as thoughe theie were made by aucthoritie of p'lament, And allso one other Acte made in the p'lament holden in the xxxiiijth yere of the Reigne of the saide late King Henry theight for the dewe execucon of the saide proclamacons, and allso all and everye br^aunche artycle and matter in the same Statut(s) and in everye of them mentioned or declared, shall fromhensfurthe be repealed and utterlye made voyde and of none effecte.

And be it enacted by thauctoritie aforesaide, that yf anny parsone or parsons at anny tyme after the first daie of Marche next cominge by open preaching expresse wordes or saying(s) doo affirme or sett furthe that the

Kinge his heires or successo^{rs} King(s) of this Realme for the tyme being is not or ought not to be supreame hed in earthe of the Churche of Englande and Ireland or of anny of them imediatlye under God, or that the Bishopp of Rome or anny other Parsone or parsons other then the King of Englande for the tyme being is or ought to be by the Lawes of God supreame hedd of the same churches or of anny of them, or that the King his heires or Successo^{rs} King(s) of this Realme is not or ought not to be King of Englande Fr^aunce and Ireland or of anny of them, Or after the saide firste day of Marche doo compasse or imagen by open preaching expresse wordes or saying(s) to depose or depryve the King his heires or successo^{rs} King(s) of this Realme from his or their Royall estate or Tytles to or of the Realmes aforesaide, or doo openlye publishe or saye by expresse wordes or saying(s) that anny other parsone or parsons other then the King his heires or successo^{rs} King(s) of this Realme of right ought to be King of the Realmes aforesaide or of anny of them or to have and enjoye the same or anny of them; That then everie suche offendo^r, being therof dewlye convicted or attaynted by the Lawes of this Realme, their aydo^{rs} comfort^{rs} abetto^{rs} procurers and counsailo^{rs} for his or their suche firste offence shall loose and forfaicte to the Kinge all his and their good(s) and Cattell(s) and allso shall have and suffer emprysonement of his and their bodies at the King('s) Will and pleasure; And yf anny parsone being ons convicted or attaynted of anny of the saide Offences shall after his saide conviction or attayndo^r eftsones comitt or p'petrate anny of the Offenc(s) before mentioned, other then suche as be expressed in the saide Estatute made in the saide xxvth yere of [the] Kinge Edwarde the Thirde, and shalbe therof dewlie convicted or attaynted by the Lawes of this Realme, That then everie suche offendo^r their aydo^{rs} comfort^{rs} abettors procurers and Counsailo^{rs} for his or their saide Seconde offence or offences shall lose and forfaicte to the King the hole Issues and proffitt(s) of all his and their Landes Ten't(s) and other hereditament(s) benefices prebend(s) and other spuall promocons for tearme of the Life of suche offendo^r and offendo^{rs}, and allso shall lose and forfaicte to the King all his and their good(s) and cattall(s) and allso suffer during his and their Lyfes p'petuall Imprisonement of his and their bodies: And yf anny psone being twoo tymes hereafter convicted or attaynted of anny of the same offences, shall after his saide Seconde conviction or attayndo^r eftsones comitte or p'petrate againe anny of the saide offences, and be therof dewlie convicted or attaynted by the Lawes and Statutes of this Realme, That then everie suche thirde offence or offences shalbe demed and adjudged Highe Treasone, and the offendo^r and offendo^{rs} their aydo^{rs} comfort^{rs} abetto^{rs} procurers and counsailo^{rs} being therin convicted or attaynted according to the Lawes and Statut(s) of this Realme shalbe demed and adjudged Highe Trayto^{rs}, and shall suffer paynes of

Deathe and lose and forfaicte all their Good(s) and Cattall(s) Landes and Tent(s) to the King as in caces of Highe Treasone.

And be it further enacted by thauctoritie aforsaide, that yf anny parsone or parsons at anny tyme after the saide first daye of Marche next cominge by writing prynting overt dede or acte doo affirme or sett furthe that the King of this Realme for the tyme being is not or ought not to be supreame hed in erthe of the Churche of Englande and Irelande or of anny of them imediatelye under God, or shall by writing prynting overt dede or acte after the saide first daye of Marche affirme or sett furthe that the Bisshopp of Rome or anny other parsone or p'sons other then the Kinge of Englande for the tyme being is or ought to be by the Lawes of God or otherwise the supreame hed in earthe of the same [Churche] or anny of them, or doo after the saide first day of Marche compasse or imagyne by writing prynting overt dede or acte to depose or deprive the King his heires or successo^{rs} King(s) of this Realme from his or their Royall estate or tytles of the King of Englande Fr^aunce and Irelande or of anny of them, or by writing prynting overt dede or acte doo affirme that anny other parsone or p'sons other then the King his heires and successo^{rs} is or of right ought to be King of the Realmes of Englande Fr^aunce or Irelande or to have and enjoye the same or anny of them, That then everye such Offence and Offenc(s) shalbe demed and adjudged Highe Treasone, and the Offendo^r and Offendo^{rs} their aydo^{rs} comforto^{rs} abbetto^{rs} procurers and counsailo^{rs} therin convicted or attaynted according to the Lawes and Statut(s) of this Realme shalbe demed and adjudged High Trayto^{rs} and shall suffer paynes of deathe and lose and forfaite all their good(s) and catall(s) landes and tent(s) to the King as in cases of Highe Treasone.

Document 4

John Fowler was a Groom of the Privy Chamber, who was examined in January 1549 concerning his dealings with Lord Thomas Seymour, the Protector's brother. Seymour was violently jealous and conspired to undermine the Protector's position. One aspect of this was to ingratiate himself with the king, using John Fowler as an intermediary. He did this successfully in gaining Edward's consent to his marriage with Catherine Parr, a match which his brother opposed. "Mr. Sharrington" was Sir William Sharrington, convicted of embezzlement from the Bristol mint. John Philpot and Robert Maddox were also Grooms of the Privy Chamber.

Document 4: The depositions of John Fowler. January(?) 1549 *Calendar of State Papers, Domestic, Edward VI*, no. 185.

1. At St James's, where the king was, the lord admiral called me to his chamber. After dismissing his servants he enquired after the king and if he lacked anything. I said not. He asked if the king ever asked for or about him: I said he would sometimes ask for him, but nothing else. I asked him what the king should ask and he said nothing unless why he did not marry. I said I never heard him ask such questions. He paused and asked me, if I had communication with the king soon, to ask him if he would be content he should marry, and if so whom. I agreed, and that night when the king was alone I said I marvelled that the admiral did not marry. He said nothing. I asked him if he was content he should do so and he agreed. I asked him whom and he said Lady Anne of Cleves, and then he said no, but he should marry his sister Mary to turn her opinions. So he went away. 2. Next day the admiral came again to St James's and called me to him in the gallery. I told him all the king had said. He laughed and asked me to ask the king if he would be content for him to marry the queen and if he would write in his suit. I agreed and did so that night. Next day the admiral came to the king: I cannot tell what communication they had, but the king wrote a letter to the queen and the admiral brought one back from her. 3. Shortly afterwards the admiral came to St James's and, meeting me in the gallery, went into the inner chamber and talked with [Sir Thomas] Wroth, the king being at school. When he came out I followed him into his chamber. He dismissed his men and asked me whether his brother had been there since he last was himself. I said not. He told me that the protector had fallen out with him concerning the admiralty, and took his part before his. I prayed him bear with his brother, but he said the protector would have his head under his girdle. I protested: he paused and said we should do well enough for all this. He asked me to tell the king or [John] Cheke, or he would tell him himself, lest the protector should do so. He said if the protector told him he would be impartial and say that the two should agree as brothers. I said I would tell the king, and did so.

The admiral said he would pray Mr Cheke to do the same, as I think he did, also Mr Wroth. **4.** Shortly before going into the country with the queen the admiral came to court at Westminster and called me to his chamber. He said that since he would do nothing to which the king was not privy, he prayed me tell him he would sue the protector for certain jewels which the late king gave the queen, including her wedding ring, which he thought legally hers. I lamented that jewels or worldly muck should begin a new matter with his brother. He trusted the protector would be content. Then he called for boats to Hanworth, bidding me send to him and nobody else if the king lacked anything. He often wished me to remind the king of him. **5.** Since his last coming to court he frequently came to the privy buttery to drink alone and ask me whether the king spoke of him. I answered not. He would wish the king were five or six years older. He often asked me to tell him when the king was rising, which I did. **6.** When the king was at St James's (I am unsure if it was the last time or not) the admiral came about 9 a.m. into the gallery where I was playing the lute. He said there was slender company about the king - no-one in the presence chamber and not a dozen in the whole house. I thanked God we were in a quiet realm and the king loved, or a hundred men could make foul work. He replied that a man might steal away the king now, for he came with more men than were in the house. He went into the inner gallery and thence to the king, with whom he talked for a while (of what I know not) and went home for dinner, saying he had guests. **7.** After Mr Sharington was arrested I came at night to the admiral's chamber at court and asked him what he had done. The admiral told me he had heard no great charge yet. Someone had accused him for coining testons since the command to the contrary, but he denied it. He said if Sharington were false he would never trust anyone for his sake. He was sure the late king trusted him. There was, he said, never anyone of the council who spoke for him, but he thought they would take his part. I then reminded him that about a year before he had willed me, if I lacked money for the king, to send in his absence to Mr Sharington. When [the admiral] was at Enfield I had written to [Sharington] for £20; if that letter were found I would be undone, and would need to tell the truth to the protector for my discharge. The admiral doubted if Sharington would have kept the letter. I said I doubted it; that I was once in the protector's displeasure, and if I fell into it again I should never recover his favour. He said I might say he gave it to me. He told me to devise an answer, but I refused and prayed him to devise to save me. He agreed and I left. **8.** Four or five nights after New Year's Day he came to the privy chamber after the king was in bed, and took bread and drink. He told [John] Philpot, [Robert] Maddox and me that he had not remembered us since New Year, but would. **9.** When he went to the country he much desired remembrances from the king. I procured the king to write several times, but only two or three lines of recommendation to him and the queen. Sometimes I wrote myself with them for money, and once had answer to receive £40 of [Anthony] Bowcher, the queen's receiver, and so did. Many other times I had answer that if I lacked money I should have £40 of Mr Locke at London, for he had caused Bowcher to write to him to deliver me as much as I sent for. **10.** So I confess he made me a minister to allure the king with money and praise of his liberality, to make the king fond of him [and cause the king to do all that he should require the protector to do]. Be a means to the protector to have mercy on me, not justice.

Money received by John Fowler of the lord admiral: at Westminster shortly after the coronation - £10; from [Arthur] Sturton last Lent at Westminster - £20 or £40; at his own house in London - £10; by letter from him to the queen's receiver at Hampton Court at the beginning of the progress - £40; another letter from Hampton Court enclosing a letter from the queen's receiver to Mr Locke of London - £40; from Mr Sharington a week before Christmas a year ago - £20; shortly before parliament, at Hampton Court - £10; since the king's coming to London, from Sturton - £20; at New Year a year ago at Hampton Court - £5; last New Year's Day after breakfast in the privy buttery at Westminster - £3; at Hampton Court, Westminster, St James's and Greenwich - £5, 20 nobles and £10; shortly before his marriage - a cap of aiglets and a brooch.

Signed.
SP 10/6, no. 10

Document 5

It was quickly reported in the early months of Edward's reign that the Council was planning sweeping changes in religion. Protector Somerset was very anxious not to allow such rumours to create political instability, and denied them vigorously, although they were substantially accurate. This proclamation also seeks to protect the Council from defamation, which would undermine its authority, by invoking the ancient law of *scandalum magnatum*. Proclamations were a favourite instrument of the Protector's administration.

Document 5:   Proclamation enforcing statutes against seditious rumours, 24th May, 1547. *Tudor Royal Proclamations* ed. P. L. Hughes and J. F. Larkin, I, no. 281.

Forasmuch as the King's highness, the Lord Protector, and the residue of the King's majesty's council is informed that there hath been now of late divers lewd and light tales told, whispered, and secretly spread abroad by uncertain authors, in markets, fairs, and alehouses, in divers and sundry places of this realm, of innovations and changes in religion and ceremonies of the Church feigned to be done and appointed by the King's highness, the Lord Protector, and other of his highness' Privy Council, which by his grace or them was never begun nor attempted; and also of other things and facts sounding to the dishonor and slander of the King's most royal majesty, the Lord Protector's grace, and other the King's most honorable council, and no less to the disquietness and disturbance of the King's highness' loving subjects, contrary to divers wholesome laws[1] and ordinances, upon grave and weighty considerations heretofore made and ordained by the King's highness' most noble progenitors to reform, punish, and chastise all manner of lewd and vagrant persons telling and reporting false news and tales to the disquieting and disturbing of the King's highness, his nobles, and subjects of this realm:
     The King's most royal majesty, by the most circumspect and laudable advice of his most dearly beloved uncle Edward, Duke of Somerset, Lord Protector of the King's majesty's realms, dominions and subjects, and governor of his most royal person, and other of his highness' Privy Council, considering and graciously pondering the great hurt, damage, loss, and disquietness amongst his grace's subjects which might ensue of such false and slanderous tales and news, and that nothing is more necessary than to provide and see that good and wholesome laws be put in ure and full execution, to the intent no manner of person may or shall have justly any occasion to surmise, invent, or disperse any kind of false tales or news to the discord or disturbance of the subjects of this realm, straightly chargeth and commandeth all manner of officers, ministers, and justices, that the said former laws and statutes be earnestly put in execution; that is to say, that no

manner of person from henceforth be so hardy to find, say, or tell any false news, messages, or other such false things, whereof discord or occasion of discord or any slander might arise within this realm between the King, his people, or the nobles; and he that so doeth shall be kept in prison until he have brought in him which was his author of the tale.

And further his majesty, by his former gracious advice of the said Lord Protector and his said Privy Council, straightly chargeth and commandeth all manner of persons, of what estate, degree, or condition he or they be, hearing, reading, knowing or witting any such false tales or news to be by any manner of person, of and upon the King's highness, the Lord Protector or any of his said majesty's most honorable council, or other nobles of the realm, reported, told, written, or otherwise published and spread about within the King's highness' realms and dominions, immediately and without all delay, all other business set apart, either to repair and declare the same to his dearly beloved uncle, the Lord Protector, or some other of his majesty's Privy Council, if that do he may conveniently; or else at the least do declare and show the same to the justice of the peace next inhabiting. The which justice also, the King's majesty most straightly commandeth, after the hearing thereof immediately to apprehend the said person, and after he be apprehended to put the said person in jail or safe custody, so to remain unto such time he hath brought forth the author of the said tale or news who told the same to him; and so then to make further search from person to person, so much as lieth in them, to search forth and get out the first author and beginner of the said tales and news; and of their diligence done herein, and the knowledge by them gotten, to certify without delay, under their seals in writings, the King's highness' said dearly beloved uncle, upon pain of incurring, as well concerning the same party so hearing, reading, knowing, or witting, and not immediately declaring as is abovesaid, as concerning the justice of peace, so hearing and not immediately giving knowledge thereof, as is abovesaid, of extreme danger of his grace's laws and imprisonment of his or their bodies, and as he and they will further answer for the grievous attempts in that behalf at his grace's pleasure.

And whosoever shall reveal, bring to light, and utter the first inventor and author of such false news, untrue tales, and lies, which tend to the slander and reproach of the King's most royal person, the Lord Protector's grace, and other of the King's highness' honorable council, and other of his nobles, or else to the disturbance of the peace and quietness of these his grace's realms, dominions, or subjects, shall have not only his majesty's great and worthy thanks, but also convenient and good reward for faithfully doing his most bounden duty therein.

[1.] 3 Edward I, c. 34 (Westminster I), 1275, *SR I*, 35; 2 Richard II, st. I, c. 5, 1378, *SR 2*, 9; 12 Richard II, c. 11, 1388, *SR 2*, 59; 37 Henry VIII, c. 10, 1545, *SR 3*, 997.

Document 6

Henry's last parliament in 1545 had passed an act dissolving chantries and other foundations whose chief function was intercessory prayer, on the grounds of the king's urgent financial needs. Because of the king's death the act was never implemented, and Edward's first parliament passed another act to the same effect. On this occasion, however, in addition to financial necessity, the Council adduced the superstitious nature of intercessory prayer as a reason for the action. All foundations with an intercessory purpose were theoretically at risk, but in practice craft and merchant guilds, which had a different primary purpose, and academic institutions such as the colleges of Oxford, Cambridge, Eton, Winchester and others, were exempt.

Document 6: An Act concerning chantries. 1 Edward VI c. 14. *Extracts*.

The King('s) moste lovinge Subject(s) the Lordes sp'uall and temporall and the Comons in this p'nt p'lament assembled, consydering that a greate p'te of Superstition and Erro^{rs} in Christian Religion hath byn brought into the myndes and estimacon of men, by reasone of the Ignor^{a}unce of their verie trewe and p'fecte salvacon throughe the deathe of Jesus Christ, and by devising and phantasinge vayne opynions of Purgatorye and Masses satisfactorye to be done for them which be departed, the which doctryne and vayn opynion by nothing more is mayntayned and upholden then by the abuse of Trentall(s) Ch^{a}untries and other provisions made for the contynuance of the saide blyndness and ignor^{a}unce; And further considering and understanding that the alteracon chaunge and amendement of the same, and converting to good and godlie uses, as in erecting of Gramer Scoles to the educacon of Youthe in vertewe and godlinesse, the further augmenting of the Universities and better provision for the poore and nedye, can not in this p'nt p'lament be provyded and convenyentlie doon, nor can not ne ought to anny other manner parsone be comitted then to the King('s) Highnes, whose Ma^{te} with and by thadvise of his Highnes moste prudent Counsaile can and will moste wiseleye and beneficiallye bothe for the honno^r of God and the weale of this his Ma^{tes} Realme order alter converte and dispose the same; And calling further to their remembr^{a}unce that in the p'lament holden at Westmestre the xxxvijth yere of the Reigne of o^r late Soveraigne Lorde King Henry theight, father to our moste drad and naturall Soveraigne Lorde the King that now is, It was ordeyned enacted and established, amongst other thing(s), that all and singuler Colleges free Chappell(s) Chauntyres Hospitall(s) Fraternityes Brotherhedd(s) Guylds and other promocons, mentioned in the saide former Acte, had or made to have contynuaunce in p'petuitie for ever, and then being or that had or ought to be contributorye or chargeable to the payment of the First Fruict(s) and Tenthes according to the Lawes and Statut(s) in that bihalfe had and made, by what name surname degree or corporacon theye or anny of them were founded ordeyned established erected named called or knowen, and al and singuler the Mansyon howses Manno^{rs} Orchard(s) gardens landes tenement(s) pastures woodes waters rent(s) revercons s^{r}vices comons tythes pencons porcons Churches Chappell(s) advousons no'iacons p'ronages annuityes Right(s) Interest(s) entrees condicons Leetes Court(s) libertyes privileges Fr^{a}unchesies and other heredytament(s) what so ever, then appertayninge or belonging or that did appertayne or belonge or were assigned or appointed to anny suche College Free Chappell Chauntry Hospitall Fraternitye brotherhed guylde Stipendarye Preist or other the saide promocons, or to anny of them, or accepted knowen or taken as p'te p'cell or membre of them or anny of them, and to the saide Colleges Ch^{a}untries Freechappell(s) Hospitall(s) Fraternities brotherhed guylde Stipendarye preist(s) or other promocons or to anny of them untyed or annexed, wch bitwene the iiijth daye of Februarye in the xxvijth yere of the saide late late King('s) Reigne and the xxvth daye of Decembre in the xxxvijth of his Graces Reigne, by reasone of anny entree expullsyon bargayne Sale Feoffament Fyne recoverye Lease or other conveyance therof made were dissolved determyned or relinquished by anny of the Waies meanes or conveyaunces mentyoned in the saide Acte or otherwise, other then suche of them as then were in the possession of the saide late King, or that were gr^{a}unted or assured by his Lycence agrement consent or l'tres patent(s) to anny p'sone or p'sons, or then had ben lawfullie obteyned or recovered by anny parsone by anny former right or Tytle without fraude or covyne, or by the King('s) Lycence, shoulde from thensfurthe by aucthoritie of the same former Acte be adjudged and demed and allso be in the verie actuall and reale possession and seasone of the saide late King and of his heires and Successo^{rs} for ever, in as large and ample manner as the saide preist(s) Wardens ministers gouverno^{rs} [or] Rulers or other Incumbent(s) or anny of them, or the Patrons dono^{rs} or founders of anny of them, at anny time sithens the saide fourthe daye of Februarye in the xxvijth Yere aforesaide had occupyed or enjoyed or then had occupyed or enjoyed the same, and as thoughe all and singuler the saide Colleg(s) Ch^{a}untries Hospitall(s) Free Chappell(s) Fraternities brotherhedd(s) Guyldes and other the saide promocons and the saide Manno^{rs} Landes Tent(s) heredytament(s) and other the premisses what so ever theie be and everye of them, had ben in the saide former Acte specyallye p'ticulerlye and certaynlie rehersed named and expressed by expresse wordes names surnames corporations tytles and faculties and in their naturall Kyndes and qualities; The saide entrees expulsions bargaynes Sales fynes feoffament(s) Recoveries or other assuraunce and conveyaunce what so ever they were had or made, (excepte before in the former Acte excepted) to the contrarie notwithstanding: And where allso it was enacted and gr^{a}unted to the saide late King by the saide former Acte, that the same late King during his naturall Life might make and direct his Comission and Comissions, under his greate Seale, to enter into all and singuler suche and as manny Ch^{a}untries freechappell(s) Hospitall(s) Colleges and other the promocons mentioned in the saide former Acte, and into all and singuler suche Manno^{rs} Mansions howses meases Landes Tenement(s) pastures Wood(s) Waters Rent(s) revercons S^{r}vices possessions and other heredytament(s) what so ever, or into anny p'te or p'cell therof, in the name seasone and possession of all the heredytament(s) annexed untyed belonging or appertayninge to anny Ch^{a}untrie Hospitall free Chappell College Fraternitye brotherhed Guylde or other the saide promocons, or wherof anny Preist(s) Provost(s) Governo^{rs} Rulers or other Incumbent(s) of them or any of them, by what name surname degree tytle or corporacon theye and everye of them or anny of them were founded erected ordeyned established named called or knowen, then had or enjoyed or that [hereafter] shoulde have or enjoye to the saide Ch^{a}untries Hospitall(s) Freechappell(s) Colleges Fraternityes brotherhedd(s) guyldes or other the saide promocons, that then were chargeable to the payment of the First Fruict(s) and Tenthes, and all Colleges that were chargeable or not chargeable to the saide payment of the First Fruict(s) and Tenthes as is aforesaide, or to anny of them, as shoulde be named expressed and appointed in the saide comission or comissions and to seise and take the same Ch^{a}untries Hospitall(s) Colleges Freechappell(s) Fraternityes brotherhedd(s) Guyldes, and other the saide promotions Manno^{rs} Landes Tent(s) and other the Premises mentyoned in the saide Comission or Comissions and in everye of them, and every p'te p'cell and membre of the same into the King('s) possession and handes; To have and to holde the same to the saide late King and to his heyres and Successo^{rs} for ever; as by the saide former Acte amongst other thing(s) more at large apperethe: It is now ordeyned and enacted by the King o^r Soveraigne Lorde with thassent of the Lordes and Comons in this p'nt p'lament assembled and by thauctoritie of the same, that all manner of Colleges Free Chappell(s) and Ch^{a}untries, having being or in esse within five Yeres next before the firste daye of this p'nt p'lament, which were not in actuall and reall possession of the saide late King, nor in the actuall and reall possession of the King o^r Soveraigne Lorde that now is, nor excepted in the saide former Acte in fo^{r}me abovesaide, other then suche as by the King('s) Comissions in fo^{r}me hereafter mentyoned shalbe altered transposed or chaunged, And all Manno^{rs} Landes Tenement(s) Rent(s) Tythes pencons porcons and other heredytament(s) and thing(s) above mentioned belonging to them or anny of them, and allso all Manno^{rs} Landes Tenement(s) Rent(s) and other heredytament(s) and thing(s) above mentyoned, by anny manner of assuraunce conveyaunce will devise or otherwise had made suffred knowledged or declared, given assigned lymited or appoynted to the fynding of anny Preist to have contynuance for ever, and wherewth or whereby anny Preist was susteyned mayntayned or founde, within five Yeres next before the first daye of this p'nt p'lament, which were not in the actuall and reall possession of the saide late King, nor in the actuall and reall possession of o^r Soveraigne Lorde the King that now is, and allso all annuall Rent(s) profitt(s) and emolument(s), at anny tyme within fyve yeres next before the begyninge of this p'nt p'lament employed payed or bestowed towarde or for the mayntenaunce supportacon or fynding of anny Stipendary Preist intended by anny Acte or Writing to have contynuaunce for ever, shall by thauctoritie of this p'nt p'lament, imediatelie after the feast of Easter next cominge, be adjudged and demed and allso be in the verie actuall and reall possession and seasone of the King o^r Soveraigne Lorde and his heires and Successo^{rs} for ever; without anny Office or other Inquisicon therof to be had or founde, and in as large and ample manner and fo^{r}me as the Preists Wardens Masters Ministers Gouverno^{rs} Rulers or other Incumbent(s) of them or anny of them at anny tyme wthin five Yeres next before the begyninge of this p'nt p'lament had occupyed or enjoyed or now hath occpyethe or enjoyethe the same; and as thoughe all and singuler the saide Colleges Free Chappell(s) Ch^{a}untries Stipend(s) Salaries of Preist(s) and the saide Manno^{rs} Landes Tenement(s) and other the premisses what so ever theye be, and everye of them, were in this p'nt Acte speciallye p'ticularlye and certaynelie rehersed named and expressed, by expresse wordes names surnames corporacons tytles and faculties, and in their natures Kyndes and Qualities.

Document 7

Although cast in the form of a proclamation, this document is in fact a full text of the Royal Injunctions of 1547, upon which the first Edwardian visitation was based. The Articles are largely the same as those of 1538, and do not go much beyond them in terms of enforcing reformed practices. They are primarily concerned with the conduct of worship and the behaviour of the clergy. The later attack on images is clearly forshadowed, but many of the traditional practices deplored were supposed to have been discontinued years earlier.

Document 7: Proclamation announcing Injunctions for religious reform. *Tudor Royal Proclamations*, I, no. 287. 31st. July, 1547. *Extracts*.

The King's most Royal Majesty, by the advice of his most dear uncle, the Duke of Somerset, Lord Protector of all his realms, dominions, and subjects, and governor of his most royal person, and the residue of his most honorable council, intending the advancement of the true honor of Almighty God, the suppression of idolatry and superstition throughout all his realms and dominions, and to plant true religion, to the extirpation of all hypocrisy, enormities, and abuses, as to his duty apperraineth, doth minister unto his loving subjects these godly Injunctions hereafter following; whereof part were given unto them heretofore by the authority of his most dearly beloved father King Henry VIII of most famous memory, and part are now ministered and given by his majesty; all which Injunctions his highness willeth and commandeth his said loving subjects, by his supreme authority, obediently to receive and truly to observe and keep, every man in their offices, degrees, and states, as they will avoid his displeasure and the pains in the same Injunctions hereafter expressed.

The first is that all deans, archdeacons, parsons, vicars, and other ecclesiastical persons shall faithfully keep and observe, and as far as in them may lie, shall cause to be observed and kept of other, all and singular laws and statutes made as well for the abolishing and extirpation of the Bishop of Rome, his pretensed and usurped power and jurisdiction, as for the establishment and confirmation of the King's authority, jurisdiction, and supremacy of the Church of England and Ireland. And furthermore, all ecclesiastical persons having cure of soul shall to the uttermost of their knowledge, and learning, purely, sincerely, and without any color or dissimulation, declare, manifest and open, four times every year at the least in their sermons and other collations, that the Bishop of Rome's usurped power and jurisdiction, having no establishment nor ground by the law of God, was of most just causes taken away and abolised, and that therefore no manner of obedience or subjection, within his realms and dominions, is due unto him; and that the King's power, within his realms and dominions, is the highest power under God, to whom all men within the same realms and dominions, by God's laws, owe most loyalty and obedience, afore and above all other powers and potentates in earth.

Besides this, to the intent that all superstition and hypocrisy crept into divers men's hearts may vanish away, they shall not set forth or extoll any images, relics, or miracles, for any superstition or lucre, nor allure the people by any enticements to the pilgrimage of any saint or image; but reproving the same they shall teach that all goodness, health, and grace ought to be both asked and looked for only of God, as of the very author and giver of the same, and of none other.

Item, that they, the persons above rehearsed, shall make or cause to be made in their churches and every other cure they have, one sermon every quarter of the year at the least wherein they shall purely and sincerely declare the word of God, and in the same exhort their hearers to the works of faith, mercy, and charity specially prescribed and commanded in Scripture, and that works devised by man's phantasies, besides Scripture, as wandering to pilgrimages, offering of money, candles, or tapers to relics or images, or kissing and licking of the same, praying upon beads, or such like superstition, have not only no promise of reward in Scripture for doing of them, but contrariwise, great threats and maledictions of God, for that they be things tending to idolatry and superstition, which of all other offenses God Almighty doth most detest and abhor, for that the same diminish His honor and glory.

Item, that such images as they know in any of their cures to be, or have been, so abused with pilgrimage or offerings of anything made thereunto, or shall be hereafter censed unto, they (and none other private persons) shall, for the avoiding of that most detestable offense of idolatry, forthwith take down, or cause to be taken down, and destroy the same, and shall suffer from henceforth no torches nor candles, tapers, or images of wax, to be set afore any image or picture, but only two lights upon the high altar before the Sacrament; which for the signification that Christ is the very true light of the world they shall suffer to remain still, admonishing their parishioners that images serve for no other purpose but to be a remembrance whereby men may be admonished of the holy lives and conversation of them that the said images do represent; which images, if they do abuse for any other intent, they commit idolatry in the same, to the great danger of their souls.

Item, that every Holy Day throughout the year, when they have no sermon, they shall immediately after the Gospel openly and plainly recite to their parishioners, in the pulpit, the Pater Noster, the Credo, and the Ten Commandments, in English, to the intent the people may learn the same by heart; exhorting all parents and householders to teach their children and servants the same, as they are bound by the law of God, and in conscience to do.

.....

Also, that they shall provide within three months next after this visitation one book of the whole Bible, of the largest volume, in English; and within one twelve months next after the said visitation the *Paraphrases* of Erasmus, also in English, upon the Gospels; and the same set up in some convenient place within the said church that they have cure of, whereas their parishioners may most commodiously resort unto the same and read the same; the charges of which books shall be ratably borne between the parson or proprietary and the parishioners aforesaid; that is to say, the one half by the parson or proprietary and the other half by the parishioners. And they shall discourage no man (authorized and licensed thereto) from the reading of any part of the Bible, either in Latin or in English, but shall rather conform and exhort every person to read the same as the very lively word of God and the special food of man's soul that all Christian persons are bound to embrace, believe, and follow if they look to be saved; whereby they may the better know their duties to God, to their sovereign lord the King, and their neighbor; ever gently and charitably exhorting them, and in his majesty's name straightly charging and commanding them, that in the reading thereof no man to reason or contend, but quietly to hear the reader.

....

Also, if they do or shall know any man within their parish, or elsewhere, that is a letter of the word of God to be read in English, or sincerely preached, or of the execution of these the King's majesty's Injunctions, or a fautour of the Bishop of Rome's pretended power, now by the laws of this realm justly rejected, extirped, and taken away utterly, they shall detect and present the same to the King or his council, or to the justice of peace next adjoining.

Also, that the parson, vicar, or curate, and parishioners of every parish within this realm, shall in their churches and chapels keep one book or register, wherein they shall write the day and year of every wedding, christening, and burial made within their parish for their time, and so every man succeeding them likewise; and also therein shall write every person's name that shall be so wedded, christened, or buried. And for the safekeeping of the same book the parish shall be bound to provide, of their common charges, one sure coffer, with two locks and keys, whereof the one to remain with the parson, vicar, or curate, and the other with the wardens of every parish church or chapel wherein the said book shall be laid up. Which book they shall every Sunday take forth and, in the presence of the said wardens or one of them, write and record in the same all the weddings, christenings, and burials made the whole week before; and that done, to lay up the book in the said coffer as afore. And for every time that the same shall be omitted, the party that shall be in the fault thereof shall forfeit to the said church *3s. 4d.* to be employed to the poor men's box of that parish.

....

Also, that they shall instruct and teach in their cures that no man ought obstinately and maliciously break and violate the laudable ceremonies of the Church, by the King commanded to be observed, and as yet not abrogated. And on the other side, that whosoever doth superstitiously abuse them doth the same to the great peril and danger of his soul's health as in casting holy water upon his bed, upon images, and other dead things; or bearing about him holy bread, or Saint John's Gospel; or making crosses of wood upon Palm Sunday in time of reading of the Passion; or keeping of private Holy Days, as bakers, brewers, smiths, shoemakers, and such other do; or ringing of the holy bells, or blessing with the holy candle, to the intent thereby to be discharged of the burden of sin, or to drive away devils, or to put away dreams and phantasies; or in putting trust and confidence of health and salvation in the same ceremonies when they be only ordained, instituted, and made to put us in remembrance of the benefits which we have received by Christ. And if he use them for any other purpose he grievously offendeth God.

Also, that they shall take away, utterly extinct, and destroy all shrines, covering of shrines, all tables, candlesticks, trindles or rolls of wax, pictures, paintings, and all other monuments of feigned miracles, pilgrimages, idolatry, and superstition, so that there remain no memory of the same in walls, glasses, windows, or elsewhere within their churches or houses. And they shall exhort all their parishioners to do the like within their several houses. And that the churchwardens, at the common charge of the parishioners, in every church shall provide a comely and honest pulpit to be set in a convenient place within the same, for the preaching of God's word.

....

Also, because through lack of preachers in many places of the King's realms and dominions the people continue in ignorance and blindness, all parsons, vicars, and curates shall read in their churches, every Sunday, one of the *Homilies* which are and shall be set forth for the same purpose by the Kings authority, in such sort as they shall be appointed to do in the preface of the same.

Also, whereas many indiscreet persons do at this day uncharitably contemn and abuse priests and ministers of the Church because some of them, (having small learning), have of long time favored phantasies rather than God's truth, yet forasmuch as their office and function is appointed of God: the King's majesty willeth and chargeth all his loving subjects, that from henceforth they shall use them charitably and reverently for their office and ministration's sake, and especially all such as labor in the setting forth of God's holy word.

....

Document 8

Protector Somerset inherited an unfinished war in Scotland, which had been pursued by Henry for the purpose of enforcing Scottish compliance with the treaty of Greenwich of 1543. By that treaty the Scots had agreed to a marriage alliance between their young Queen, Mary, and Prince Edward. The agreement was unpopular in Scotland, and was repudiated by the Scottish parliament in 1544. This reaction had provoked the war, known as the 'rough wooing', which Somerset continued by invading, as here described, in September 1547. The result was the battle of Pinkie Cleugh, and the subsequent intervention of France on the Scottish side. Grafton is hostile to the Scots, and flattering both to the Protector's motives and his achievments.

Document 8: The Scottish campaign of 1547, and the battle of Pinkie Cleugh. From Grafton's *Chronicle*, pp. 500 - 504.

These thinges done, the sayd Lord Protector, with the rest of the counsayle, calling to minde the euill vsage and daliaunce of the Scottes concerning the matter of mariage betweene the kinges maiestie and the Ladye Mary heire of Scotlande which as you haue before heard in the xxxv. yere of king Henry the eyght, was concluded by parliament in Scotland, thought it not for the kinges honor to be in such maner deluded by them. Considering therefore how honorable and profitable it should be for the quyetnesse and safetie of both the realmes, that these two princes might ioyne in matrimonie did deuise sondry wayes and meanes to bringe the same to passe, and the rather for the charge which kinge Henry before his death (as it is sayd) had geuen them. But the Lordes of Scotland were so corrupted by the French king and abused by the Scottish clergy, & namely by Cardinall Beton, that they fledde from all that they had before promised. Wherefore nowe was prepared a great and puyssaunt army to passe by land into Scotlande vnder the conduction of the Lord Protector as generall, and the Erle of Warwike Lieuetenaunt of the armye. And in like manner was appoynted a nauie to passe by Sea, whereof the great Galley and xxiiij. tall shippes were well furnished with men and munitions for the warre, besides many Merchants shippes and other smaller vesselles which serued for the caryage of vittayle. And of this fleete the Lord Clynton was Admirall, and sir Thomas Woodhouse Viceadmirall.

Now assone as the Army by land was in a readinesse and set forward to be by a daye appoynted at Berwicke, the Lord Clinton with his nauie set also forward by Sea, and by Goddes helpe had so good passage that they arriued in safetie at Barwicke in time conuenient, and there attended upon the armie which went by lande and passed along the sea coast in such maner as the army passed by land. So that alwayes as the army by land lacked vittaylles, the shippes were at hand to vittayle them.

The armie that trauayled by land marched out of Barwicke the fourth day of September, and in good array passed forwarde into Scotlande fiue daies iourney, before they could vnderstand of any army assembled in Scotland. And in their passage they tooke and rased downe to the ground certain Castles and holdes, as Douglasse, Anderwicke, Thonetone and the towne of Hadington, which towne of Hadington, was afteruard fortefied and kept with a garrison of souldiers as in the course of this history shal after appere.

In thys meane season the Scottes had assembled a puyssant host, estemed to the number of thirtie thousand men, who to forstalle our armie from further inuasion into the countrie, encamped themselues vpon a streight nere to a litle riuer called Eske, foure miles on this side the Citie of Edenborough, minding there to attende our comming, because there was none other way conuenient for our armie to passe.

The ix. day of September both the armies came within the sight of eche other, not distaunt by estimation aboue two myles, the riuer of Fryth liyng on the East, and a hill called Fauxcide Bray on the West, whereon standeth a litle Castle, and the Scottysh campe north from vs vpon the Riuer of Eske aforesayde within foure miles of Edenborough.

And at this time our men were in no readinesse to fight, nor did not then think they should haue battaile. Insomuch that the Duke of Somerset lord Protector, standing and viewing the Scottes how they aduaunced themselues towardes battayle, sayde vnto the Erle of Warwicke who then was with him, that for his life the Scottes ment nothing lesse then to fight at that time.

....

But now to returne againe to the battaile, ye heard that the Armies on both sydes approched so nere that the one was in the others sight: ye heard also that the Lorde Protector was of opinion, that it was not ment of the Scottes to fight at that tyme, but onely that they made a shewe of themselues, which he termed to be but a Scottishe bragge, howbeit it proued farre otherwise. For sodainly the Scottes beyng encamped in a valey by the riuer of Eske, arose and made great hast vp the hill, mindyng to haue obteyned the hill, the wind, and the sonne, which if they had gotten, then our men had bene much hindred, the which thing the Englishmen perceyued, who as then were not in good array, neither could their armie of footemen come so soone to the recouerie of the hill as they would. Wherefore to stop the Scottes of their purpose, the Lorde Gray beyng Capitain of the horsemen, was forced (partly out of order) to set forward, and to geue the onset vpon the Scottes, onely to stay them from the hill. The which English horsemen nobly and valiauntly encountered with the Scottes footemen, but the Scottes stoode so close, and were so defended with their Pykes, that our men coulde not enter. By reason whereof diuers of the Englishe Gentlemen that gaue the onset were ouerthrowne and slaine, the which when they that folowed perceyued, they reculed, and in runnyng backe, ranne through a peece of the English armie of footemen (which by this tyme had recouered the hill, and were behinde the Englishe horsemen) and hurt many of them, howbeit the footemen brake not their array, but stood still in good order in the face of the

Scottes. The Scottes perceiuing the English footemen to haue recouered the hill, and seyng the whole armie readie to geue them the onset, and the vawarde marchyng towardes them, sodainly (of what occasion no man certainly can tell) they forsakyng their weapons, and their former places fled, the which when our men perceyued, they with a great shoute cryed they flie, they flie, & therewithall they fled in dede spedily, and our men pursued after in chase as fast, namely our horsemen, and folowed so egerly and with such fiercenesse, that they ouertooke many and spared in dede but fewe. And the chase continued almost the length of fiue myles, and al the way was couered with dead men, Pikes, Iackes, Skulles, Swords, Bucklers, Daggers, & other weapons, and the riuer made red with bloud. And at this battail called Musklebrough field, nere vnto a place called Pinkerslough, there were slaine, as some of the Scottes themselues confessed xiiij. thousand Scottes, among the which number as it was well knowne by credible report, there were slaine of noble men, Lordes, Lardes, and Gentlemen xxvj. hundred and aboue, and there were taken prisoners of the Scottes xv. hundred, whereof many were Gentlemen. And among other the Erle of Huntley was one, who was taken by sir Raufe Auane. And within lesse then two yeres folowyng, he made his escape, and gat again into Scotland. And of the Englishmen there were slaine not aboue one hundred persons.

....

The next day after this battaile, the Lorde Protector with the armye marched forward to the towne of Lithe, where they remayned x. or xii. dayes, and there began to make Trenches and fortifications: But because Winter approched, & the season of the yere serued not, it was thought good in tyme to returne home to the Borders. And in their returnyng, first they tooke a Castell called Lowthair, and placed for Capitaine thereof sir Hugh Willoughby. And from thence they marched to the Castell of Hunes, where was shewed some face of resistance, but when the Englishmen had planted their ordinaunce and artillary, they yelded, and there was placed Capitaine Edward Dudley esquier, sonne and heyre to the Baron Dudley. And from thence they passed to the Castell of Rokesborough, which beyng a place very meete to kepe frontire warre, the same beyng yelded, was forthwith by the Englishmen fortified, & there was made Capitain, sir Raufe Bulmer, and so he returned vnto Barwicke, and thether came vnto him, these Lardes and Gentlemen of Scotland, and submitted themselues vnto the King of Englandes obedience and tooke their othe, whose names folow.

The Larde Cefford	The Lard of Huntley	The Lard of Malesteines
The Lard of Fernyhurst	The Lard of Markston	The Lard of Warmdsey
The Lard of Grencechard	The Lard of Boniworth	The Lard of Linton
The Lard of Huntill	The Lard of Ormeston	The Lard of Egerston
The Lard of Marton	Robert Carre of Greidan	Thomas Carre
The Lard of Mowe	Adam Kirton	Water Holiburton
The Lard of Ryddell	Androw Meither	Richard Hangaside

The Lard of Remersyde	Saundyr Sporenose	Androw Carre
Gentlemen:	Marke Carre	Iames Douglas
George Trombill	George Carre	Iames Carre
Iohn Holyburton	Alexander Mackdowell	Iohn Carre
Robert Carre	Charles Rothirford	

A Lard in Scotland, is a degree next vnder a knight, which we call an Esquier, or such a one as is Lord of a towne.

Document 9

Protector Somerset was determined to discharge what he saw as his duty by enforcing the existing statutes against enclosure. He set up several commissions to report on the extent of the problem, and this is an extract from the report of one of them, dealing with the town of Cambridge. The complaints are representative of several such returns. In sending out such commissions, the Protector was seen by some of his aristocratic critics as encouraging the commons to take the law into their own hands. That was never his intention, but it is not an unfair description of what was to happen in the summer of 1549.

Document 9: Presentments before the enclosure commissioners, 1548. *Tudor Economic Documents*, **ed. R. H. Tawney and Eileen Power, I, pp. 44-7.**

Complayntes at the Insurrection

In primis, we fynde that ther be iiii Awmessehowses decayed in Jesus Lane whych owght to be upholden and mayntayned by Mr. Thomas Hutton.

Item, we fynde that the Master and Fellows of Jesus College have let ther ferme hollye with all commodities together, and the fermor thereof hathe letten the lande to certeyne persons and betwyxt Jesus College grownde and Myhell howse grownde, and he hath dyched it at both endes.

Item, we fynde that he hath eared upp a lyke bawlk in lyk manner, lying betwixt the Kynges hall grownde and Myhell howse grownde.

Item, we fynde also that the said Mr. Bykardyck hath taken in and inclosed a portyon of the common hyghewayes at both endes of the sayde bawlke.

Item, we fynde there is another bawlke enclosed at both endes and plowed uppe, that leadeth from the forenamed bawlke, dyrectlye crossing the hyghewaye unto Barnwell cawsey and Jesus Grene.

*   *   *

Item, we fynde that one pece of common is inclosed now in the handes of Mr. Mores, which hath been accustomed to lye common at Mydsomer.

Item, we fynde one berne now in the tenure of William Bradlye buylded on St. Thomas lease, which was accustomed and owght to lye common at lamas.

Item, we fynde that a ferme howse called cotton hall, now in the tenure of Mr. Fanne, is dekayed and fell downe abowt xx^{ti} yeres agon, not inhabyted and hath iiii^{xx} acres of lande longinge thereunto, and is letton for v^{li} bye yere.

Item, we fynde that beyonde Styrbrydge chappell, Dytton men have pulled downe a brydge, stopped the water, drowned the commons, and so enter upon Cambridge common.

Item, we fynde that Mistress Lacys of Barnwell hathe severed the lande and the shepe gate of her ferms, and that bayley Genings and John Bernes have done the lyke in ther fermes.

Item, we fynde that Mr. Kymbalde hath walled and dyched upon the hyghwaye in Barnwell, wherbye the sayd waye is much straytened.

Mem. of a common balk throwe a pasture ground adjoyning next to Rutlands howse in little St. Marys nowe inbabited bi R. Tomlynson, which balke shulde be a weye to go to Thomas leyes and so forth on balkes to Jesus Grene, &c., which pasture is now purchased bi the town, &c.

....

Document 10

Francois Van der Delft was the Imperial ambassador in England, and a reasonably well informed observer of events. His report on the risings of 1549 is brief but objective. He also acted as the protector and adviser of Princess Mary, on behalf of his master. In reporting her tribulations he is very well informed but not at all objective, as this despatch makes clear. M. de Granvelle is the Bishop of Arras, the Emperor's chief minister, and the King of the Romans is Ferdinand, the Emperor's younger brother.

Document 10: Ambassador Van der Delft to the Emperor, 19th July 1549. *Calendar of State Papers, Spanish*, IX, pp. 405-9.

Sire, the revolt of the peasants has increased and spread, so that now they have risen in every part of England, asking for things both just and unjust: that they may enjoy the land that used to be public property once, that all victuals shall be sold at reasonable prices, and that the land hired out to them on leases (*en ammodiation*) shall be considered to be of the same value now as in the time of King Henry VII. This last request is very difficult to meet. In Kent and Essex the risings had subsided because victuals had been taxed at a reasonable price, and the King's proclamation to that effect printed and posted up, with a pardon for past offences; but they have risen again now, because a few of the prisoners were kept in the Tower, and they seem more dangerous than before. They have come as far as Elton near Greenwich and pulled down (the enclosures of) one of the King's parks. They are threatening to come to London to get their prisoners; and this would be disastrous, considering that the town is over full of people who ask for nothing better than an opportunity of sacking it. In Norfolk, where the Lady Mary is now, there are over eight thousand of them. They partly pulled down the enclosure of her park, but did not molest her in any way. On the contrary, they asserted that she was kept too poor for one of her rank. There is no mention of religion made among them, except in Cornwall and Norfolk, where they are in greater numbers. The Council are in great perplexity, as is clearly shown by the printed answer they made to the Cornish men, who asked for the mass, matins, confirmation and other observances to be restored to the condition they were in at the time of the late King's death, because, they said, nothing should be changed during the King's minority. The Lord Privy Seal who was sent out to them, has not succeeded in quieting them. It is said that if the threats contained in the printed answer made to them referred to above, to treat them as Turks and infidels unless they disband, has no effect upon them, then my Lord Grey who is gone to assist the Lord Privy Seal with a great number of noblemen and foreign troops, such as Germans and Albanians, and some field artillery, will fight them. Things are in a very bad way here, and all the worse because the people are angry that Dimock's infantry and other foreign troops are employed against the Engish; and they are so resentful that they say they won't leave a foreigner alive in England.

Heaven watch over us! London is very closely guarded; there is artillery at the gates and outlets, and Hacfort's band, which was to remain at Guines, and in the Boulonnais, was suddenly sent for to come to England. Presumably it is intended to guard the King, who has been at Richmond up to now and, they say, is going to Windsor to-day.

Sire, I wrote lately how certain servants of the Lady Mary had been sent for to go to court, and that I was expecting to hear from them an account of what took place before the Council, to inform your Majesty of it immediately. The Lady Mary has since written to me, confirming what her controller had told me himself, that great pressure was put upon him to undertake to persuade the said lady to accept the new laws and religious practices, and conform with the King. He refused to accept such a task, and made application to be relieved of it; for it was nowise suitable that a servant should act otherwise than in obedience to his mistress's orders, and discharge of his domestic duties. I put off writing to your Majesty until I might hear what was happening about the lady's chaplain who was sent for at the same time, and was detained longer. He has at last gone back to the Lady Mary, with letters of which she promised to send me a copy. I am expecting it hourly. But as it seemed to me that she was being worried over much by the pressure put upon her old servants, and by the inhibition made to other worthy people not to join her service, under pretext that they (these people) were the King's servants, and all because of her religion, I determined to speak to the Protector, not on her behalf, but on account of the common reports about the affair: for in truth people are talking a great deal. I went yesterday to see him. I told him I had heard the rumour that he intended to worry the Lady Mary and induce or compel her to change her religion. This I said, would be in absolute contradiction to his former assertions, and could not fail to displease your Majesty; who, by your last letters, had charged me again to make the observation to him that because of the close relationship between you and her and the perfect friendship that your Majesty had always borne her, you could not desist from attempting to encompass her immunity from vexation, and her freedom to practice and observe the old religion. I urged him to consider how much better it would be to leave the Lady Mary her liberty in religious matters until the King came of age, as he had formerly told me he intended to do, though rumour now affirmed the contrary. He might well suppose, I said, that your Majesty and the King of the Romans would be displeased if she were either openly or indirectly pressed to change her religion; for as I had told him before, I knew well that even if she were wholly inclined to change, your Majesty would look for means of preventing her, and not see the spectacle of so near a relative falling away from our holy faith and the general practices prescribed by the Church. I added that I had had letters from your Majesty on this subject the very day Paget came to bid me farewell but I had put off speaking to him, believing I should have no necessity to do so, particularly as I put my trust in his (the Protector's) word. But as things were going differently, according to public rumour, I could not forbear from fulfilling my duty and laying what I had just said before him, so that the matter might be arranged without bitterness; for your Majesty would undoubtedly be greatly displeased to see the Lady Mary in distress in the cause of religion. To this he answered: "I remember well what I said to you on this subject;" and he repeated everything he had said to me on other occasions; but, slurring over the point I have so often made, that your Majesty would not countenance her changing her religion through inducements or other means, he repeated that he hoped her prudence and wisdom would make her yield to the arguments of learned and lettered men, and conform her practice with the King's, and with his laws. He said that since our last interview, the Chancellor and Secretary Petre had been sent to see her, and he gave me an accurate account of all that passed, as I had heard it from her, and written it to your Majesty.

....

London, 19 July, 1549

Document 11

By September 1549 a substantial number of Privy Councillors were convinced that the Protector would have to be overthrown. Who began the plot is not known; it may have been the Earl of Arundel, or it may have been the Earl of Warwick. Somerset's religious policy appears to have been one of the targets, and Mary was approached to act as regent. She declined, but a confrontation nevertheless ensued in early October. Richard Grafton describes the subsequent events from the point of view of a reasonably well informed Londoner. He does not know what happened at Windsor, and exaggerates the role of Sir Philip Hoby.

Document 11: The coup of October 1549. From Grafton's *Chronicle* pp. 521-24.

After these hurly burlyes were pacefied and quieted, many of the Lords of the realme, as well counsaylors as other mislyking the gouernement of the Protector, began to withdrawe themselues from the Courte, and resorting to London, fell to secret consultation for redresse of things, but namely for the displacing of the sayde Lorde Protector, and sodainely of what occasion many maruayled and fewe knewe, euery Lorde and Counsaylor went thorowe the Citie weaponed, and had their seruauntes likewise weaponed attendyng vpon them in newe lyuerings to the wondering of many. And at the last, a great assemble of the sayde Counsaylors was made at the Erle of Warwikes lodging then at Ely place in Holborne, whether all the Confederates in this matter came priuily armed, and finally concluded to possesse the Tower of London, which by the pollecie of Sir Wylliam Paulet Lord Treasorer of Englande was peaceably obteyned for them, who by order of the sayde Confederates immediatly remoued Sir Iohn Markam then Lieutenant of the Tower, and placed in that rome syr Leonard Chamberleyne. And after that the sayde counsayle was broken vp at Ely place, the Erle of Warwike remoued forthwith into the Citie of London, and laye in the house of one Iohn Yorke Citezen of London, who was then chiefe mayster of the Mynt in Southwarke in Suffolke place, which Yorke as shortly after by the ayde of the sayde Erle of Warwike made by the king knight, by the name of syr Iohn Yorke.

The Lorde Protector hearing of the maner of the assembly of this counsaile, & of the taking of the Tower which seemed to him verie straunge and doubtfull, did presently the saide night remoue from Hampton Court, taking the king with him vnto the Castell of Wyndsore, and there began to fortifie the same.

The Lordes of the Counsayle beyng then in London as aforesaide conferred with the Maior of London and his brethren, first wylling them to cause a good and substantiall watch by night, and a good warde by daye to be kept for the safegarde of the Citie, and the portes and gates thereof, which was consented vnto: and the Companyes of London in their turnes warned to watch and warde accordingly.

Then the sayd Lords and counsaylors demaunded of the Lord Maior and his brethren fiue hundred men to ayde them to fetch the Lorde Protector out of Wyndsore from the king. But thervnto the Maior aunswered that he could graunt no ayde without the assent of the common counsayle of the Citie. Wherevpon the next daye, a common counsayle was summoned to the Guyldhall in London.

But in this meantime, the sayde Lordes of the counsayle assembled themselues at the Lorde Maiors house of London, who then was syr Iohn Amcotes Fishemonger, and William Locke Mercer, and syr Iohn Aileph Shiriefes of the sayde Citie. And there the sayde Counsaile agreed and published a proclamation forthwith agaynst the Lorde Protector, the effect of which proclamation was as foloweth.

First, that the Lord Protector by his malicious and euill gouernement was the occasion of al the sedition that of late had happened w^{t}in the realme.

The losse of the kings peeces in Fraunce.

That he was Ambicious and sought his awne glory, as appered by his building of most sumpteous and costly houses, and specially in the time of the kings warres, and the kings souldiours vnpayde.

That he esteemed nothing the graue counsayle of the Counsaylors.

That he sowed sedicion betwene the nobles, the gentlemen & commons.

That the nobles assembled themselues together at London for none other purpose, but to haue caused the Protector to haue liued within lymits, and to haue put suche order for the kings maiestie as apperteyned, whatsoeuer the Protectors doings were, which, (as they sayde) were vnnaturall, ingrate and Trayterous.

That the Protector slaundered the counsayle to the king, and did that in him laye to cause variaunce betwene the king and his nobles.

That he was a great Traytor, and therefore the Lordes desired the Citie and the commons to ayde them to take him from the king. And in witnesse and testimonie of the contentes of the sayde proclamation, the Lordes subscribed their names and tytles, beyng sixtene in number.

After the aforesayd proclamation was proclaymed, the Lordes or the most part of them continuing and liyng in London, came the next day to the Guyldhall during the time that the Lord Maior & his brethren, sate in their court or inner chamber, and entred and commoned a long while with them, and at the last, the Maior and his brethren came forth vnto the comon counsayle, where was read the kinges letter sent vnto the Maior and Citezens, commaunding them to ayd him with fiue hundred men, and to send the same to his Castell at Windsore: and to the same letter was adioyned the kinges hand and the Lorde Protectors. On the othersyde by the mouth of the Recorder, it was requested that the Citezens would graunt theyr ayde rather vnto the Lordes, for that the Protector had abused both the kinges maiestie and the whole Realme, and without that he were taken from the king, and made to vnderstand his folly, this realme was in great hasard, and therfore required y^t the Citezens would willingly assent to ayd the Lordes with fiue hundred men, herevnto was none other answere made but scilence. But the Recorder (who at that time was a worthy gentleman called Maister Brooke) still cryed vppon them for aunswer. At the last stepped vp a wise and good Citezen and sayd, in this case it is good for vs to thinke of thinges past to auoide the daunger of thinges to come. I remember, sayth he, in a story written in Fabians Chronicle, of the warre betweene the king and his Barons, which was in the time of king Henry the third, and the same time the Barons as our Lordes do now demaunded ayde of the Maior and Citie of London, & that in a rightfull cause for the common weale, which was for the execution of diuers good lawes, whervnto the king before had geuen his co'sent, and after would not suffer them to take place, and the Citie did ayde the Lords, & it came to an open battayl, wherin the Lordes preuayled and toke the king and his sonne prisoners, and vpon certayne condycions, the Lordes restored againe the king and his sonne to their liberties. And among all other condicions, this was one that the king should not only graunt his pardon to the Lords, but also to the Citezens of London, which was graunted, yea and the same was ratefied by act of parliament. But what followed of it? was it forgotten? no surely, nor forgeuen during the kinges life, the lyberties of the Citie were taken away, Straungers appoynted to be our Heades and Gouernors, the Citezens geuen away bodye and goodes, and from one persecution to another, were most miserably afflicted, suche it is to enter into the wrath of a prince, as Salomon sayth, the wrath & indignation of a Prince is death. Wherefore forasmuch as this ayde is requyred of the kinges maiestie, whose voyce we ought to hearken vnto, for he is our high shepherd, rather then vnto ye Lords: and yet I would not wish the Lords to be clerely shake' off, but that they with us, and we with them may ioyne in sute and make our most humble peticion to the kinges maiestie, that it woulde please his highnesse to heere such complaynt against the gouernement of the Lorde Protector as maye be iustly alleged and proued. And I doubt not, but this matter will be so pacefied, that neither shall the king, nor yet the Lordes haue cause to seeke for further ayde, neyther we to offend any of them both. After this tale, the commons staied, and the lord Maior and his brethren for that time brake vp, and afterwarde commoned with the Lordes.

The Lordes sate the next daye in counsayle in the Starre Chamber and from thence they sent Sir Phillipe Hobby, with their letter of credence to the kinges maiestie, beseching his highnesse to geue credite to that which the sayd Sir Phillip should declare vnto his maiestie in their names: and the king gaue him libertie to speake, and most gently heard all that he had to saye. And truely he did so wisely declare his message, and so grauely told his tale in the name of the Lordes, but therewithall so vehemently and so grieuously against the Protector, who was also there present by ye king, that in the ende, the Lord Protector was commaunded from the kinges presence and shortly was committed to ward in a Tower within the Castel of Windsore called Beauchampes Tower. And sone after were staied Sir Thomas Smith, Maister Whalley, Maister Fissher, and many other Gentlemen that attended vpon the Lorde Protector. And the same daye, the Lordes of the Counsayle came to Wyndsore to the king, and the next day they brought from thence the Lorde Protector and the other that were there stayed, and conueied them through the Citie of London with as much wonderment as might be vnto the Tower, where they remayned prisoners.

Document 12

The defeat of Kett's rebellion in August 1549 left behind a legacy of fear and bitterness. In addition to continuing anger against the gentry and against the city authorities of Norwich, there was much settling of private scores; denunciations and counter denunciations. The Mayor and Aldermen were understandably apprehensive, and alert for signs of further trouble. At the same time there was no shortage of people who were willing to get their neighbours into trouble. The brave talk of another "camping summer" was probably no more than whistling in the dark, but it was obviously felt that no chances could be taken, and many hours were consumed in this type of investigation.

Document 12: The aftermath of Kett's rebellion in Norfolk. *Tudor Economic Documents*, I, pp. 47-53.

Made the XXI^t daye of September in the thredde yere of the rayne of our sovereign lorde King Edwarde the syxte. Edmunde Warden and Thomas Dorye Churchewardens of the parishe of St. Gregory demanded certen ornaments out of thands of Robert Burnam being our pariche clerke for dyvers considerations, and ded advyce him to turne his harte and become a newe man. And he sayed he had offended no man But that he was hable to answere. Then sayed I unto him That I harde a gentylman saye when he was in pryson that he was not affrayed of his lief of no man but of the seide Burnam. Thenne answered the seide Burnam and sayed: There are to many gentylman in Englande by Fyve hundred. Thenne saied I agayne, if thowe spekiste suche a worde agayne thowe shalte go to pryson.

The seide Robert Burnam hathe spoken theis worde sythens in the precence of certen of thaldermen: Mr Mayour, ye do me wrong to kepe me here without any cause; whereunto Mr Mayor answered and sayed, noo Burnam, I kepe the not here, and he sayed, yes, ye skrybes and pharisies, ye seke innocente bloude, But if I cannot have justice here I shall have it of better men, and I aske no favour at your handes.

Made the last day of September anno R.R. Edwardi VI*ti*. tercio. Mary [?] Chapman, the wief of Alexander Chapman, went to the house of William Mutton, he being sicke, there [s]he founde with him doctor King, and he ded aske him howe he ded, and he sayed, sickelye, and the same Doctor King desired him to be of a good chere, exhorting him to be a newe man, and to be sorry for thoffences that he had done; whereunto the saide Mutton answered and sayed that he had don nothyng that he wolde repent him of. Then sayed the wief of Mr Chapman unto him, Mutton, you must be sorry for one thing that ye have doon, he demanded what that was; whiche [s]he declared unto him was for breking downe of the Pentess in Norwiche. And he sayed he never repented him for that thing, for there was muche dysceyte; and he sayed it was no dysceyte for he never boughte ware of any man, But he myghte have had the same into the strete to loke uppon it. And further [s]he sayed it shalbe a greate hinderaunce to you, for men woll not nowe sette you in their worke; where unto he seide he wolde never work more, For the lorde have inoughe for us all....

The sayeng of one Ralphe Claxton to Thomas Wolman, witnes Henry Musored [?] Mens. November.

Firste he sayed that he ded well in keping in Ketts campe and so he wolde saye, and thenne I asked him what he ded thinke by Kette; and he sayed, nothing but well that he knewe, and after that he sayed that he trusted to see a newe daye for suche men as I was.

Thexamynation of Robert Syphat of Norwiche, sworne and examyned before Thomas Codes, Mayor of the Cittie of Norwiche, and others the xvii day of January anno R.R. Ed. sexti tercio.

The same Roberte sayeth that as on Munday last paste at nyne of the cloke at nyghte, at John Chandlers house there, John Oldman and James Cowell with other sayed unto Candelers wief, let him in who so ever he be, we care not for them; and afore that they sayed, that they wolde have no more lieng camp but a ronnyng camp.

*   *   *

The examynacion of John Redhedde before Thomas Codde Mayor of the cittie of Norwiche, and others the xii th day Februarye anno R.R. Ed. sexti quarto.

John Redhead of Norwiche, of the parisshe of St. Marten, worsted wever, sayeth and confesseth: that uppon a market daye not a monthe passed, whether it was Wednesdaye or Saterdaye he certenly knoweth not, being in the market uppon his busynes to bye his victualle, walking there he saw twoo or three persons men of the contrithe stonding together having conversation betwixte themselves. He harde the une of them speke to thother loking uppon Norwiche castell towarde Kette thies wordes, viz. Oh Kette god have mercye uppon thy sowle, and I trust in God that the Kings Maiestie and his Counsall shalbe enformed ones betwixte this and Mydsomer even, That of their owne gentylnes thowe shalbe taken downe by the grace of god and buryed, and not hanged upp for wynter store, and sette a quyetnes in the realme, and that the ragged staffe shalbe taken downe also of their owne gentylnes from the gentylmens gates in this cittie, and to have no more Kings Armes but one within this cittie under Christe but King Edwarde the syxte, god save his grace; Whiche persones he saytthe he never knewe them, nor cannot name them.

Witness examyned of and upon certen wordes spoken by William White broughte before Mr Robert Rug, Mayor of Norwich, Thomas Cawdy, Recorder, John Corbet, Esquyer, Augusten Stywarde, Thomas Dodde, and other Aldermen and Justices etc, XIIII. Junii anno R.R. Ed. VI^ti Quarto.

Robert Ederych of Wroxham, of thage of xxiiii[ti] yere, sworn and examyned saith and deposeth by vertu of his othe: That one John Whyte, of St. Augustens parishe in Norwiche, wollen wever, being at Wroxham the weeke before Pentecoste last past in his owne worke in this deponents loom, whiche he doth hyere by the weeke there, had brought some certen thromes, and at his comyng home sayed to this examynate that he coulde tell him tydings, and this deponent saith he demande[d] what that was; and the sedde John White spake and declared to him thies wordes: That by the Mass we shall have as hoote a somere as ever was, and also sayed that this somere shuld be as evell and busy as the last somer was. And this deponent then requyred the seide John to attende to his worke and meddell with no suche mattier, and the seide John White answered and sayed That he was out of worke and coulde not worke, nor by the masse he wolde not worke for he knew well it shulde be trewe, For he have harde bookes speke thereof, and if it prove not so, he wold be hanged for it; at the which tyme was present the wief of thies examynate and Thomas Godfrey. And further he saith that the seide John White is a very slanderous creature and further cannot depose.

Thomas Godfrey of Wroxham, of thage of xx[ti] yere, sworne and examyned saith and deposeth uppon his othe: that the deposicion of Robert Ederech before deposed and taken is trewe in all things and further cannot saye.

....

Document 13

Richard Scudamore was Hoby's London agent, Hoby having returned abroad after his intervention at Windsor in October. He clearly had well informed friends at court, and provides the nearest thing to an eye-witness account of the political tensions which followed the Protector's overthrow. The editor's notes explain the detailed allusions in this letter.

Document 13: Richard Scudamore to Sir Philip Hoby, 5th. December
1549. *Camden Miscellany*, **XXXIX, ed. Susan Brigden,**
pp. 95-99.

It may please yow to be advertesyd that upon ffryday at nyght[1] very late I delyuered yor letter unto my lord of Warrewyck after the departurc from thens of all the kynges most honorable Counsell who sate ther yn the Counsell, for that my lord of Warrewyck kepyth yett his chamber. And after that my lord had perused yor long letter, seyd unto me that he wold answeare yow yn certayn poyntes therof, comaundyng me to attend upon his lordshyp on the morrowe, accordynge unto whos appoyntment I wayted ther Setorday, Sonday, & Mondaye, but by occasion that my lord was troubled with his disease kept his bedd ij dayes. And on the monday[2] all the Counsell came thether exept the Erle of Arrundell, the cause of whos absens I can not lern. And the Erle of Sowthampton who abydeth styll syke yn his howse.[3] And that nyght I, fearing lest my seyd lord of Warrwyck shold iudge slacknes in me for not geavyng good attendaunce upon him, found the meanes to come to his speche, puttyng hym yn remembraunce of his former pleasure, who seyd that he had not as yett wreten but he wold shortlye, seyng ffurther thatt the kynges hyghnes with all his most honorable Counsell had seen yowre hole discours. And yor doyng theryn they much comendyd, allowyng both yor dylygent servyce and also yor good intellygence. And my lord of Warrewyck dyd geave unto yow a very good reporte, promysyng unto yow all such ffavor or pleasure as shall lye yn hym either for yor affayres abowte the Courte, the marches of Walys or elles wheare.[4]

Thearfore it may please yow to consyder his lordshyp with yor letters of thankes as ye shall haue occasyon to wryte unto hym. The dischardge of yor statute is sygned by the kynges maiestye and remayneth yn the custodye of my lord great master, but I ame promysed to haue it as to

---

[1] 29 November

[2] 2 December

[3] The Earls of Southampton and Arundel were conspiring against Warwick to win control of the Council and Court. Wriothesley had ceased to attend Council meetings after 22 October: Hoak, *King's Council*, pp. 59-60, 246-51.

[4] Warwick owed Hoby favour after his part in the October *coup*.

morrowe to sett it to the sygnet and privey seale, and afterwardes to the greate seale. And then I must bryng the greate seale to my lord greate master, whearfore I do entend to sue oute a duplycat, that is to haue it doble wreten to the greate seale and then to kepe the one. The ouer charge of the suyng furth of the same wilbe the more by ffoure nobles or ther abowtes. Ye shall ffurther understand that I haue receauyd CCxxiiij li for yor dyett money, more throwe the gentlenes of Mr Williams' clerk then of hym self,[5] the which money I wyll not delyuer oute before Symons retorne, at which tyme I trust yor pleasure shalbe knowen. I have put my lord lysle[6] yn remembraunce for the chase dogg that he promysed yow, who seyd that he merveled much thatt the dogg had not been sent unto hym before this, alledgyng further that yf it came not shortly that then he wold send a seruaunt of his owne for hym. And my lord of urmond[7] seyth that he fforgeateth yow not but that he will prouyde a hownd for yow as sone as he can. Vpon Setorday last ther was certeyn nues brought to the Counsell of a certeyn stere that was begon at newborye yn Berkeshyre, to the acquyetyng of the whych the capytayn of the garde wt all his men and lx of the garde weare appoynted to goo thetherwardes, but that appoyntment beyng alteryd Sir John Williams, Sir Thomas Carden[8] and dyuers other gentlemen wear sent immedyatly awey for the redresse therof, but to whate ende it is come to I knowe not. But onles God doth extend his great mercy ouer us to kepe the Counsell yn an unytye and amytye, and to indue them with the grace to be very circumspect yn theyr doynges, the rage of the beastlye commons is such that it will (I feare) very shortly brast oute. Ther was sworn ynto the pryve Counsell vpon ffryday last the lord marqwess of Dorcett, and the Bushopp of Elye,[9] the which putteth all honest hartes yn good coumfort for the good hope that they haue of the perseueraunce of Goddes woord. Yett that notwithstondyng ther be some wyse men yn a great perplexite of mynde theryn for that the brute goeth so openly of so ernest sute made for the [fo.* 53ᵛ] delyveraunce of the late duke of Norfolke, the which was almost brought to passe by the ernest suytt of my lady of Rychmond,[10] but by whom she receauyd ffyrst comfort theryn I knowe not. Many of the Counsell were perswaded that the late Duke was become as good a chrystyan as eny was yn england, but I am much

---

5   Sir John Williams, treasurer of the Court of Augmentations.

6   John Dudley, son of the Earl of Warwick

7   Thomas Butler, Earl of Ormond

8   Sir Thomas Cawarden, Hoby's Protestant friend, was Sheriff of Surrey

9   Henry Grey, third Marquess of Dorset, and Thomas Goodrich, Bishop of Ely, rose to prominence at the height of the struggle between Warwick and Wriothesley for control of the Council. Protestants were admitted to counter the admission of Catholics. BL, Add. MS 48126, fos. 15ᵛ-16ʳ; Hoak, *King's Council*, pp. 54-7, 245-6, 248-9

10   Thomas Howard, third Duke of Norfolk, had been attainted for treason on 27 January, 1547. His daughter was the widow of Henry VIII's son, Henry Fitzroy, Duke of Richmond

affrayed that god hath not yett called hym. By the which perswasyon the most parte of the Counsell that favoreth goddes worde weare become almost his ffryndes, so much that his comyng furth was shortelye loked for, but I trust that God hath so reveled his cloked relygyon with much dissymulacyon that at this present the solycytors of his suytt are not yn so much comfort as they weare three dayes past, I trust this be the workyng of god for it can be judged non otherwyse, but the begynnyng of this suytt was pryvely procured by some of the old sort to the entent to make theyre part the stronger.[11] Ther was also a brute (and not amongst the meane sort) that master Courtney shold come at lybertye.[12] My lord Cobham arryved at London upon Setorday last, with whom I have ben twyse sence his comyng, puttyng his lordshyp yn remembraunce of yor request unto hym, who answeared that he wold withyn ffewe dayes take a tyme for it. Me semyth it shall not be so ernestlye performed as it was with wordes promysed. I have also spoken with Mr Arnold,[13] who promysed to paye unto my handes iiij^{xx} crownes or the value therof to the vse of his brother[14] as sone as his man cometh oute of Gloucester shyre, but when that wilbe he knoweth not the tyme certeyn. I can perceaue nothyng that they do yn the parliament howse but, as I by my last letters aduertesyd yow of, the remyssyon of a parte of the relyef, whos name is turned yn to a subsydye, and one payment more graunted than was before with the restoryng of the payment of ffee ffermes to the kyng ageyn immedyatly after the next payment payd.[15] This parlyament is called the styll parlyament. It is not misnamed for they do almost nothyng but geave the lokyng ther one ouer thother. Upon Sonday last ther was admytted ynto the ordre of the Garter the lord delaware, and Sir William Harbart. And Mr Pagett is created lord pagett of Beaudesert,[16] by the meanes whearof he is oute of his controllershypp, ynto whose Roome is placed Sir Anthony Wyngfeld.[17] And Sir Thomas Darcye appoynted vyce Chamberleyn and

---

[11] Catholic councillors were attempting to win control in Council and, allegedly, to make Princess Mary Regent of England: BL, Add, MS 48126, fo. 15^V; Hoak, *King's Council*, pp. 246-9

[12] Edward Courtenay, Earl of Devonshire, had been imprisoned in the Tower in November 1538 and attainted in 1539 for treason. He was released upon Mary's accession

[13] Nicholas Arnold of Gloucestershire, a Gentleman Pensioner. He was another of Hoby's Protestant friends, and Scudamore's cousin. *House of Commons, 1509 1558*

[14] Richard Arnold of Gloucestershire. Scudamore would be the principal beneficiary and executor of his will. *House of Commons, 1509-1558*

[15] 3 & 4 Edward VI, cc. 23, 18; *SR* iv, pp. 122-4, 118-19

[16] Paget, who had been with Somerset at Windsor, was influential in attaining his peaceful submission. This was his reward. Tytler, *England under the reigns of Edward VI and Mary*, i, pp. 223-7, 239-43

[17] Wingfield had been aligned with the London Lords against the Protector, and had been sent to arrest him. *DNB*

Capt. of the garde.[18] Ye shall further perceaue that my lord of Warrewyck is nomynated to be Marques of pembroke, and also shalbe lord Treasorer of England. And the Erle of Arrundell shalbe lord greate Chamborleyn, and that my lord pagett shalbe lord Chamberleyn.[19] The admyssyon of all the seyd dygntyes stayeth, as it is seyd, of my lord of Warrwyckes comyng to the Courte. I have solycyted Mr Chauncellor[20] for thallowance of the reparacyons of Stanwell,[21] who declared unto me that he had yow yn remembraunce but he requyred me to bere with hym theryn untyll the parlyament be fynysshed. And then he wold take an order therof. Mr Phelpott hath receauyd none answeare oute of the contrey as yett consernyng yor hors, but he loketh daylye for the same. Mr Wroth sayeth that he will burden yow with unkyndnes for that he hath receauyd no letter from yow sence yor departyng.[22]

And wheare as I aduertesyd yow by my last letters of the comyttyng of Sycell and Whalley to the Towre, ye shall perceaue that on the morrow after theyr comyng to the Towre they had both the lybertye of the Towre, and Sycell lyeth at Cornelys howse.[23] Mr Kelway is ageyne at lybertye, but ffulmoston remayneth as yet yn sauffe kepyng at my lord of Warrewyckes. And on ffryday last pynnock of Worcester shyre was brought up, and that nyght he was comytted to the fllete wheare he remayneth.[24] Thus haue I heapyd together such thynges as I do knowe although it be not yn good ordre, but for as much as my ignoraunce is to yow well knowen I haue good hope that yow wyll take it yn good parte. Nowe hauyng none other thyng worthye of aduertyesment (but that yor rent of Yorke shyre is receauyd) do beseche the lord to prospere yow yn all yor procedynges. I have stayed the sendyng of this letter by the space of iiij or v dayes bycause my lord of Warrewycke told me upon monday last that a post shold be dispatched to come unto yow. Wreten at the Blake ffryers the vth day of december by yor most bounden seruaunt.

---

[18] Darcy replaced Wingfield in these important Household posts: Hoak, *Kings Council*, pp. 82-3

[19] False rumours

[20] Sir Edward North, Chancellor of the Court of Augmentations

[21] Hoby had been made chief steward of the manor of Slanwell in Middlesex in 1545: *VCH, Middlesex*, iii, pp. 37, 46-7

[22] Sir Thomas Wroth was appointed one of the four Principal Gentlemen upon the reorganisation of the Privy Chamber at Somerset's fall. He was another of Hoby's Protestant friends. *APC* ii, pp. 344-5; *Travels and Life*, pp. 116, 117, 120

[23] Cecil was released from the Tower on 25 January upon a recognisance of 1,000 marks. John Cornelius was a gunfounder in the Tower. *APC* ii, p. 372; *House of Commons*, 1509-1558 (John Cornelius)

[24] William Pynnock Of Hanley Castle, Worcestershire, was bound in recognisance for £100 on 18 December *APC* ii, p. 367

Yet may please yow that Mr fflemmyng[25] and John lymes hath declared unto me that a gonners Roome of xijd by the day is ffallen voyed by the deth of a gonner that was taken at Seynt Andrewes and lately dyed, the which Roome is stayed untyll yor pleasure be knowen theryn. For as much as John lymes hath ben a sutor unto yow yn that behalf; yn consyderacyon that his Roome is paynefull and hether to he hath had small recompence for his servyce, that it may stand with yor pleasure to directe yor letters to Mr lyeffetenant with spede declaryng yor pleasure yn that behalf, and yef I myght with yor ffavor comend eny man unto yow I do judge John Lyems both for his honestye and his dylgens to be worthye for the same.

Rychard Scudamore

---

25 Sir Frances Fleming was Lieutenant of the Ordnance

Document 14

Images were the *bêtesnoirs* of the protestant evangelists. Any suspicion of an image was deemed to be idolatrous, and a campaign had been mounted since 1548 for their total removal from churches. This statute was the final enactment of that campaign. At the same time the introduction of the Prayer Book had been passively resisted in many places, and the rich variety of the old rites often continued. This act is intended to put an end to such traditional practices by insisting upon the destruction of all the obsolete service books. To judge from the expense and time required to re-equip such churches in the following reign, it must have been fairly effective.

Document 14: An Act for the abolishing of Images. 3 & 4 Edward VI, c. 10.*Statutes of the Realm*, IV, i, pp. 110-111.

An acte for the abolishinge and puttinge awaye of div'se Bookes and Images.

Wheare the King('s) most Excellent Majestie hathe of late setforthe and established by auctoritie of Parliament an unyforme quyett and godlye ordre for comon and open Prayer, in a Booke intituled, The Booke of Comon Prayer and Admynistracon of the Sacrament(s) and other Rytes and Ceremonyes of the Churche after the Churche of Englande, to be used and observed in the saide Churche of Englande, agreable to thordre of the prymative Churche, moche more conformable unto his lovinge Subject(s) then other div'sitye of s'vice as heretofore of longe tyme hathe bene used, beinge in the saide Booke ordeyned nothinge to be redd but the verie pure worde of God, or whiche is evidentlye grounded upon the same, And in the other thing(s) corrupte untrue vayne and sup'sticious, and as it were a p'paracon to sup'sticon, whiche for that they be not called in but p'mytted to remayne undefaced, doe not onlye give occacon to suche parverse p'sons as doe ympugne the ordre and godly meanynge of the King('s) saide Booke of Comon Prayer to contynue in their olde accustomed supsticious s'vice, but also mynister great occacon to div'sitye of opynions rytes ceremonyes and s'vices: Be it therefore enacted by the Kinge our Soveraigne Lorde the Lordes sp'uall and temporall and the Comons in this p'sent Parliament assembled, that all Book(s) called Antyphons Myssales Scrayles P'cessionalles Manuelles Legends Pyes Portuyses Prymars in Lattyn or Inglishe Cowchers Journales Ordinales, or other book(s) or writing(s) whatsoever heretofore used for s'vice of the Churche, written or prynted in the Inglishe or Lattyn tongue, other then suche as are or shalbe settforthe by the King's Majestie, shalbe by auctoritie of this p'sent Acte clerelye and utterlye abollished extinguished and forbidden for ever to be used or kepte in this Realme or elles where within any the King('s) D'nions.

And be it further enacted by thauctoritie aforesaide, that yf anye parson or parsons of what estate degree or condicon soever he she or theye be, bodie Polytique or Corporate, that nowe have or hereafter shall have in

his her or their custodye anye the Book(s) or writing(s) of the sort(s)
aforesaid, or anye Images of Stone Tymbre Alleblaster or Earthe graven
carved or paynted, whiche heretofore have bene taken out of anye Churche
or Chappell, or yet stande in anye Churche or Chappell, and doe not before
the laste daye of June next ensuynge deface and destroye or cause to be
defaced and distroyed the same Imag(s) and everie of them, and delyver or
cause to be delivered all and everie the same Bookes to the Mayor Baylief
Constable or Churche wardyns of the Towne where suche Book(s) then
shalbe, to be by them delyvered over openlye within thre monethes next
followinge after the saide deliverie to the Archebusshopp Busshoppe
Chauncellor or Comyssarie of the same Dioces, to thintent the saide
Archebusshoppe Busshoppe Chauncellor or Comyssarie and everie of them
cause them ymediatlye eyther to be openlye brent or otherwayes defaced and
destroyed, shall for everie suche Booke or Book(s) willinglye retayned in his
her or their hand(s) or custodye within this Realme or elswhere within anye
the King('s) D'nyons, and not delivered as ys aforesaide after the saide laste
daye of June, and be thereof laufullye convicte, forfeyte and loose to the
Kinge our Soveraigne Lorde for the fyrst Offence twentie shilling(s) and for
the seconde Offence shall forfeyte and lose beinge thereof laufullie convicte
fower poundes, and for the thirde Offence shall suffre ymprisonment at the
King('s) will.

And be it further enacted by thauctoritie aforesaide, That yf anye
Mayors Bayliefes Constables or Churche Wardyns doe not, within thre
monethes after the receipte of the same book(s), deliver or cause to be
delivered suche book(s) soe by them receyved to the Archebusshoppe
Busshoppe Chauncellor or Comyssarie of their Dioces, and yf the saide
Archebusshoppes Busshoppes Chauncellors or Comyssaries do not within
fourtye dayes after the receipte of suche book(s), burne deface and distroye
or cause to be burned defaced or destroyed the same book(s) and everie of
them, that then they and ev'y of them so offendinge shall lose and forfeyte to
our Soveraigne Lorde the Kinge, beinge therefore laufullye convicte, fourtye
poundes; Thone halfe of all suche forfeytures shalbe to anye of the King('s)
Subject(s) they will sue for the same in anye of the King('s) Court(s) of
Recorde by bill playnte action of debte or informacon, in whiche accon noe
essoyne p'teccon wager of lawe or other delaye shalbe allowed.

And for better execucon of the same Acte, Be it enacted by
thauctoritie aforesaide, That aswell Justic(s) of Assise in Circuyte as Justices
of Peace within the lymytt(s) of their Comyssion in the gen'all Sessions, shall
have full power and authoritie to enquyre of thoffenc(s) aforesaide and to
heare and determyne the same, in suche forme as they maye doe in other
suche lyke cases.

Provyded alwaye and be it enacted by thauctoritie aforesaide, That
any p'son or P'sons maye use kepe have and reteyne any Prymars in the
Englishe or Lattyne tongue set forthe by the late Kinge of famous memorie
Kinge Henrie theight; so that the sentenc(s) of Invocacon or Prayer to

Sainct(s) in the same prymars be blotted or clerelye put out of the same; any thinge in this Acte to the contrarye notwithstandinge.

Provyded alwayes, That this Acte or any thing therin conteyned shall not extende to any Image or Picture sett or graven upon anye Tombe in any Churche Chappell or Churche Yarde, onelye for a Monument of any Kinge Prince Nobleman or other dead pson, whiche hath not bene comonly reputed and taken for a Saincte; but that suche Pyctures and Imag(s) maye stande and contynue in like manner and fourme as yf this Acte had never bene had nor made; anye thinge in this Acte to the contrarie in anye wise notwithstandinge.

Document 15

Latimer was a powerful advocate of the Christian stewardship of wealth, and one of the most effective protestant preachers. His direct and forceful style, and his strong advocacy of social responsibility are well exemplified in this extract. Latimer was a strong believer in order and obedience, and refrained from the more violent denunciations of the wealthy, which had helped to spark off the social violence of 1549. He was consequently unintimidated by the reaction which followed that outbreak.

Document 15: The social teaching of Hugh Latimer. Fifth sermon on the Lord's Prayer, 1552. From *Sermons by Hugh Latimer*, ed. G. E. Gorrie, Parker Society, pp. 406-10.

Remember this word "our": what it meaneth I told you. And here I have occasion to speak of the proprieties of things: for I fear, if I should leave it so some of you would report me wrongfully, and affirm, that all things should be common. I say not so. Certain it is, that God hath ordained proprieties of things, so that that which is mine is not thine; and what thou hast I cannot take from thee. If all things were common, there could be no theft, and so this commandment, *Non facies furtum*, "Thou shalt not steal", were in vain. But it is not so: the laws of the realm make *meum et tuum*, mine and thine. If I have things by those laws, then I have them well. But this you must not forget, that St. Paul saith, *Sitis necessitatibus sanctorum communicantes*; "Relieve the necessity of those which have need". Things are not so common that another man may take my goods from me, for this is theft; but they are so common that we ought to distribute them unto the poor, to help them, and to comfort them with it. We ought one to help another; for this is a standing sentence: *Qui habuerit substantiam hujus mundi, et viderit fratrem suum necessitatem habere, et clauserit viscera sua ab eo, quomodo caritas Dei manet in eo?* "He that hath the substance of this world, and shall see his brother to have need, and shutteth up his entire affection from him, how dwelleth the love of God in him?" There was a certain manner of having things in common in the time of the apostles. For some good men, as Barnabas was, sold their lands and possessions, and brought the money unto the apostles: but that was done for this cause,- there was a great many of christian people at that time entreated very ill, insomuch that they left all their goods: now, such folk came unto the apostles for aid and help; therefore those which were faithful men, seeing the poverty of their brethren, went and sold that they had, and spent the money amongst such poor which were newly made Christians. Amongst others which sold their goods there was one Ananias and Saphira his wife, two very subtle persons: they went and sold their goods too; but they played a wise part: they would not stand in danger of the losing of all their goods; therefore they agreed together, and took the one part from the money, and laid it up; with the other part they came to Peter, affirming that to be the whole money. For they thought in their hearts, like as all unfaithful men do, "We cannot tell how long this religion shall abide; it is good to be wise, and keep somewhat in store, whatsoever shall happen." Now Peter, knowing by the Holy Ghost their falsehood, first slew him with one word, and after her too: which indeed is a fearful example, whereby we should be monished to beware of lies and falsehood. For though God punish thee not by and by, as he did this Ananias, yet he shall find thee; surely he will not forget thee. Therefore learn here to take heed of falsehood, and beware of lies. For this Ananias, this wilful Ananias, I say, because of this wilful lie, went ot hell with his wife, and there shall be punished world without end. Where you see what a thing it is to make a lie. This Ananias needed not to sell his lands, he had no such commandment: but seeing he did so, and then came and brought but half the price, making a pretence as though he had brought it all, for that he was punished so grievously. O what lies are made now-a-days in England, here and there in the markets! truly it is a pitiful thing that we nothing consider it. This one example of Ananias and Saphira, their punishment, is able to condemn the whole world.

.....

But you will say, "Here is a marvellous doctrine, which commandeth nothing but 'Give, give:' if I shall follow this doctrine, I shall give so much, that at the length I shall have nothing left for myself." These be words of infidelity; he that speaketh such words is a faithless man. And I pray you, tell me, have ye heard of any man that came to poverty, because he gave unto the poor? Have you heard tell of such a one? No, I am sure you have not. And I dare lay my head to pledge for it, that no man living hath come, or shall hereafter come to poverty, because he hath been liberal in helping the poor. For God is a true God, and no liar: he promiseth us in his word, that we shall have the more by giving to the needy. Therefore the way to get is to scatter that that you have. Give, and you shall gain. If you ask me, "How shall I get riches?" I make thee this answer: "Scatter that that thou hast; for giving is gaining." But you must take heed, and scatter it according unto God's will and pleasure; that is, to relieve the poor withal, to scatter it amongst the flock of Christ. Whosoever giveth so shall surely gain: for Christ saith, *Date, et dabitur vobis.* "Give, and it shall be given unto you." *Dabitur*, "it shall be given unto you." This is a sweet word, we can well away with that; but how shall we come by it? *Date*, "Give." This is the way to get, to relieve the poor. Therefore this is a false and wicked proposition, to think that with giving unto the poor we shall come to poverty.

....

Document 16

The nth. round in the long running battle between Mary and the Council over her indulgence to hear private masses. The Princess complained bitterly about how she was treated by her brother's councillors, and appealed repeatedly to the Emperor's ambassador. The Council in turn accused her of abusing her privileges, and of setting a public example of defiance to lawful authority. This interview was presumably included in the council records in order to demonstrate that the government was treating the Princess with respectful restraint, but that she was not reciprocating.

Document 16: A Privy Council delegation visits the Princess Mary, 29th. August 1551. *Acts of the Privy Council*, III, pp. 347-52.

Wyndsour, the xxix[th] of August, 1551.

> The Duke of Somersett; the Lorde Chauncellour; Lorde Thresaurer; Lorde Pryvey Seale; Marques of Northampton; therle of Huntingdon; Lorde Cobham; Mr. Comptroler; Master of thorse; Mr. Secretary Peter; Mr. Hobby.

The Lorde Chauncellour, Mr. Comptroller and Mr. Secretary Peter being returned from the Lady Maryes Grace, made suche reporte of thexecucion of their charge and of her Grace's aunswer as followeth:

> A note of the reporte of the message doone to the Ladye Maryes Grace by us, the Lord Riche, Lorde Chauncellour of England; Sir Anthony Wingfeld, knight of thorder and Comptroler of the Kinges Majesties moste honorable Howshold; and Sir William Peter, knight, oone of his Majesties two Pryncipal Secretaryes; and of her Grace's aunswers to the same, reported by us all thre to the Kinges Majestie and the Lordes of his Majesties Pryvey Counsell at Wyndsour, the xxix[th] of August, 1551.

First, having receyved commaundement and instruccions from the Kinges Majestie, we repayred to the sayd Lady Maryes howse at Copthall in Essex on Fryday laste, being the xxviij[th] of this instant, in the morning, where, shortly after our cummyng, I, the Lord Chauncellour, delyvered his Majesties lettres unto her, which she receyved uppon her knees, saying that for thonour of the Kinges Majesties hand wherwith the said lettres were signed she would kysse the lettre and not for the mattier conteyned in them, for the mattier (sayed she) I take to procede not from his Majestie but from you of the Counsell.

In the reading of the lettre, which she did rede secretely to her self, she sayd thies wordes in our hearing, "*Ah! good Master Cecyll tooke muche payne here.*"

When she had red the lettres we began to open the mattier of our instruccions unto her, and as I, the Lorde Chauncellour, began, she prayed me to be shorte, for (sayed she) I am not well at easse, and I will make you a short aunswer, notwithstanding that I have alredy declared and wrytten my mynde to his Majestie playnely with myn owne hande.

After this we told her at good length how the Kinges Majestie, having used all the gentle meanes and exhortacyons that he might to have reduced her to the rightes of relygeon and order of Devyne Servyce sett forthe by the lawes of the realme, and fynding her nothing conformable, but styll remayning in her former errour, had resolved, by thole estate of his Majesties Pryvey Counsell and with the consent of dyvers others of the nobyllity, that she shuld no longer use the pryvate Masse nor any other Devyn Service then is sett forthe by the lawes of the realme; and here we offred to shew her the names of all those which were present at this consultacion and resolucion, but she sayd she cared not for any rehersall of their names, for (sayd she) I knowe you be all of one sorte therin.

We tolde her further that the Kinges Majesties pleasure was we shuld also gyve strayte charge to her chaplayns that none of them shuld presume to say any Masse or other Devyne Servyce then is sett forthe by the lawes of the realme, and like charge to all her servantes that none of them shulde presume to here any Masse or other Devyne Servyce then ys afforesaid. Hereunto her aunswer was this; first she protested that to the Kinges Majestie she was, ys and ever wolbe his Majesties moste humble and most obedyent subject and poore sister, and wold most willingly obey all his commaundementes in any thing (her conscyence saved); yea, and would willingly and gladly suffer death to do his Majestie good, but rather than she will agre to use any other servyce than was used at the death of the late King her father, she would laye her hed on a block and suffer death; but (sayed she) I am unworthy to suffer death in so good a quarrel. When the Kinges Majestie (sayed she) shall come to suche yeres that he may be able to judge thies thinges himself, hys Majestie shall fynde me redy to obey his orders in religyon; but now in thies yeres, although he, good, swete King, have more knowledge then any other of his yeres, yet is it not possible that he can be a judge in thies thinges. For if shipps were to be sent to the sees, or any other thing to be doone touching the pollycye and gouvernement of the realme, I am sure you would not think his Hieghnes yet able to consider what were to be doone, and much lesse, sayd she, can he in thies yeres decearne what is fyttest in mattiers of Devynity. And if my chaplayns do say no Masse I can heare none, no more can my poore servantes. But as for my servantes, I knowe it shalbe againste their willes, as it shalbe agayllst myne, for if they could comme where it were sayd they would heare it with good wyll. And as for my priestes, they knowe what they have to doo. The payne of your lawes is but emprysonnement for a short tyme, and if they will refuse to saye Masse for feare of that emprisonment, they may do therin as they will; but none of your nue Service (said she) shalbe used in my howse, and if any be sayd in it I woll not tary in the howse.

And after this we declared unto her Grace according to our instruccions for what causes the Lordes of the Kinges Majesties Counsell had appointed Rochester, Inglefeld, and Walgrave, being her servantes, to open the premisses unto her, and how yll and untruly they had used themselfes in the charge committed unto them, and besydes that, how they had manifestly disobeyd the Kinges Majesties Counsell, &c. To this she sayd it was not the wysest counsell to appoint her servantes to comptrolle her in her owne howse, and that her servantes knew her mynde therin well ynough, for of all men she might wurst endure any of them to move her in any suche mattiers, and for their punyshement my Lordes may use them as they think good. And if they refused to do the message unto her and her chaplaynes and servantes as afforesayd, they be (sayed she) the honester men, for they shuld have spoken agaynst their owne conscyences.

After this, when we had at good length declared unto her the effect of our instruccions touching the promisse which she claymeth to have been made to themperour, and besydes had opened unto her at good length all suche thinges as we knewe and had hard therin, her aunswer was that she was well assured the promisse was made to themperour, and that the same was ones graunted before the Kinges Majestie in her presence, then being there seven of the Counsell, notwithstanding the denyall therof at my last being with his Majestie. And I have, quoth she, themperour's hand testyfying that this promisse was made, which I beleve better then you all of the Counsell; and though you estyme litle themperour, yet shuld you shewe more favour to me for my father's sake, who made the more parte of you almost of nothing. But as for themperour (sayd she), if he were dede I would say as I do, and if he would gyve me now other advise I would not followe it; notwithstanding, quoth she, to be playne with you, hys Ambassadour shall knowe how I am used at your handes.

After this we opened the Kinges Majesties pleasure for oone to attende uppon her Grace for the supply of Rochester's place during his absence, &c., as in thinstruccions. To this her aunswer was that she would appointe her owne officers, and that she had yeres sufficyent for that purpose; and if we lefte any suche man there she would go out of her gates, for they two would not dwell in one howse. And (quoth she) I am sickly, and yet I will not dye willingly, but will do the best I can to preserve my lief; but if I shall chaunce to dye I will protest openly that you of the Counsell be the causes of my death. You gyve me fayre wordes, but your dedes be always ill towardes me. And having sayd thus, she departed from us into her bedchamber and delivered to me, the Lorde Chauncellour, a ryng uppon her knees moste humbly, with very humble recommendacions, saying that she would dye his true subject and suster, and obey his commaundementes in all thinges except in thies mattiers of relygion touching the Masse and the new Service, but yet, saide she, this shall never be told to the Kinges Majestie.

After her departing we called the chaplayns and the rest of her howshold before us, geveng them strayte comaundement, uppon payne of their allegeance, that neither the pristes should from hensforth say any Masse or other Devyne Service then that which ys set forth by the lawes of the realme, nor that they, the resydewe of the servantes, shuld presume to heare any. The chaplayns, after summe talke, promised all to obey the Kinges Majesties comaundement sygnified by us.

We gave like commaundement to them and every of them, uppon their allegeaunce, to gyve notyce to somme one of the Counsell at the least, if any Masse or other Devyne Service then that which ys sett forth by the lawes of this realme shulde be hereafter sayed in that howse.

Fynally, when we had sayd and doone as ys afforesaid and were goone out of the howse, tarying there for one of her chaplayns who was not with the rest when we gave the charge afforesaid unto them, the Lady Maryes Grace sent to us to speake with her one worde at a wyndowe. When we were comme into the courte, notwithstanding that we offred to come upp to her chamber, she would nedes speake out of the wyndowe, and prayed us to speake to the Lordes of the Counsell that her Comptroler might shortly returne; for, sayd she, sythens his departing I take thaccoumpt myself of my expenses, and learne how many loves of brede be made of a busshel of whete, and ywys (*sic*) my father and my mother never brought me up with baking and bruying, and to be playne with you, I am wery with myn offyce, and therfore, yf my Lordes will send myn officer home they shall do me pleasure; otherwise, if they will send him to pryson, I beshrewe him if he goo not to it merely and with a good will. And I pray God to send you to do well in your sowles and bodies to, for somme of you have but weake bodyes.

Document 17

Aggressive evangelicals could be a nuisance and a liability to a government which was trying to move steadily and retain a degree of consensus. Preachers like Hancock were invaluable as spearheads against conservative resistence, but by persistently trying to force the pace of change they provoked antagonism and made its implementation more difficult. Thomas Hancock, from whose autobiography these extracts were taken, had graduated B.A. from Oxford in 1532, and subsequently become curate at Amport in his native county of Hampshire. In 1546 he had been suspended for attacking the sacrificial character of the mass. At this time he was so vehement against transubstantiation that he ran the risk of contravening the statute against revilers of the sacrament.

Document 17: A Preacher's story: autobiographical extracts by Thomas Hancock, 1547. *Narratives of the Days of the Reformation*, ed. J.G. Nichols. Camden Society, Old Series, LXXVII, pp. 72-8.

The first year of the reign of King Edward VI, I the said Thomas, having licence of Bishop Cranmer, preached at Christchurch Twinham [Hampshire] where I was born, Mr. Smythe, vicar of Christchurch and bachelor of divinity being present; where I, taking my place out of the 16 *St. John*, v. 8, [said]...Here doth our Saviour Christ say that he goeth to the Father and that we shall see him no more. The priest being then at mass, I declared unto the people that [what] the priest doth hold over his head [the consecrated bread and wine] they did see with their bodily eyes, but our Saviour Christ doth here say plainly that we shall see him no more. Then you that do kneel unto it, pray unto it and honour it as God, do make an idol of it, and yourselves do commit most horrible idolatry. Whereat the said vicar, Mr. Smythe, sitting in his chair in the face of the pulpit, spake these words, 'Mr. Hancock, you have done well until now and now have you played an ill cow's part, which when she hath given a good mess of milk, overthroweth all with her foot, and so all is lost', and with these words he got him out of the church...

This done, I rode from Salisbury unto my Lord of Somerset his Grace, who lay at that time at Syon. I requested his Grace that I might have his letter for the discharge of them that were bound for me: he caused my Lord Treasurer his honour that now is, who then was Master of the Requests [William Cecil] to write to my Lord Chief Justice for the discharge of the bond. Which letter, whilst I was with my Lord [Chief Justice] at Hampton [Southampton] to deliver, the bell rang to the sermon. My Lord asked me whether I minded to preach. I answered yea. My Lord said unto me that Hampton was a haven town, and that if I should teach such doctrine as I taught at Sarum [Salisbury], the town would be divided, and so should it be a way or a gap for the enemy to enter in; and therefore he commanded me that I should not preach there. I answered that I would not take that for a forbidding, but that forsomuch as the people resorted to the church at the ringing of the bell to hear the word of God, they should not return home again void of God's word. My Lord said again unto me that I should not preach, and that there was one in the Tower (meaning Bishop Gardiner) that he would believe before 400 such as I was. I answered him that he spake those words betwixt him and me, but if I had record of them, he would not speak them.

So my Lord sent for the Mayor and his brethren. Mr. Mayor asked me whether I would be content that another should supply the room for me. I answered, yea, and that I was as willing to hear the word as to preach myself. So did Mr. Mayor send to one Mr. Griffith, who did preach; and my Lord being present, he challenged him that he, being Chief Justice of the Law did suffer the images in the church, the idol hanging in a string over the altar [in the vessel known as the pyx], canldlesticks and tapers on them upon the altar, and the people honouring the idol, contrary to the law; with much other good doctrine. I praised God for it. And thus were my friends of Sarum that were bound for me discharged their bond.

This trouble being overcome, another followeth, for after this I was called the same year, which was the first year of King Edward, to be the minister of God's word at the town of Poole, in County Dorset, which town was at the time wealthy, for they embraced God's word; they were in favours with the rulers and governors of the realm. They were the first that in that part of England were called Protestants; they did love one another, and every one glad of the company of the others, and so God poured his blessing plentifully upon them; but now I am sorry to set my pen to write it, they have become poor; they have no love to God's word...

I being minister of God's word in that town of Poole, preaching the word upon some Sunday in the month of July, inveighed against idolatry and covetousness, taking my place out of the 6th of *Timothy*...The brightness of the Godhead is such that it passeth the brightness of the sun, of angels and all creatures, so that it cannot be seen with our bodily eyes, for no man hath seen God at any time and liveth. The priest at that time being at mass, if it be so that no man hath seen God, nor can see God with these bodily eyes, then that which the priest lifteth over his head is not God, for you do see it with your bodily eyes: if it be not God, you may not honour it as God, neither for God. Whereat old Thomas Whyte, a great rich merchant and a ringleader of the papists, rose out of his seat and went out of the church, saying, 'Come from him, good people; he came from the devil and teacheth unto you devilish doctrine.' John Notherel, alias John Spicer, followed him, saying, 'It shall be God when thou shalt be but a knave.' [Hancock describes further clashes with Whyte and his adherents, who threatened to disembowel him in the church and reviled the Mayor of Poole when the latter came to his aid. After the accession of Mary, he was excepted from the Queen's general pardon, and fled with his wife and son to Geneva.]

Document 18

Mary of Hungary was the Emperor's half sister, and Regent of the Netherlands. In this extract she is speculating to the Emperor's chief minister about the possibility of using Mary, and her special dependence upon Charles, as a means of forcing a way into England. Her cynicism, and the contempt in which she holds the English government, make this a very revealing document in terms of English foreign policy. The Emperor would probably not have endorsed such predatory sentiments, but his poor health meant that he was not always in control.

Document 18: Mary of Hungary to the Bishop of Arras, 8th October 1551. *Calendar of State Papers, Spanish*, **X, pp. 378-9.** *Extracts.*

As for England, I think we must find out what we are to look for from that country. In order to do this it would be necessary to have an intelligent ambassador there, such as Renard, who has just returned from France, or another who would do his utmost to keep up friendly relations there and at the same time find out how our merchantmen and warships are going to be treated, and how they are going to behave towards French shipping. It is quite certain that the possession of one port there, if we managed to seize one, would enable us to protect our shipping; but our vessels would be exposed to a thousand dangers if they had nowhere to run into in case of storm. We must therefore have a port in that country at our disposal, either by force or through friendship. Many people are of opinion that the kingdom of England would not be impossible to conquer, especially now that it is a prey to discord and poverty. It seems that there are three persons who might try their fortune, conquer the country, and marry our cousin if she is able to hold out with his Majesty's favour, under colour of taking the King out of the hands of his pernicious governors, as the late King's dying recommendation to his Majesty might be taken as an invitation to do. If they had already got rid of the King, we could intervene with the pretext of avenging him, or some other excuse easily to be devised. Of those who might be suited for this enterprise, the first is the Archduke Ferdinand; but in that case his Majesty would have to stand the expense, for little help would be forthcoming from the King (of the Romans). In the second place there is the Infante Don Luis of Portugal, who might look for assistance from his brother, the King, in a task so good as the restoration of an important kingdom to the fold of the Church, not to mention the chance of winning it for his brother. Third, comes the Duke of Holstein, who might undertake it with the hope of marrying our cousin, or if she were to fail us, one of our nieces, daughters of the King of the Romans. He might be assisted by his brother, the King of Denmark, for the Danes claim England, have often invaded it, and have actually held it for a number of years. And if we were able to win in England a fine, commodious port such as there are there, we might reinforce the invader with our fleet and also deprive the French of the use of English harbours, lacking which they are unable to keep up a dangerous fleet. It is very true that all this would call for money, and it would be hard to find enough. But this is a juncture at which we must use all our power and get together money by our subjects' assistance and all other means possible, using our credit for all it is worth in all quarters, inside the Empire and out. In any case it would be well to apply for the half-fruits of the Low Countries, and I pray you to take the necessary steps to obtain them. We had better proceed, obtaining all the money we can and making our plans accordingly.

Document 19

Northumberland's attitude towards the church was always ambivalent. In this letter he starts off by wishing to bring the radical preacher John Knox south as Bishop of Rochester, in order to force the pace of evangelical change. But in the second half he is speculating about how much profit the king can make out of the recent dissolution of the see of Durham. His ideas of how two new dioceses can be cheaply funded show extensive ignorance of the real affairs of the old see. This attitude helps to explain the deterioration in his relations with the protestant bishops which preceded the crisis of July 1553.

**Document 19: The Duke of Northumberland to Sir William Cecil, 28th.
October 1552.** *Calendar of State Papers, Domestic, Edward VI*, **no. 747.**

I would the king might appoint [John] Knox to the bishopric of Rochester; he would be a whetstone to sharpen the archbishop of Canterbury and confound the Anabaptists lately sprung up in Kent; he would not continue the ministration in the north, contrary to this set forth here; the Scots inhabiting Newcastle for his fellowship would not continue there. Ask the lord chamberlain or vice-chamberlain to help, for God's service and the king's. If the dean of Durham is appointed bishop with 1,000 marks more than his deanery, the houses he now has in the city and country will serve honourably - so may the king receive the castle, which has a princely site, and the other stately houses the bishop had in the country. The chancellor's living to be converted to the deanery and an honest man placed in it; the vice-chancellor to be turned into the chancellor, the suffragan,* who is placed without the king's authority, and has a great living, may be removed, being neither preacher, learned, nor honest, so pernicious that the country abhors him. The living, with a little more to its value - 100 marks - will serve the erection of a bishop of Newcastle. Thus the king may place godly ministers in these offices and receive £2,000 a year of the best lands in the north; it will be 4,000 marks a year of as good revenue as any in the realm. Order should be taken for [Thomas] Gower. Then must the treasurer be proceeded into for abusing his office, to the king's great detriment. Scribbled in bed, as ill as I have ever been.

* Thomas Sparke, suffragan bishop of Berwick.   SP
10/15, no. 35

Document 20

Robert Wingfield wrote this highly circumstantial and very partisan account of Edward's death and Mary's accession within a few weeks of the events. It was written in Latin, and reflects the experience of a man who was very close to the action, at least in East Anglia. The dedication to Edward Waldegrave, also an East Anglian gentleman and probably known to the author, was no doubt intended to win him preferment. There is no record that it did. Wingfield's account of Edward's last speech should be seen as a rhetorical embellishment, in the manner of the classical historians - evidence of the author's humanist credentials.

Document 20: Robert Wingfield on the succession crisis of 1553. Extract from the 'Vita Mariae Anglia' ed. and trans. D. MacCulloch, *Camden Miscellany*, XXVIII, pp. 245-250.

[*f.7r*] Robert Wingfield of Brantham, to the most illustrious Edward Waldegrave, councillor of the queen's majesty, and keeper of the royal wardrobe.

Although, excellent Maecenas, I cannot but confess myself unequal to the burden of recording history, a burden heavier than Etna to my feeble shoulders, yet with no ill forebodings, thanks to the lustre of my noble reader, I will not fear first to make these few remarks to you as excuse for my boldness, lest I might be accused of presumption for meddling in the renowned exploits of sacred Mary. When, on the most holy queen's first bid for or approach to her hereditary throne, I gave myself freely to the service of her Highness, I began assiduously and carefully to note almost all of the more remarkable occurrences from her first claim to the throne to the present day. And since these events were not only marvellous but worthy of note, I have resolved to bring them together in this little treatise, lest the famous deeds of such a godly Queen remain unknown to many. I freely admit that I did this not to be taken as the author of a new history, but rather that I might offer material to Christopherson, Ascham or to some other initiate of more accomplished literary composition. I therefore tell you that my efforts, whatever they are, will be submitted to your scrutiny or consideration, so that with the support and authority of your name they may succeed more readily. Now I am bringing my preface to a close so as not to detain you any longer with my trifling work when you are occupied with weightier matters, and I pray for lasting happiness and long life for you and those near to you. London, 20 May, in the first year of Queen Mary.

Yours if he may serve,
Robert Wingfield.

[*f.8r*] When King Edward, the sixth of his name, had attained the age of fifteen and was in the seventh year of his reign, he was almost wasted away with a long and lingering disease, and at first sight showed to everyone who

had the opportunity of seeing his royal majesty, manifest and eloquent tokens
of his imminent death, almost as if it were within the gates, as they say. The
man best aware of and acquainted with this was John Dudley, or as others
will have it, Sutton; he was famous for the renown of his exploits and was
duke of Northumberland, but he was an ambitious man descended of an
ambitious father. After a notable victory on Norwich heath against the
peasants, who had been stirred up against the better sort by idle men, he
sought with excessive impudence to control both the king and the kingdom,
and because the nobility entrusted him with just such a task, he did indeed,
alas, succeed. However, afterwards the leading men dealt a heavy but
deserved punishment for this his shameful crime, which was to prove
especially calamitous for the young king and fatal to Northumberland
himself, as the following narrative will demonstrate more clearly in the
appropriate place.
....

The unhappy king - born to disaster, and subject to abuse and
plunder from both his guardians, first by his dearest uncle, the duke of
Somerset, then as if from the frying-pan into the fire, by Northumberland -
dared not make any protest, but fell in with the duke's wishes; he soon
ordered the most skilled lawyers to be called to note his will, or rather that of
Northumberland, and to write it with all the ancient legal elaboration.
Meanwhile Northumberland was far from idle, but assiduously attended to
his own designs, for he was exceedingly worried that he might let slip his ill-
gotten reins of power, or be accused of extortion or of lese-majesty; so he
made every effort to call the most learned legal minds to draw up the royal
will. Among the lawyers that he called (to publicize the more memorable
individuals) were Cholmeley, chief justice of England, Montague, chief
justice of the Common Pleas; Bromley and Hales, both justices, the latter of
the Common Pleas, the former of the King's Bench; Staunford [f.9v] and
Dyer, advocates, or to use the more customary form, serjeants-at-law;
together with other distinguished representatives of the same profession.
After these came John Baker, an important and distinguished lawyer; John
Gosnold, procurator or solicitor of royal causes, a most honourable man,
born to good breeding and deserving of general commendation; Lucas and
Cooke, both puisne judges of the king's court; and other men of importance
and notable learning whose names I here omit for the sake of brevity.

All these readily appeared on the summons, and the dying king
addressed them after this fashion:

'Trusty and well-beloved, I have been pondering the fleeting nature
of human life and my own illness, which is becoming more and more
serious. To prevent death from striking me unexpectedly while I am
unprovided and unprepared, I have had a care to have you summoned, not
only that you may help me with your advice and pains in drawing up this my
new will, but also that I may more clearly outline and explain the secrets of
my plan to stablish, and as far as in me lies, to strengthen this kingdom after
my death, to you, my faithful servants, and to the other noblemen' (for

Northumberland and the other conspirators were standing close by). 'I desire this all the more ardently to prevent my death from providing our beloved country with an occasion or profferred opportunity for civil war. Therefore, to cut a long story short, since I am convinced that my sister Mary would provoke great disturbances after I have left this life, and would leave no stone unturned, as the proverb says, to gain control of thus isle, the fairest in all Europe, my resolve is to disown [f.10r] and disinherit her together with her sister Elizabeth, as though she were a bastard and sprung from an illegitimate bed. For indeed my sister Mary was the daughter of the king by Katherine the Spaniard, who before she was married to my worthy father had been espoused to Arthur, my father's elder brother, and was therefore for this reason alone divorced by my father. But it was the fate of Elizabeth, my other sister, to have Anne Boleyn for a mother; this woman was indeed not only cast off by my father because she was more inclined to couple with a number of courtiers rather than reverencing her husband, so mighty a king, but also paid the penalty with her head - a greater proof of her guilt. Thus in our judgement they will be undeservedly considered as being numbered among the heirs of the king our beloved father.

'Therefore, to avoid the kingdom being weakened by such shame, it is our resolve, with the agreement of our noblemen, to appoint as our heir our most dear cousin Jane. She is the grand-daughter of our aunt Queen Mary, who was taken from her first marriage-bed, that of King Louis of France, and subsequently married Charles Brandon, duke of Suffolk, a mighty man; she is a girl distinguished both by her noble lineage and her beauty, and only a few days ago, with our consent, she married Guildford Dudley, one of the sons of our guardian, the duke of Northumberland, and a man, unless I am mistaken, born to achieve celebrity; from him you may expect great things, if it please the gods.

'For if our sister Mary were to possess the kingdom (which Almighty God prevent), it would be all over for the religion whose fair foundation we have laid, not without your support and agreement. Therefore to avert such a great and imminent evil, make all speed to lend your support, so that while I am still drawing breath, this my last will may be [f.10v] perfectly drawn up with your resources, which I most eagerly desire; then, with our proclamation to give it especial strength, it may be published openly to the people.'

....

The most godly king indeed died without waiting for parliament on 6 July at his manor of Greenwich, at the age of fifteen years, six months and a few weeks. This prince was tall and of a healthy constitution for a boy in middle youth, [f.12r] but his manner was so gracious and his countenance so modest and pleasant that he charmed observers into an exceptional love and an extraordinary devotion towards their sovereign. Moreover, his endowments of intellect were so much more outstanding and admirable than his good looks that not without reason might the English reproach the fates for being unjust and utterly envious in carrying off a future leader of such promise. He was the third and last male Tudor to reign after Richard III, the last Plantagenet king, who so notably tyrannized his people that he seemed not merely to equal but even to surpass the savagery of the Ottomans. And since I can hardly see a more fitting opportunity in all this treatise to set down the descent of such illustrious houses, it is appropriate to deal with their genealogies here.

From a reading of ancient histories I am able to conclude that for its immense antiquity, the House of Tudor is second to none in all Europe, for it traces its origin from Cadwallader, the last king of the Britons before the Saxons became lords of this island. After many centuries his descendants, as if claiming their birthright (perhaps by God's will), regained their ancestral glory with all possible good fortune in Henry VII.

....

Select Reading List

1. Bibliographies

Conyers Read, *Bibliography of British History, Tudor Period 1485-1603* (before 1959)
H.J. Creaton, *Writings in British History* (1960-1974)
G.R. Elton, D.M. Palliser et al., *Royal Historical Society Annual Bibliography of British History* (since 1975)

2. Sources

Calendar of State Papers, Domestic, Edward VI, ed. C. Knighton (1992)
Calendar of State Papers, Spanish, Vols. IX, X, XI. ed. Royall Tyler et al. (1862-1954)
Calendar of State Papers, Venetian, Vol. V. ed. Rawdon Brown et al. (1864-1898)
Acts of the Privy Council, Vols. II, III, IV. ed. J.R. Dasent et al. (1890-1964)
Chronicle and Political Papers of Edward VI, ed. W.K. Jordan (1966)
Grafton's Chronicle, ed. Henry Ellis (1809)
Statutes of the Realm, ed. A. Luders et al. (1810-28)
Tudor Royal Proclamations, ed. P.L. Hughes and J.F. Larkin (1964-69)
Liturgies of the Reign of Edward VI, ed. J.F. Ketley (1844)
Visitation Articles and Injunctions 1536-1559, ed. W.H. Frere and W.M. Kennedy (1910)
Original letters relative to the English Reformation, 1531-58, ed. Hastings Robinson (1910)
Tudor Economic Documents, ed. R.H. Tawney and Eileen Power (1924)
The Commonwealth of the Realm of England, ed. E. Lamond (1950)
The Report of the Royal Commission of 1552, ed. W.C. Richardson (1974)
"An Eyewitness's account of the Coup d'Etat of October 1549," ed. A.J.A. Malkiewicz, *English Historical Review*, 70 (1955)
"Documents relating to the Treaty of Boulogne, 1550," ed. D.L. Potter, *Camden Miscellany*, XXVIII (1984)

"The Vita Mariae Angliae of Robert Wingfield of Brantham," ed. D. MacCulloch, *Camden Miscellany*, XXVIII (1984)

"The Letters of Richard Scudamore," ed. S. Brigden, *Camden Miscellany*, XXX (1990)

The Reigns of Edward VI and Mary, ed. J.F. Tytler (1839)

The Reformation of the Ecclesiastical Laws of England, 1552, ed. J.C. Spalding (1992)

Martin Bucer and the Book of Common Prayer, E.C. Whitaker (1974)

Literary Remains of Edward VI, Roxburgh Club (1857)

3. Secondary works

J.D. Alsop, "The Revenue Commission of 1552," *Historical Journal*, 22 (1979)

J.D. Alsop, "A regime at sea: The Navy and the 1553 succession crisis," *Albion*, 24 (1992)

M. Aston, *England's Iconoclasts* (1988)

B.L. Beer, *Northumberland; the Political career of John Dudley, Earl of Warwick and Duke of Northumberland* (1973)

B.L. Beer, *Rebellion and Riot; popular disorder in England during the reign of Edward VI* (1982)

B.L. Beer, "Episcopacy and Reform in Mid-Tudor England," *Albion* 22 (1991)

H.S. Bennett, *English Books and Readers, 1475-1557* (1952)

G.W. Bernard, *The power of the early Tudor nobility; a study of the fourth and fifth earls of Shrewsbury* (1985)

W.G. Bittle and R. Lane Todd "Inflation and philanthropy in England; a reassessment of W.K. Jordan's data," *Economic History Review*, 29 (1976)

I.S.W. Blanchard, "Population change, enclosure and the early Tudor economy," *Economic History Review*, 2nd series, 23 (1970)

M.L. Bush, "The Lisle-Seymour land disputes; a study of power and influence in the 1530s," *Historical Journal*, 9 (1966)

M.L. Bush, *The government policy of Protector Somerset* (1975)

J. Cornwall, *Revolt of the Peasantry, 1549* (1977)

J. Cornwall and D. MacCulloch, "Debate: Ketts rebellion in context," *Past and Present*, 93 (1981)

C.S.L. Davis, "Slavery and Protector Somerset; the vagrancy Act of 1547," *Economic History Review*, 2nd series, 19 (1966)

J.F. Davies, *Heresy and Reformation in the South East of England, 1520-1559* (1983)

M. Dewar, *Sir Thomas Smith; a Tudor intellectual in office* (1964)

A.G. Dickens, *Lollards and Protestants in the Diocese of York* (1959)

F.C. Dietz, *English public finance, 1485-1558* (1964)

E. Duffy, *The Stripping of the Altars*, (1992)

G.R. Elton, "Mid-Tudor Finance," *Historical Journal*, 20 (1977)

G.R. Elton, *Reform and Reformation, England 1509-1558* (1977)

F.J. Fisher, "Influenza and Inflation in Tudor England," *Economic History Review*, 2nd series, 18 (1965)

S.R. Gammon, *Statesman and Schemer; William, first Lord Paget* (1973)

J.J. Goring, "Social change and military decline in Mid-Tudor England," *History* 60, (1975)

J.D. Gould, *The Great Debasement; currency and the economy in Mid-Tudor England* (1970)

M.A.R. Graves, *The House of Lords in the Parliaments of Edward VI and Mary; an institutional study* (1981)

J.A. Guy, *Tudor England* (1988)

C. Haigh (ed.), *The English Reformation Revised* (1987)

C. Haigh, *The English Reformations* (1993)

A.D.K. Hawkyard, "The enfranchisement of constituencies, 1504-1558," *Parliamentary History*, 10 (1991)

R.W. Heinze, *The Proclamations of the Tudor Kings* (1976)

D.E. Hoak, "Rehabilitating the Duke of Northumberland; politics and political control," in J. Loach and R. Tittler, *The Mid-Tudor Polity c.1540-1560* (1980)

D.E. Hoak, "The King's Privy Chamber, 1547-1553," in D.J. Guth and J.W. McKenna (eds.) *Tudor Rule and Revolution* (1982)

D.E. Hoak, "The secret history of the Tudor Court; the King's coffers and the King's purse, 1542-1553," *Journal of British Studies* 26 (1987)

D.E. Hoak, *The King's Council in the Reign of Edward VI* (1976)

R.A. Houlbroke, *Church courts and the people during the English Reformation* (1979)

P. Hughes, *The Reformation in England* (Vol. 2, 1952)

E.W. Ives, "Henry VIII's will; a forensic connundrum," *Historical Journal* 35, 4, (1992)

H. James, "The aftermath of the 1549 coup, and the Earl of Warwick's intentions," *Historical Research*, 62 (1989)

W.R.D. Jones, *The Tudor Commonwealth* (1970)

W.K. Jordan, *Edward VI: the young king* (1968)

W.K. Jordan, *Edward VI: the threshold of power* (1970)

E. Kerridge, *Agrarian problems in the sixteenth century and after* (1969)

J.M. King, "Freedom of the press, protestant propaganda, and Protector Somerset," *Huntingdon Library Quarterly*, 40 (1976)

M.M. Knappen, *Tudor Puritanism* (1939)

A. Kreider, *English chantries; the road to dissolution* (1979)

S.K. Land, *Ketts rebellion* (1977)

J. Loach, *Protector Somerset* (1993)

D.M. Loades, *The Tudor Court* (1986)

D.M. Loades, *Revolution in Religion...1530-1570* (1992)

D.M. Loades, *The Mid-Tudor Crisis, 1545-1565* (1992)

I. Luxton, "The reformation and popular culture," in F. Heal and R. O'Day (eds.) *Church and Society in England* (1977)

J.K. McConica, *English Humanists and reformation politics* (1965)

D. MacCulloch, "Ketts rebellion in context," *Past and Present*, 84 (1979)

D. MacCulloch, *Suffolk and the Tudors* (1986)

R.B. Manning, "Violence and Social conflict in Mid-Tudor rebellions," *Journal of British Studies*, 16 (1977)

G.J. Mayhew, "The progress of the reformation in East Sussex, 1530-1559; the evidence of wills," *Southern History*, 5 (1983)

H. Miller, "Henry VIII's unwritten will; grants of land and honours in 1547," in E.W. Ives, R.J. Knecht, and J.J. Scarisbrick, eds. *Wealth and Power in Tudor England* (1978)

J.A. Muller, *Stephen Gardiner and the Tudor Reaction* (1926)

R. O'Day, "Hugh Latimer; a prophet of the Kingdom," *Historical Research*, 65 (1992)

J.E. Oxley, *The Reformation in Essex to the death of Mary* (1965)

G.J.R. Parry, "Inventing the Good Duke of Somerset," *Journal of Ecclesiastical History*, 40 (1989)

M.T. Pearse, "Freewill, dissent and Henry Hart," *Church History* 58, 1989

J. Phillips, *The Reformation of Images: Destruction of Art in England 1535-1660* (1973)

W.C. Richardson, *The History of the Court of Augmentations* (1961)

J. Ridley, *Thomas Cranmer* (1966)

G.R. Redworth, *In Defence of the Church Catholic; a biography of Stephen Gardiner* (1990)

F. Rose-Troup, *The Western Rebellion of 1549* (1913)

J.J. Scarisbrick, *The Reformation and the English people* (1984)

W.J. Sheils, *The English Reformation*, 1530-1570 (1989)

P.Slack, "Social policy and the constraints of government, 1547-1558," in J. Loach and B. Tittler, *The Mid-Tudor Polity*

A.J. Slavin, "The fall of Lord Chancellor Wriothesley; a study in the politics of conspiracy," *Albion*, 7 (1975)

A.G.R. Smith, *The Emergence of a nation state, 1529-1660* (1984)

L.Stone, "Patriarchy and Paternalism in Tudor England; the Earl of Arundel and the Peasants revolt of 1549," *Journal of British Studies*, 13 (1974)

R. Whiting, *The Blind Devotion of the people* (1989)

D. Willen, *John Russell, First Earl of Bedford: one of the King's men* (1981)

C.H. Williams, *English Historical Documents, 1485-1558* (1976)

P.H. Williams, *The Tudor Regime* (1979)

K.S.H. Wyndham, "Crown lands and royal patronage in mid-sixteenth century England," *Journal of British Studies*, 19 (1980)

J.A. Youings, "The South Western Rebellion of 1549," *Southern History* 1, (1979)

INDEX